The Social Construction of the Ocean

CAMBRIDGE STUDIES IN INTERNATIONAL RELATIONS

Series list continues after index

The Social Construction of the Ocean

Philip E. Steinberg

CAMBRIDGE
UNIVERSITY PRESS

PUBLISHED BY THE PRESS SYNDICATE OF THE UNIVERSITY OF CAMBRIDGE
The Pitt Building, Trumpington Street, Cambridge, United Kingdom

CAMBRIDGE UNIVERSITY PRESS
The Edinburgh Building, Cambridge CB2 2RU, UK
40 West 20th Street, New York, NY 10011-4211, USA
10 Stamford Road, Oakleigh, VIC 3166, Australia
Ruiz de Alarcón 13, 28014 Madrid, Spain
Dock House, The Waterfront, Cape Town 8001, South Africa

http://www.cambridge.org

First published 2001

Printed in the United Kingdom at the University Press, Cambridge

Typeface Palatino 10/12.5 pt.   *System* LATEX 2$_\varepsilon$ [TB]

A catalogue record for this book is available from the British Library.

ISBN 0 521 80443 4 hardback
ISBN 0 521 01057 8 paperback

Contents

Illustrations

Tables

Acknowledgments

It is perhaps expected that every book reflecting upon the meaning of the sea will begin with a pithy quote from Melville. As one might gather from the frequent references throughout this book, I am a greater fan of Verne. Indeed, I would like to think that Captain Nemo's continuing vacillation between stubborn independence and selfless communitarianism better reflects both my personality and the process of writing this book than does the tortured angst of Captain Ahab. Nonetheless, like Ishmael in *Moby Dick*, I still am not exactly certain how it was that my intellectual journey took me to the sea. I sometimes wake in the morning to find a book of maritime art or *The Oxford Companion to Ships and the Sea* by my side, not quite sure how I arrived at this point from my initial plans to study urban planning politics and development theory. I can only hope that this book is more coherent than the path by which it was conceived.

There is no way to do justice to the numerous individuals who – by providing me with odd facts, literature reviews, encouraging words, insightful questions, or even outlets for aggression – helped me in forging that path. My former professors and fellow graduate students at the Graduate School of Geography at Clark University played a critical role (in both senses of the word!), as did later colleagues at Bucknell and Florida State universities. Although encouragement from my dissertation advisor, Dick Peet, was characteristically skeptical (his first written comment on my ocean project: "As to your dissertation topic on 'Territoriality and the Sea' – at first I thought 'Oh no!' But as I read your outline I changed my mind (something I do only rarely)"), it also was characteristically heartfelt and encouraging. At Florida State, Jan Kodras has lent me advice, inspiration, and, during frequent times of department budgetary crisis, toner cartridges, while Basil Savitsky's couch has been a steady source of comfort when I've needed midday therapy sessions. I am grateful to other faculty members and graduate students in the Department of Geography at FSU for offering a thoughtful ear, even as they made the grievous error of encouraging my ocean puns. Mary Burke and John Reynolds, respectively of the Economics and Sociology departments at Florida State, provided the dual services of ensuring that I maintain a multidisciplinary perspective while (equally importantly) providing cat-care for Raster and Vector while I engaged in field expeditions. Donna Jo Hall helped me get in touch with my marine self by accompanying me on frequent trips to Florida's gulf coast, even when she would have preferred to be heading toward the mountains.

Beyond FSU, the ad hoc "Fish 'n' Ships" geography specialty group has been there for me time and again, letting me know that I am not *quite* alone in my effort to bring geographic theory to the sea, and I am grateful to them for having let me know when they've thought that I was on to something (and for letting me know when they've thought that I was off the wall). Countless other individuals have inspired me along the way, but Gavin Bridge, George Clark, Martin Lewis, Steve McDowell, Carol Moeller, Karen Nichols, Sunita Reddy, Freddie Robles, Allan Sekula, Neil Smith, Genese Sodikoff, Carolyn Trist, and Barney Warf in particular stand out as mentors, critics, collaborators, editors, and academic pen pals who were willing to engage my work with their own and use our shared knowledge and complementary approaches to suggest routes for improvement. During the final stages of this project, Paolo Aluffi provided crucial translation assistance, Heidi Recksiek cleared up a few issues in US coastal law, and Mike Pryce-Jones read through the entire manuscript, providing some extremely valuable comments as well as assistance with index preparation. The anonymous reviewers of the manuscript also provided exceptionally useful advice.

Financial and logistical support for this book came from several sources. A dissertation grant from the Association of American Geographers helped support the project early on. I could not have completed the sections on the papal bulls of 1493 and the Treaty of Tordesillas of 1494 (Chapter 3) were it not for a summer 2000 fellowship from the American Geographical Society Collection at the University of Wisconsin-Milwaukee. Institutional support from the American Society of International Law and the International Institute for Environment and Development helped facilitate my attendance at meetings at the United Nations in 1994.

Acknowledgments

Portions of this book are derived from articles and book chapters that appeared previously in print. These include "Three historical systems of ocean governance: a framework for analyzing the law of the sea" (*World Bulletin*, 1996); "Transportation space: a fourth spatial category for the world-system perspective?" (in P. Ciccantell and S. Bunker, eds., *Space and Transport in the World System*, Greenwood, 1998); "The maritime mystique: sustainable development, capital mobility, and nostalgia in the world-ocean" (*Environment and Planning D: Society & Space*, 1999); "Lines of division, lines of connection: stewardship in the world-ocean" (*Geographical Review*, 1999); "Navigating to multiple horizons: toward a geography of ocean-space" (*The Professional Geographer*, 1999). Editors and anonymous reviewers for each of these articles played an important role in fine-tuning some of the ideas that are contained within this book.

I had the good fortune to be assigned Philippa Youngman as copy editor. She went far beyond the call of duty to tutor me on subjects as diverse as English history and Latin vocabulary. Finally, John Haslam at Cambridge University Press made the entire process less painful, shepherding me through the intricacies of permissions and reproductions while patiently and promptly fielding my pleas for time and logistical assistance.

Introduction: From Davy Jones' locker to the Foot Locker: the case of the floating Nikes

On May 27, 1990, 600 miles south of Anchorage, Alaska, the Seattle-bound container ship *Hansa Carrier* encountered heavy storms, and twenty-one containers were lost overboard. Inside five of these containers were some 80,000 Nike sneakers, hiking boots, and sandals, with a retail value of approximately $2.5 million. Four of the five Nike containers opened, and 61,280 shoes began a long journey eastward to the coast of North America. Over the next two years, more than 1,600 Nikes were recovered on the beaches of British Columbia, Washington, and Oregon.

West Coast residents soon discovered that the shoes, although somewhat stiff after a year or two in the ocean, were wearable after a thorough washing in warm water. Unfortunately for the sneaker scavengers, Nike had shipped the shoes untied, and so pairs of like models, colors, and sizes did not wash ashore together. Beachcombers responded by holding "swap meets" in West Coast beach towns throughout 1991. One particularly enterprising beachcomber, Oregon artist Steve McLeod, reported earning $568 by collecting, matching, cleaning, and selling washed-up Nikes. Meanwhile, two Seattle-based oceanographers, Curtis Ebbesmeyer and James Ingraham, took advantage of the spill, calibrating shoe recovery data and the release site to existing ocean-current models to gain new insights into the variability of ocean currents (Ebbesmeyer and Ingraham 1992, 1994; Powell 1992; Reuters 1991; Sullivan 1992).

This story provides a fitting beginning for a narrative about the various ways the world-ocean has been perceived, constructed, and managed

Davy Jones is nautical slang, dating back to at least the mid-eighteenth century, for the spirit of the sea. Thus, Davy Jones' locker refers to "the bottom of the sea, the final resting place of sunken ships, of articles lost or thrown overboard, of men buried at sea" (Kemp 1988: 232).

1

under modernity. For the Nike Corporation, the sea represented the least expensive means of transporting commodities from point of production to point of sale. It enabled the company to reproduce geographical hierarchy and the global division of labor. By utilizing the sea for transporting a commodity, Nike was able to move the labor and capital embedded in each shoe from a low-wage region (Asia) to a high-wage region (North America), permitting profit realization. The sea, for Nike, was a space of distance, a space across which shoes had to travel so that their sale could generate a profit for corporate shareholders. For Leonhardt & Blumberg, the Hamburg-based shipping firm that operated the *Hansa Carrier*, the sea also was a surface to be crossed, and its distance similarly presented profit-making opportunities.

For residents of the West Coast, including beachcombers like McLeod and his customers, the sea was a provider. It was the means by which goods arrived to satisfy North American footwear needs. For these North Americans, the sea was more than just a space across which goods traveled; it was the entity that *brought* low-cost goods to the consumer. The sea provided the resource of connection. In this particular instance, the role of the sea as resource provider is especially clear, since the sea itself (not a ship) "carried" the shoes and they arrived decommodified, like a "natural" resource. Essentially, however, the sea would have performed a similar "provider" function had the containers not fallen overboard. Once the sneakers had been extracted from the ocean, McLeod performed a service similar to more conventional Nike distributors, adding labor-value to the product by packaging it and bringing it to the customer.

While Nike and Leonhardt & Blumberg saw the ocean as a transportation surface and McLeod and his customers saw it as a resource provider, the oceanographers viewed the ocean as a set of discrete locations: places of ocean currents, storm centers, coastlines, islands, past message-in-bottle releases, and so on. These places, each with its own distinct nature, related to one another to make the ocean one grand physical system. Leonhardt & Blumberg's insurer similarly perceived the ocean as a space of discrete places and events, each of which might interfere with the transport-surface construction favored by Nike and Leonhardt & Blumberg.

Each actor in the Nike drama perceived the ocean as an arena of both predictability and unpredictability. Even as it constructed the ocean as a predictable, formless transport surface, Nike and Leonhardt & Blumberg were aware that the ocean was not totally "frictionless"; this is why Nike required Leonhardt & Blumberg to retain insurance on the vessel. Nike and its customers pay for this unpredictability of the sea in the price of every sneaker, a portion of which covers shipping insurance. For McLeod, the sea, while a provider, was an exceedingly capricious one. He could not know whether his time spent combing the beaches or the "swap meets" would result in his finding a matched pair of sneakers. His customers paid for this unpredictability of the sea in that the price of each pair compensated McLeod for time spent wandering the beaches and not finding any shoes. The oceanographers and the insurers, meanwhile, were attempting to conquer the unpredictability of the ocean by fine-tuning models of ocean-current variability and calculating the degree to which the ocean's features might interfere with its transport-surface properties. Indeed, if the oceanographers were to succeed in rendering the ocean totally predictable, much of the uncertainty facing the other actors would disappear: Leonhardt & Blumberg would be able to redirect its ships to safe routes and cancel its insurance policy; McLeod would know exactly where shoes would wash ashore; and Nike would benefit from lower transportation costs, which it then could pass on to the consumer by lowering the price for its sneakers.

Of course, the Nike case is exceptional. The vast majority of ocean-transported goods arrive safely. Yet the story demonstrates succinctly how the ocean is perceived and used by various social actors. Furthermore, it shows how each of these uses is characterized by that combination of predictability and unpredictability that reproduces cycles of capital speculation and investment, whether on the scale of a multinational insurance firm, the Nike Corporation, or Steve McLeod. The story of the floating Nikes demonstrates how multiple constructions of the ocean serve to maintain the concentrations and movements of wealth that characterize modern capitalism.

One could take this scenario one step further and speculate how each actor might favor certain ocean policies (which in turn would imply further perceptions and constructions of the ocean) so as to strengthen their specific interests. The insurance firm, working with the oceanographers, might seek to restrict navigation to calm regions and times. Nike, Leonhardt & Blumberg, and the consumers, on the other hand, would favor a regime that preserved for each ship the right to weigh risks on a case-by-case basis and choose the least costly and quickest route for each trip from South Korea to Seattle. McLeod too would favor an absence of regulation. As a non-traditional Nike distributor, McLeod has a direct interest in the ships embarking on high-risk journeys, but even if he were a more typical Nike retailer he could be expected to favor low-cost wholesale goods that would enable him to resell the shoes at a competitive price.

The various parties also would differ on whether or not individual entities should be permitted to claim exclusive access (or exclusive use privileges) to specific areas of the sea. McLeod would probably favor a mechanism whereby he could obtain property rights (or at least exclusive usufruct) to areas of the beach and coastal waters that he had prospected and found to be sneaker-rich. Likewise, Leonhardt & Blumberg might favor a means by which it could gain exclusive access to specific ocean routes. McLeod and Leonhardt & Blumberg then would find themselves supporting some degree of militarization of the sea in order to exclude others from their domains. By contrast, the insurer, Nike, and the consumers would probably oppose this territorial division of the sea. Militarization would increase the risks associated with each shipment, something that Nike and the insurer would seek to avoid. Additionally, these increased risks – especially when combined with the monopolization of shipping routes that would be facilitated by the territorialization of the sea – would increase cost, which would negatively impact Nike and the consumers. Ebbesmeyer and Ingraham, the oceanographers, would also oppose this territorialization of the sea, since it would probably interfere with their research.

If each actor were to pursue its strategy, the result would be a set of social institutions, attitudes, and norms that would reproduce the construction of the ocean as unclaimable transport surface, claimable resource space, a set of discrete places and events, *and* a field for military adventure. The balance between these often contradictory constructions would shift from time to time, as the power of the actors varied and as the need for certain ocean uses waxed and waned, but the overall competition among the various actors would serve to reproduce the ocean as a uniquely constructed space with a complex regime designed to serve a multiplicity of functions.

The narrative presented in this book resembles that of the Nike story, with the number of actors, the geographical extent, and the time frame greatly extended to encompass the whole of the modern era, roughly from 1450 to the present. Through a historical narrative, it is argued that each period of capitalism, besides having a particular spatiality on land, has had a complementary – if often contrapuntal – spatiality at

Table 0. *The Nike story: characteristics of key actors*

Actor	Conception of sea's function	Conception of sea's physical properties	View on regulations and restrictions to limit risk	View on militarization/ possession/ territorialization
Nike	Transport surface	Featureless and placeless	Against	Against
Leonhardt & Blumberg	Transport surface	Featureless and placeless	Against	For
Insurer	Transport surface	Contains distinct features and places	For	Against
Steve McLeod	Resource provider	Contains distinct features and places	Against	For
Sneaker consumers	Resource provider	Featureless and placeless	Against	Against
Ebbesmeyer and Ingraham	Arena for physical processes	Contains distinct features and places	For	Against

sea, with specific interest groups during each period promoting specific constructions of ocean-space. As is the case with land-space, the contradictions and changes within each period's construction have been intertwined with contradictions and changes in that period's political–economic structures. The ever-changing uses, regulations, and representations of ocean-space have been as much a part of each period's spatiality as have the spatial constructions of land-space.

To make this case, Chapter 1 presents the book's theoretical perspective. In contrast to most studies of marine areas, wherein the ocean is viewed as a *resource* space used *by* society, this chapter develops a constructivist perspective wherein the ocean is viewed as a *social* space, a space *of* society. Specifically, this chapter outlines a *territorial political economy* perspective in which attention is directed to the spatial structures of the political–economic system prevalent during a given period and, within that context, the institutional mechanisms implemented by individual actors to define, bound, govern, police, and communicate with distinct territories. It is shown that this process of spatial construction occurs at sea as well as on land, and that ocean-space is thus an arena of social conflict.

Chapter 2 explores the range of options available in ocean-space governance and territoriality, and their association with specific political–economic spatialities. To illustrate these options, this chapter considers three non-modern ocean governance systems: the Indian Ocean prior to large-scale European influence, Micronesia prior to very recent times, and the Mediterranean under Roman rule. In particular, attention is drawn to the Mediterranean construction, as this construction of the sea as a space beyond territorial possession but amenable to stewardship by land-based societies has had a strong impact on the various constructions of ocean-space that have prevailed during the modern era.

Chapters 3 to 5 use the territorial political economy perspective to analyze the social construction of ocean-space during the modern era, across three historical periods: merchant capitalism (*circa* 1450–1760), industrial capitalism (*circa* 1760–1970), and the transition to postmodern capitalism (*circa* 1970 to the present). Within each period, attention is drawn especially to the tension between capital's need for spatial fixity and its need for spatial mobility – two essential and contradictory properties of capitalist spatiality – and analysis is focused on how this tension has resolved itself in a variety of ocean-space constructions.

Chapter 6 considers future territorial constructions, not just of ocean-space, but also of other domains of mobility, such as cyberspace and inner- and outer-atmospheric airspace, that increasingly are likely to face problems of territorial governance similar to those historically encountered at sea. Because the social constructions of these spaces are inherently unstable, these seemingly marginal spaces are identified as potential arenas for generating social change.

1   Territorial political economy and the construction of ocean-space

The significance of ocean-space

It is difficult to overstate the role of the ocean in the rise of the modern world-system. As Braudel notes,

> The great technological "revolutions" between the fifteenth and eighteenth centuries were artillery, printing and ocean navigation . . . Only the third – ocean navigation – eventually led to an imbalance, or "asymmetry" between different parts of the globe.
>
> (Braudel 1981: 385)

Similarly, Hugill has remarked,

> The Portuguese cannon-armed caravel of the mid-1400s was the first ship that could sail anywhere on this planet, defend itself against piracy, pose a threat to those unwilling to trade, and carry enough trade goods to be profitable. The range, security, and profitability of shipping are the subsequent keys to European success and to the hegemony of whichever polity found the best combination of the three.
>
> (Hugill 1993: 16)

In fishing too it has been argued that early modern Europe's development of a system for regularly harvesting and trading distant cod stocks "changed the world" (Kurlansky 1997).[1]

Even today, while the decline of sea travel and diminished dependence on self-supplied food sources has removed the maritime world

---

[1] This is not to say that, at the dawn of the modern era, European navigation and fishing technologies were superior to those of other parts of the world. Rather, advances in technology were combined with inter-state competition and a utilitarian perspective on the sea, and this enabled Europe to mobilize sea power, trade, and resource extraction in an integrated manner that supported systemic dominance (see Chapters 2 and 3).

from the realm of most landlubbers' everyday experiences, the sea remains a crucial domain for the resources and processes that sustain contemporary life. Since World War II, global fish catch has increased tenfold (FAO, *various years*) as has total tonnage shipped by the world cargo fleet (ISEL, *various years;* OECD, *various years*; UNCTAD, *various years*). Similarly, offshore petroleum extraction has increased rapidly since the first commercial well was sunk in 1937; today, over 20 percent of the world's petroleum is derived from offshore sources and the ocean presents a host of other mineral extraction opportunities (Couper 1989; Earney 1990). Tourism promotion too has taken a leading role in many countries' development plans, and this activity frequently involves further human interaction with the sea (Orams 1999). Biologists are turning to the sea as the next frontier for genetic and pharmacological research (Norse 1993), and with this increased attention to marine biota has come a heightened awareness of marine ecosystems' fragility and the connections between the health of marine environments and that of terrestrial environments (Berrill 1997; Earle 1995; Safina 1998). Combining all of the resources provided by the ocean, economists have calculated that the sea provides services to humanity valued at twenty-one trillion dollars, as opposed to only twelve trillion dollars provided by land (Costanza *et al.* 1997).

The recognition that the ocean should be studied as a space of society is not new. Almost 2,000 years ago, the Greek geographer Strabo wrote:

> We are in a certain sense amphibious, not exclusively connected with the land, but with the sea as well . . . The sea and the land in which we dwell furnish theaters for action, limited for limited actions and vast for grander deeds. (cited in Semple 1931: 59)

More recently, Semple admonished:

> Universal history loses half its import, remains an aggregate of parts, fails to yield its significance as a whole, if it does not continually take into account the unifying factor of the seas. Indeed, no history is entitled to the name of universal unless it includes a record of human movements and activities on the ocean, side by side with those on the land. Our school textbooks in geography present a deplorable hiatus, because they fail to make a definitive study of the oceans over which man explores and colonizes and trades, as well as the land on which he plants and builds and sleeps. (Semple 1911: 294)

And still more recently, Hartshorne, reflecting on the US geopolitical situation after World War II, wrote:

> As long as we limit our attention to land areas and associate these together in terms of large land units, referring to the seas only as an afterthought, we inevitably etch deeper the impression given by our maps, that the seas are negative in human relations and hence form the great barriers between peoples ...
>
> The fundamental error in popular geographic thought is that of regarding the land masses of the continents as the basic divisions of the world. You and I know that this is false. Since the time of Columbus and Magellan, the oceans have aided, rather than opposed, the spread of settlement, economic connections, cultural penetration and military action. Because the oceans are nearly empty, they do divide, but they do not separate.   (Hartshorne 1953: 386)

Most recently, the International Geographical Union launched its OCEANS program, dedicated to holistic study of the ocean as an integrated system (Vallega 1999; Vallega *et al.* 1998), *The Geographical Review* (1999) devoted an issue to the Oceans Connect program which is built around the idea that oceans define world regions rather than divide them, and *The Professional Geographer* (1999) devoted a focus section to the geography of ocean-space wherein it is urged that the social and physical aspects of the sea be analyzed with reference to each other and to the land-based processes that interact with marine phenomena.

Nonetheless, despite the past and present significance of the world-ocean to modern society, and despite these calls for a holistic geographical accounting of human interactions with the sea, relatively little research has been conducted on the historical geography of the ocean as a space that, like land, shapes and is shaped by social and physical processes. Within the discipline of geography per se, most marine research has been of an empirical and applied nature (for reviews, see Psuty *et al.* 2002; Steinberg 1999d; West 1989). Within the social sciences more generally, the bulk of research has focused on one or another use of the marine environment, but not on the ocean as an integrated space that is a product of – as well as a resource for – a variety of human uses. Following a review of traditional perspectives on the ocean, this chapter presents a *territorial political economy* approach for analyzing the geography of ocean-space.[2]

---

[2] The term *ocean-space* is used throughout this book to emphasize parallels between the aquatic and the terrestrial realms; that is, between ocean-space and land-space. Like

Traditional perspectives on human–marine interactions

Three perspectives form the basis for most studies of human–marine interactions: the ocean as resource provider, the ocean as transport surface, and the ocean as battleground or "force-field". Embedded in each of these three analytical perspectives is a certain conception of ocean-space.

International regime and resource management perspectives

The perspective most often applied in academic studies of marine issues is that of the ocean as a space of resources. The ocean is perceived as akin to other resource-rich spaces, and its management is characterized by similar dilemmas: How can the maximum sustainable yield be calculated and how should portions of that yield be allocated to competing users? How can traditional tenure systems and production practices be integrated with emerging resource needs, political power differentials, and technological advances? How can one adjudicate between the needs of users of one ocean-space resource and those who wish to use the same area for a different, incompatible resource use? How can one implement comprehensive, binding management of a space expressly defined as outside state territory when the key actors in building institutions of global governance are territorially bounded states?[3]

Students of resource management regimes note that in recent decades there have been dramatic increases in the rates of extraction of both non-living and living resources from marine environments. While petroleum is the best known and, to date, most important non-living resource extracted from the ocean floor, significant quantities of sand and gravel also are taken from marine space, and since the 1960s there has been strong interest in other marine minerals, including coal, polymetallic sulphides, metalliferous sediments, phosphorite nodules, and, most notably, polymetallic manganese nodules (Earney 1990). Since World War II, the quantity of fish harvested from marine areas has risen at an average growth rate of 3.6 percent per annum, increasing from 17.3 million metric tons (t) in 1948 to 61.7 million t in 1970 to 91.9 million t in 1995

land-space, ocean-space is constructed by a variety of actors as they respond to and reproduce social processes, spatial patterns, and physical nature.
[3] Scholars writing about the ocean from this perspective utilize literature on such topics as resource management and public policy issues (Rees 1990), common property resource management (Ostrom 1990), resource economics (Pearce and Turner 1990), international relations and international regimes (Krasner 1983), and issues of global environmental governance (Haas *et al.* 1993; Young 1997).

(FAO, *various years*). Most recently, the ocean has attracted attention as an alternative source for renewable energy (Tsamenyi and Herriman 1998), while deep sea habitats have aroused the interest of biologists seeking previously unexploited genetic material (Norse 1993).

Diminishing stocks of ocean resources (especially certain fish species) have led many scholars to advocate a stronger regime for managing marine resource extraction. Some have suggested that a stronger system of ocean governance be built around enhanced international regulatory organizations (Bautista Payoyo 1994; Borgese 1986, 1998; Prager 1993). Others argue that this "tragedy of the commons" situation requires a regime based on enclosure of ocean resources, so that each producer will become a "stakeholder" with an incentive to restrict production to the ocean's maximum sustainable yield (Denman 1984; Eckert 1979). Others suggest that models for sustainable ocean governance may be found in the "traditional" tenure systems of non-Western societies (Cordell 1989; McCay and Acheson 1987; Jackson 1995; Ostrom 1990; Van Dyke *et al.* 1993), while still others promote a civil society-based partnership wherein fishers, processors, consumers, retailers, and nongovernmental organizations work together to implement a sustainable extraction system (Constance and Bonanno 2000; Steinberg 1999a).

Whichever policy proscription one adopts, the resource-centered perspective offers a limited account of the *history* of human interactions with the sea. Through the early twentieth century:

> The only [extractive] resource exploitation was fishing, and with some infrequent exceptions of inshore fisheries there were no serious problems of stock depletion until the technical modernization of fishing vessels in the twentieth century. The oceans [i.e., non-coastal areas] were used mainly as avenues of commerce and for waging war, and in the latter case military endeavors involved for the most part colonization or naval encounters. Large invasions across ocean spaces were difficult and infrequent. Therefore the major use of the oceans was essentially for the transportation of goods.
>
> (Zacher and McConnell 1990: 78)

In more recent times, the geographical limit of the "near-shore" area where most fishing takes place has been extended to the ends of the continental shelf or beyond; the 1982 United Nations Convention on the Law of the Sea gives every coastal state the right to establish an exclusive economic zone (EEZ) which extends beyond the 12 nautical mile (NM)[4]

---

[4] 1 nautical mile equals 1.15 statute miles or 1.852 kilometers. All references to "miles" are to nautical miles.

limit of territorial waters to 200 NM from the coast. Coastal states have sovereign rights to all living and non-living resources in their EEZs.[5] Although data gathered by the FAO do not reveal the percentage of marine life (either by weight or by value) caught at specified distances from the coast (Pontecorvo 1988), generally it is accepted that the majority of fish caught are found in the 8 percent of ocean-space lying above the continental shelf (FAO 1981; Rounsefell 1975) and that over 90 percent of the world's catch of fish comes from the 37 percent of the ocean lying within 200 NM of the coast (Alexander and Hodgson 1975; Eckert 1979; Friedheim 1991; Juda and Burroughs 1990; Pardo 1983; MSC 1998). Extraction of non-living marine resources (primarily oil, gas, sand, and gravel) also occurs at present entirely within EEZs or territorial waters.

Resource management questions revolve around the likelihood that unregulated exploitation without a coherent management strategy will result in the dissipation of a scarce and exhaustible resource. For a historical study of ocean-space, however, a perspective based upon the dangers of limiting destructive over-use is of only limited value. Historically, and even at present, the greater portion of ocean-space has failed to be a major provider of finite resources. The traditional uses that have been more characteristic (commerce and warfare) have not (at least until very recently) posed a significant threat to the quality of the marine environment; that is, they are not uses for which today's use degrades the value of the resources available to tomorrow's user.[6] Therefore, this history of the world-ocean turns away from perspectives derived from studies of the regulation of the extraction of finite resources and toward perspectives grounded in the more characteristic uses of the world-ocean.

Commercial history perspectives

Throughout modern (and pre-modern) history, the primary use of ocean-space has been as a surface for transportation. During the era of merchant capitalism, innovations in ocean transport were central in buttressing European domination of the world-economy (Andrews

---

[5] This 200-NM limit in most areas exceeds the boundaries of the continental shelf. In cases where the continental shelf extends beyond 200 NM, coastal states retain rights to seabed resources (but not to those in the water itself) out to the limit of the shelf.

[6] To some extent, this situation has changed in the past few decades. In the current era, military ships (e.g., nuclear submarines) and commercial vessels (e.g., petroleum supertankers) pose a threat to the marine environment.

1984; Braudel 1981; Hugill 1993), and the importance of the deep sea as transport space continues through the present. Ninety-five percent of world trade by weight, and two-thirds by value, is carried by ship (Zacher and Sutton 1996).[7] Total carriage by the world's merchant marine, as measured in ton-miles, is five times that transported by rail (Cafruny 1987). As the world economy and international trade have grown, so has the world shipping industry, with the capacity of the world ocean-going fleet increasing from 23 million deadweight tons (dwt) in 1870 to 82 million dwt in 1922 to 758 million dwt in 1996 (UNCTAD *various years*; Zacher and Sutton 1996). Outpacing overall growth in the world economy, total tonnage shipped internationally rose by an average of 8 percent per annum from the end of World War II to 1979 (Couper 1989). Although the growth of tonnage shipped remained essentially flat from 1970 to 1985, since then it has rebounded, increasing at a rate of over 3 percent per annum, for an overall increase from 996 million t in 1959 to 5,064 million t in 1998 (UNCTAD *various years*). In 1996, international shipping expenses added 5.27 percent to the cost of imported goods, bringing the shipping industry gross receipts of almost $250 billion (UNCTAD *various years*). By contrast, in 1995, global fish catch from marine areas was valued at only $100 billion.[8]

The major drawback of a perspective centered around the construction of ocean-space as a transport surface is its implication that the sea was and is an unmanaged space. If the ocean is conceived as merely a void between societies – a surface across which goods must travel so that international trade may occur – no regulation of the ocean itself is needed. According to this conception, the behavior of ships at sea still would require regulation, but the sea itself, as a formless surface across which ships sail, is beyond territorial control.

In the modern era, much of the dominant legal and political discourse on the ocean has been based upon this perspective. For instance, Bruce Harlow, a retired US navy admiral and former vice-chairman of the US

---

[7] This estimate varies. The US State Department has calculated that seaborne commerce accounts for 80 percent of world trade and 95 percent of US international trade by weight (cited in Galdorisi 1998). See Taggart (1999) for more on the importance of seaborne shipping.

[8] FAO statistics do not specifically refer to the value of fish caught in marine areas. This figure is derived from the following 1995 statistics: 42.17 percent of global fish catch (by weight) was exported; total value of fish exported was $52.034 billion; and 81.4 percent of global fish catch was from marine areas (FAO *various years*). The calculation assumes that value per weight of fish exported equals that of fish consumed domestically and that value per weight of fish caught in marine areas equals that of fish caught in inland waters.

Delegation to the Third United Nations Conference on the Law of the Sea (UNCLOS III), has written:

> For the past several centuries the world's oceans have been predominantly governed by two fundamental principles. First, the oceans can be used by all, for any peaceful ... purpose, short of a national claim to sovereignty. The only limitation to this principle, described as the "freedom of the high seas," is that the activity must be undertaken with reasonable regard for similar rights of other users ... The second principle, in contradistinction to the first, is that coastal states may exercise complete jurisdiction and control over this narrow band of water adjacent to their coast, a regime termed "territorial seas." (Harlow 1985: 1)

The sea, then, is characterized by Harlow as containing two opposing regions with contrasting governance regimes. One region, the coastal zone, is like land in that it is susceptible to being claimed, controlled, regulated, and managed by individual state-actors. In the other region, the deep sea, the only necessary (or even permissible) regulation is that which ensures that all ships will be able to travel freely across its vast surface.

This dichotomous construction of ocean-space is also reflected in the traditional legal distinction between "private" and "public" ocean law. Private ocean law (or maritime law) is the set of rules (including national legislation and international agreements) regulating the economic and commercial aspects of marine transport. Public ocean law (or the law of the sea) governs the sea itself, particularly with reference to control of ocean-space and access to its living and non-living resources. Traditionally, there has been an extensive body of private (maritime) law relating to the conduct of ships in international waters but very little public law, especially beyond the coastal zone. This evidence would appear to support Harlow's recognition of a long-standing liberal, minimalist regime for the deep sea. Yet, as Gold notes:

> This neat division [between "private" and "public" ocean law] appears nonexistent when one views the political and historical processes that have influenced ocean uses. There has hardly ever been a political or jurisdictional aspect in the law of the sea that has not had its effect on the commercial and economic use of the sea. The reverse is equally true. (Gold 1981: xx)

The historical narrative developed here confirms Gold's assertion. Despite the prevalent conception of non-coastal ocean-space as unmanaged and unmanageable, the modern era has been characterized by a series of interventions that – directly or indirectly – have regulated the oceans. Although often within the literal domain of "private" law, these interventions and regulations have reproduced and adjusted the "public" law of the sea as well. Just as many of the interventions relating to shipping have been founded upon a construction of the ocean as a formless transport surface, other interventions have been founded upon competing ocean-space constructions. Indeed, Harlow's description of the deep sea as an unregulated transport surface is itself representative of a particular era when a particular perspective on the ocean was dominant. To appreciate and analyze the full range of ocean-space constructions, their historical realizations in ocean-space regulatory regimes, and their bases and contributing roles in ongoing dialectical socio-spatial processes, one must work from a perspective richer than that of commercial history.

Military history perspectives

A third perspective frequently used for studying social uses and regulations of ocean-space is one wherein the ocean is perceived as a space of military adventures. Scholars utilizing this perspective note two distinct ways in which ocean-space is militarized: as a surface for troop movement and as a battlefield. While it seems likely that every society that used the ocean for transporting goods also discovered its utility as a surface for transporting troops, the second of these two uses has not been constructed universally; some societies that used the ocean for shipping and resource extraction failed to develop the concept of the sea battle.[9]

In modern times a third variation on the military construction of ocean-space has emerged. Said notes that in modern Britain, France, and the United States, the *idea* of projecting power across vast expanses of ocean-space to distant lands has played an important role in discourses of empire:

> The idea of overseas rule – jumping beyond adjacent territories to very distant lands – has a privileged status in these three cultures. This idea has a lot to do with projections, whether in fiction or geography or art, and it acquires a continuous presence through actual expansion, administration, investment, and commitment.   (Said 1993: xxiii)

The ideological significance of the projection of military power across and in ocean-space is revealed in one of the classic twentieth-century

---

[9] See, for instance, the examples of the non-modern societies of Micronesia and the Indian Ocean, discussed in Chapter 2.

works promoting United States overseas expansion:

> Maritime mobility is the basis for a new type of geopolitical structure, the overseas empire. Formerly, history had given us the pattern of great land powers based on the control of contiguous land masses such as the Roman, Chinese, and Russian empires. Now the sea has become a great artery of communication and we have been given a new structure of great power and enormous extent. The British, French, and Japanese empires and the sea power of the United States have all contributed to the development of a modern world which is a single field for the interplay of political forces. It is sea power which has made it possible to conceive of the Eurasian Continent as a unit and it is sea power which governs the relationships between the Old and the New Worlds.
>
> (Spykman 1944: 35)

In fact, most modern-era advocates of sea power, from Sir Walter Raleigh to Alfred Mahan and Nicholas Spykman, have combined this new, ideological value of sea power with the two more traditional uses, stressing the key role of a strong "blue-water" fleet in troop mobility, naval warfare, *and* domination of distant lands.

Much like the "transport-surface" construction of ocean-space, the construction of the ocean as a "force-field"[10] is dependent upon an idealization of the sea as an unmanaged and unmanageable surface, an idealization that resonates with the spatial assumptions that permeate realist theories of international politics. According to realists, individual societies, as embodied by spatially defined nation-states, are the repositories of order, while international relations are characterized by anarchic competition (Grieco 1990; Morgenthau and Thompson 1985). As unclaimed and unclaimable "international" space, the world-ocean lends itself to being constructed as the space of anarchic competition par excellence, where ontologically pre-existent and essentially equivalent nation-states do battle in unbridled competition for global spoils. In realist geopolitics (a subset of realist international relations theory), control of specific locations on the earth's surface is considered crucial in the competition for global power (Cohen 1973; Mackinder 1904; Parker 1985). Within this group of geopolitical realists, certain theorists have put a premium on control of portions or the entirety of the world-ocean (Mahan 1890; Raleigh 1829; Spykman 1944).

---

[10] The term "force-field" is used in preference to the word "battlefield" because the word "force-field" implies not only a space in which battles are waged but also a space across which power is projected.

17

Leaving aside for the moment any further critique of the realist conception of either the state or international relations (both of which are taken up again later in this chapter), it is argued here that the military history perspective is deficient for much the same reason as the commercial history perspective: Both perspectives are premised upon a denial of the ocean's long history as a space that continuously has been regulated and managed. Even those who study the history of sea power from an explicitly social angle – such as Modelski and Thompson (1988), who trace the rise and fall of maritime powers as indicators of world-systemic long cycles and the shifting fortunes of individual countries – fail to investigate the ocean itself as a space within which the social contest is played out. Rather than being a neutral surface across and within which states have vied for power and moved troops, the sea, like the nation-states themselves, has been socially constructed throughout history. Although in the modern era the sea has been constructed outside the territory of individual states, it has been constructed as a space amenable to a degree of governance within the state system. Indeed, as Thomson (1994) has shown, this construction of the sea has played an important role in the construction of modern norms of international relations. As was the case with Harlow's definition of the sea as unregulatable transport space, the very act of defining the sea as a space of anarchic military competition both reflects and creates specific social constructions of both ocean-space and land-space.

Attempts at fusion and the "expanded" resource regime perspective

The above presentation of three distinct perspectives on the uses of ocean-space obscures what is actually a continuum within the literature on marine uses and regulatory regimes. Many scholars, while concentrating on one use of the sea, recognize that this use takes place in a context of other uses as well.

An early analysis of the link between commercial and military uses of the sea was made by Sir Walter Raleigh (1552–1618) when he coined the aphorism:

> He who commands the sea commands the trade routes of the world. He who commands the trade routes, commands the trade. He who commands the trade, commands the riches of the world.
>
> (cited in Cafruny 1987: vii)

Likewise, one of the classic twentieth-century works on the history of sea power begins with the sentence:

> The term sea power, in its widest interpretation, must be taken to include not only the navies of nations but their total strength and interests on the sea – their extent of coast line, overseas bases and colonial possessions, merchant shipping and sea-borne trade.
>
> (Stevens and Westcott 1942: 1)

Additionally, the "environmental security" perspective, applied to the sea by Broadus and Vartanov (1994), folds resource and environment issues within a military perspective.

Scholars working from a commercial history perspective also frequently make links with other ocean-space uses. Hugill (1993) narrates a history of capitalism that revolves largely around advances in transportation technology. Because of the close tie between advances in the technology of transport ships and those of warships, Hugill touches frequently upon naval military issues. Similarly, Gold (1981) contends that the history of maritime transport can be understood only in the context of other ocean uses, including both resource extraction and military competition.

Because the international regime/resource management perspective begins with the observation that there are multiple, conflicting uses (and users) of ocean-space, this perspective especially is amenable to a more complex rethinking of the relationship between land-space and ocean-space. The "pluralist" nature of this perspective allows it to be expanded to include non-extractive "resources" provided by the ocean, including the "resources" of connection (as mobilized through shipping) and domination (as mobilized through naval power). The merging of the various perspectives on ocean-space also has been encouraged by the intensification of ocean-space uses. Juda and Burroughs (1990), for instance, have argued that extractive-, military-, and transport-oriented activities now conflict so often within any given region of the ocean that the time has come for a series of strong, regional ocean-space regimes to replace the many global single-use organizations (e.g., the International Whaling Commission) that currently prevail. This expansion of the resource management perspective amidst multiple, conflicting uses is exemplified by a "multiple use" chart published in *The Times Atlas and Encyclopaedia of the Sea*, in which navigation/communication, waste disposal/pollution, strategy/defense, research, and recreation uses and concerns are considered alongside and in interaction and competition with the extraction and harnessing of mineral/energy and biological resources (Couper 1989: 208).

Still, even this perspective fails to provide a framework for viewing ocean-space as an integral space of ongoing social processes. The "expanded" resource management perspective, like the other traditional perspectives, still implies that the ocean is a space designed and managed *by* land-based societies to *serve* land-based societies. In contrast, it is proposed here that the ocean – like land-space – is simultaneously an arena wherein social conflicts occur and a space shaped by these conflicts. The "socially constructed" ocean that results then goes on to shape social relations, on land and at sea. In short, the ocean is not merely a space used *by* society; it is one component of the space *of* society.

The territorial political economy perspective

The history of ocean-space told here is explicitly constructivist; that is, attention is drawn to the social structures, individual behaviors, institutional arrangements, and natural features that have intersected to create specific spaces, both on land and at sea. The roots of this perspective lie in the link between nature and society, a theme that was developed by some of the earliest known geographers and that provided a basis for much of human geography through the early twentieth century (Ratzel 1896; Semple 1911; Strabo 1917), wherein the natural environment was perceived as a factor limiting and enabling human behavior. For some, natural resources mandated a certain kind of social organization; for others, nature provided an environment within which humans had a limited choice of adaptation strategies; while for still others, nature directly affected a people's temperament or physical characteristics. Whatever the exact mechanism by which nature affected society, the link was conceived as predominantly unidirectional.

Twentieth-century cultural ecologists, building upon the works of Marsh (1965), have refined this thesis. They note that the link between nature and society goes in two directions: human actions shape the physical landscape, just as the landscape enables and limits human action and social formation (Sauer 1963; Thomas 1956; Turner *et al*. 1990). In recent decades, Marxist geographers also have analyzed the nature–society relationship. Expanding upon the cultural ecologists, they elaborate on how the actions by which individuals reproduce and/or transform "nature" and "places" also reproduce the hierarchies and institutions of societies (Bryant and Bailey 1997; Harvey 1996; Peet and Watts 1996; Smith 1990). Marxists utilizing this "political ecology" perspective stress how the nature–society relationship spans places and scales as, for instance, commodity speculation in Chicago can bring about land degradation in Kenya (Blaikie 1985).

Further extending the study of the social production of "nature" and "places," theorists such as Lefebvre (1991) and Soja (1989, 1996) call for analysis of the social production of *space*. Critiquing the spatial assumptions implicit in much of social theory, Soja writes:

> [The] contextual, physicalist view of space ... has imbued all things spatial with a lingering sense of primordiality and physical composition, objectivity, and inevitability. Space in this generalized and existential form has been conceptually incorporated into the materialist analysis of history and society in such a way as to interfere with the interpretation of human spatial organization as a social product ... The term typically evokes the image of something physical and external to the social context and to social action, a part of the "environment," a context *for* society – its container – rather than a structure created *by* society. (Soja 1980: 209–210)

As an alternative, Soja calls for a social theory in which "being, consciousness and action ... [exist] not simply 'in' space but 'of' space as well. To be alive intrinsically and inescapably involves participation in the social production of space, shaping and being shaped by a constantly evolving spatiality" (Soja 1985: 177).

The territorial political economy perspective continues this tradition of studying nature–society relations and the social construction of space by concentrating on three aspects of a space's social construction: its uses, regulations, and representations. As Table 2 depicts, elements of a space's social construction may be tied to the material organization of society, which itself is a function of the natural material base and the technologies and systems of social organization developed for transforming nature so as to sustain social life. The political–economic logic and structures of a given society lead social actors to implement a series of uses, regulations, and representations in specific spaces, including ocean- space. Once implemented in a particular space, each aspect of the social construction (each use, regulation, and representation) impacts the others, effectively creating a new "nature" of that space. This "second nature" is constructed both materially and discursively, and it is maintained through regulatory institutions. Finally, the social construction of space impacts the material organization of society, both directly and

Table 2. *The territorial political economy model of the social construction of space*

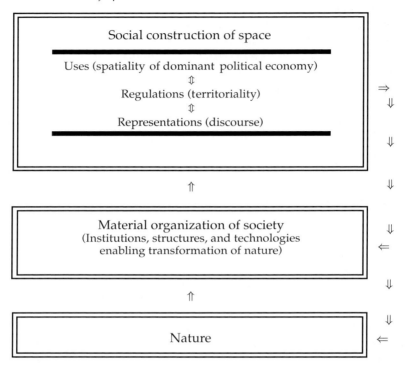

indirectly through its re-construction of the nature that provides the foundation for social organization.

Uses of ocean-space: spatiality and political economy

To trace the ways in which changing uses of ocean-space during the modern era have reflected changes in the material organization of society and contributed to the social construction of ocean-space, the territorial political economy perspective draws on three groups of contemporary scholars who have developed insights into the spatiality of capitalism: world-systems theorists, articulation theorists, and spatial dialectics theorists. Although these scholars' works vary in their emphases, they share a common thesis: Capitalism has progressed by creating places and arranging them hierarchically. These constructed places have served particular functions in reproducing the processes of capitalism and in advancing its overall trajectory. This environment of hierarchical spatial differentiation, far from being a contingent landscape upon which capitalist processes have played themselves out, has been both a necessary product and a necessary component of world capitalism. This book attempts to extend this thesis to ocean-space.

According to world-systems theory, as capitalism has expanded and proceeded through various stages and hegemonic cycles, it has created peripheral places, constructing them so that they can serve necessary functions for the capitalist world-economy. The processes that have emerged within these places, in turn, have gone on to reproduce not only those places but also the cycles and overall trajectory of the world-system (Amin *et al.* 1982; Shannon 1989; Taylor 1989; Wallerstein 1979, 1983, 1984, 1991). In world-systems theory, space (and also time) are understood to be dynamic creations of social processes rather than the background against which social activity takes place:

> Perhaps the most significant implication of this methodological approach to space and time is that they are liberated from the constraints of merely representing physical quantities and arbitrary standards of measure. Space and time need to be incorporated into the processes of the world-system itself: that is, we need to think of spatial and temporal processes.   (Bach 1982: 179; see also Hopkins 1982; Steinberg 1998)

World-systems theory also is germane to this study because of its conceptualization of a global society. Most social theories begin by assuming that the boundaries of "societies" (or at least of modern societies) are coterminous with those of territorially defined nation-states. World-systems theory, in contrast, develops an argument based upon Marx's assertion that the division and organization of labor is the key social process in a society. Since trade is the expression of a division of labor, the geographical extent of a world-system (i.e., a "society") is defined by the existence of intensive and repeated trade interactions. Thus, since around 1900, the entire globe has been incorporated within one world-system (or "society") (Wallerstein 1979).

The implication of this line of reasoning is that the uninhabited ocean-space across which extensive trade and interaction occurs is not a formless void *between* societies but rather a unique and specifically constructed space *within* society. Indeed, noting the unique role that the world-ocean has played in integrating the modern (post-1450) world-system, Modelski and Thompson proclaim, "The modern world system is, characteristically and importantly, an oceanic system"

23

(Modelski and Thompson 1988: 4). Ocean-space does not fall into any of the three categories of space commonly identified by world-systems theorists (core, semi-periphery, and periphery) and generally it has not been the object of direct attention within world-systems theory. However, it follows from the logic of the theory that ocean-space, like the three categories of land-space, serves a crucial role in the reproduction and development of the world-system and that historically it has been constructed and regulated as one unique element of social space so as better to serve the system's functions (Steinberg 1998).

A second group of theorists who influence the understanding of capitalist spatiality that informs the territorial political economy perspective are those who argue that Third World societies are characterized by transitional social formations with "articulated" modes of production. As capitalism has expanded into new areas it has constructed social formations that are characterized only partially by capitalist relations of production, and in which many of the social reproduction functions remain less than fully commodified. These partially incorporated, semi-capitalist areas serve global capitalism well; workers can be paid sub-subsistence wages while the goods they produce enter the global trade system that is dominated by capitalist countries. The transitional social formations of the Third World are creations of capitalism and they participate in the capitalist-dominated world trade network, but they are not *sensu stricto* capitalist (Brenner 1977; Foster-Carter 1978; Laclau 1971; Luxemburg 1964; Meillasoux 1981; Wolpe 1980).

Articulation theory informs this study of the social construction of ocean-space in two ways, one general and one more specific. Like world-systems theorists, articulation theorists suggest that the spatiality of the modern world, far from being contingent to fundamental capitalist processes, is a necessary component of capitalism. Locations of partial incorporation play an essential role in reproducing capitalism. While this theory does not directly address ocean-space, it raises the possibility that ocean-space, as another area that lacks definitive capitalist processes but serves a crucial role in the global economy, is in some manner a necessary and unique "place" within the capitalist-dominated world economy.

More specifically, articulationists show how First World capitalists enter a non-capitalist region and selectively buttress elements of the non-capitalist social formation so that the region, when integrated into the global trading system, is of exceptional service to the capitalists who dominate the world economy. Even as capitalists transform a Third

World region so as to be compatible with First World interests, selective non-capitalist characteristics of the region are emphasized both in reality and in representation. This selective emphasizing of non-capitalist, "non-First World" characteristics both serves to facilitate domination and to justify it. In the narrative presented here, an analogous process is revealed: First World capitalists have constructed the ocean in a manner that selectively reproduces and emphasizes its existence as a space apart from land-based capitalist society. This construction has been adjusted over time to serve specific stages of capitalism, much as the techniques of imperialism have shifted over time from plantations and trading posts to colonies to post-colonial domination. Yet through all the different definitions and social constructions of ocean-space, the ocean consistently has been a creation of capitalism even as it has lacked some of capitalism's essential characteristics, just as the Third World continually has been (re)constructed to serve capitalism even as it has remained immune from the labor system that is paradigmatic of the capitalist mode of production. Indeed, in both the Third World and the ocean, the designation of these spaces as "incomplete" (or "less developed") justifies further intervention and manipulation.

A third theory of capitalist spatiality that informs the territorial political economy perspective employed here is spatial dialectics theory. According to spatial dialectics theorists, the cycles of investment and disinvestment that characterize modern political economy are driven by the interplay of two contradictory tendencies of capital. On the one hand, capital characteristically is mobile as it seeks out new markets, low-cost inputs, and undervalued investment sites. Thus, there is a tendency toward diffusion of investment across space, eventually tending toward geographical *equalization.* On the other hand, productive investments and their supportive physical and social infrastructure frequently are immobile, and so there is also a tendency toward capital concentration as investors attempt to maximize their return on investments. This tendency toward capital concentration suggests that investments and value will be distributed highly *unequally* over space (Harvey 1982; Smith 1990).

Like world-systems and articulation theories, spatial dialectics theory holds that the spatial patterning of the world is not merely incidental to capitalist expansion; it is a result of and a necessary condition for foundational capitalist processes. The very existence of an "underdeveloped" Third World is due both to the capitalist drive toward mobility and expansion (hence the incorporation of the Third World into the capitalist-dominated trading and investment system) and the capitalist tendency toward fixity (hence the lack of comprehensive investments in the Third World that might spur Western-style "development"). Thus, the conflict between capital's two spatial tendencies is *dialectical*, and one result of this conflict is a third, long-run tendency toward systemic dysfunction: Uneven development (which results from the tendency toward capital fixity) encourages mobility which encourages equalization which, in the long-run, stymies the unevenness and mobility necessary for the continuation of capital investment and valorization.

Among spatial dialectics theorists, Manuel Castells (1996) is particularly germane because of his work on how contemporary society is being impacted by a qualitative transformation in this tension between the "spaces of flows" within which social processes of movement occur and the lived spaces of production and reproduction. Although Castells' assertion of a fundamental shift in this tension is questioned (see Chapters 5 and 6), this book is fully in accord with his argument that in order to understand the evolving spatiality of capitalism (and its social ramifications), one must study dialectical change in the spaces of flows as well as the spaces of fixity.

Regulations of ocean-space: territoriality

By positioning the history of the ocean within the spatiality of capitalism, the theoretical framework outlined above is susceptible to the three related critical charges of functionalism, economism, and determinism. As a functionalist theory, it may be interpreted as implying that an institution or historical event occurs because it must exist to serve a larger systemic function (e.g., the ocean has been constructed in a certain way because capitalism could not exist without the sea providing this function). As an economistic theory, it may imply that all non-economic components of society reflect developments in the economic sphere (e.g., antagonists in political and legal battles fought over the construction of ocean-space were representing solely economic interests). And as a deterministic theory, it may imply that the actions of individuals and institutions are determined by social forces with little contribution from individual agency (e.g., if Grotius had not written his landmark 1608 treatise on the freedom of the sea, capitalist processes would have "invented" someone else to write a similar tract).

To avoid this slippage into functionalism, economism, and determinism, the territorial political economy perspective blends its focus on abstract structural forces of capitalist spatiality with analyses of the practices of actual regimes, actors, and institutions in specific historical eras. This tactic – utilizing the historic approach as a means to implement structural theory while bypassing the trap of determinism – was adopted most notably by Marx (1967), but it has been continued by a host of authors working in the Marxist tradition. Althusser's (1971) social formations, Gramsci's (1971) historic blocs, and Lipietz' (1986) regimes of accumulation all can be characterized broadly as historic social assemblages. For each theorist, the time–space boundaries of the assemblage are defined by its institutions, social mores, cultural attributes, laws, reproductive subsystems, and technologies. The economics of capitalism provides each assemblage with its underlying logic, but it is a logic that is realized through actors who respond to historically and geographically (and even individually) contingent realities. Production activities lie at the foundation of historical assemblages (e.g., Fordist industrial capitalism) and their social or "superstructural" institutions (e.g., the welfare state), but they are not trans-historically or trans-geographically determinant. As the Gramscian international relations theorist Robert Cox notes:

> Production has . . . a certain *logical* precedence in the sense of providing the material basis for any form of state. It has no *historical* precedence; indeed, the principal structures of production have been, if not actually created by the state, at least encouraged and sustained by the state. Competitive capitalism required a liberal state in order to break through the shackles of mercantilism. Central planning was the creation of the bolshevik state and state corporatism of the fascist state. In historical time, production has been more shaped by the state than shaping of it. (Cox 1987: 5, emphasis added)

Cox pays little intellectual homage to Althusser, but one sees in this statement a rephrasing of Althusser's adage that the economy is determinant in the last instance (Cox's assertion of *logical* precedence) but that the last instance never comes (Cox's denial of *historical* precedence).

In extending this epistemological perspective to the social production of a *space*, the approach taken here resonates with Lefebvre's (1991) admonition that the production of space is not only social and dialectical, but also *political*. Spaces are both arenas and outcomes of politics, and it is because they so frequently are taken for granted as being "just there" that they are such fertile ground for implementing, reproducing, and

27

challenging systems of power/knowledge. Thus, any analysis of the social construction of a space must include not only a history of conflicts among the space's uses (what Lefebvre calls "spatial practices"), but also a history of how various social forces or actors have attempted to have their interests represented through constructions of the space (what Lefebvre calls "representations of space") and how the space itself has been mobilized as a representational sign and arena of social struggles (Lefebvre's "spaces of representation" or "representational space").[11] Put another way, the dialectic within the construction of a space as a space of production (the conflict between fixity-oriented and mobility-oriented "spatial practices") is complemented by struggles among those seeking to utilize the space as an arena for reproducing hierarchical structures of social organization and those who reproduce the space through actions of everyday life.

In practice, this book attempts to meet the twin goals of avoiding the pitfalls of functionalism, economism, and determinism *and* remaining sensitive to the multifaceted political conflicts that underlie the social construction of space by presenting a historical narrative that blends two continually intersecting but conceptually distinct sub-plots. On the one hand, there is a structural sub-plot of "logical precedence": each era of capitalism has a certain spatial logic that is reflected in a specific construction of the deep sea. Chapters 3, 4, and 5 – and the major sections of Chapter 2 – each are introduced with paragraphs establishing this structural context. Once the structural context is established, however, each chapter turns to a sub-plot of geo-historical contingency wherein the focus is directed to the manner by which individual seafarers, merchants, authors, artists, jurists, capitalists, policy makers, and governments have assessed their environment, gathered the resources available, and made their contributions to the construction of ocean-space. To develop an analytical framework for this second, parallel sub-plot, one must complement the discussion of spatiality – a structural concept – with a discussion of its behavioral counterpart: territoriality.

Whereas spatiality encompasses "the socially created spatial structures by which an historical system operates ... the integral spatial

---

[11] There is a rough correspondence between Lefebvre's division of social practices–representations of space–spaces of representation and my division of uses–regulations–representations. However, I generally restrict "uses" to *material* spatial practices (e.g. shipping, resource extraction) while I broaden the arena of "regulations" (roughly equivalent to Lefebvre's "representations of space") to include behavioral practices that have material repercussions (e.g. norms of territoriality).

'nature' of the system," territoriality is:

> a form of behaviour that uses [the] bounding of space for political advantage. Territoriality is about attempting to control both people and their activities within a delimited area and flows of people and their products in and out of an area. (Taylor 1991: 2)

Others have defined "territoriality" similarly:

> The attempt by an individual or group to affect, influence, or control people, phenomena, and relationships, by delimiting and asserting control over a geographic area. (Sack 1986: 19)

> A behavioral phenomenon associated with the organization of space into spheres of influence or clearly demarcated territories which are made distinctive and considered at least partially exclusive by their occupants or definers. (Soja 1971: 19)

> The process by which individual and collective social actors define, bind, reify and control space as a means toward some social end.
> (Steinberg 1994a: 3)

In his history of territoriality, Sack (1986) discusses the "tendencies" and "combinations" of territoriality implemented by three types of social groupings: "classless–primitive" societies, "pre-modern" civilizations, and "modern capitalism." While comprehensive, the number of "tendencies" and "combinations" identified by Sack makes the application of his typology somewhat unwieldy. The history of territoriality developed by Sack suggests that a simpler typology may be constructed (Table 3).

In classless–primitive societies, territoriality played only a limited role. Territoriality was used to define possession and differential rights

Table 3. *A simplified history of territoriality (after Sack 1986)*

Level of society	Primary aspects of territoriality
Classless–primitive society	Territoriality used to define possession and differentiate access
Pre-capitalist civilization	Territoriality used for above functions *and* to (re)produce hierarchy, domination, group identity, and uneven social power
Modern capitalist civilization	Territoriality used for above functions *and* to define space as "conceptually emptiable"

of access. This function became considerably more important with the origin of agriculture, as productive resources began to occur "relatively predictably and densely in space and time" (Sack 1986: 59). But these societies did not use territoriality to define who was inside or outside the community or to support hierarchical or impersonal relations within the community.

With the rise of pre-modern civilizations, territoriality took on new functions appropriate to the social structure of these societies. Territoriality began to be used by the ruling classes to define which people and resources belonged under their control and to define exactly what that relationship of control should be. Territoriality was used to create and enforce hierarchical social relations within the society. Limiting certain people's access to certain spaces came to serve as a means toward the end of reproducing social hierarchy. Territories were constructed as molds for other social relationships, not necessarily pertaining to the direct relationship between people and place. Additionally, territoriality began to be used for classification purposes: whether one lived within a society's territory and whether one controlled (owned) a portion of that territory had social implications transcending land-use and land-access issues.

The development of territoriality continued with the advent of capitalism and modernity. Already under hierarchical civilizations, territoriality occasionally had been utilized to reify impersonal bureaucratic relationships and to obscure sources of power. These uses of territoriality became more prevalent and more refined under capitalism. Most significant, though, was the way in which territoriality under capitalism became constructed in such a way as to support the concept of abstract, "emptiable" space:

> The repeated and conscious use of territory as an instrument to define, control, and mold a fluid people and dynamic events leads to a sense of abstract, emptiable space. It makes community seem to be artificial; it makes the future appear geographically as a dynamic relationship between people and events on the one hand and territorial molds on the other. And it makes space seem to be only contingently related to events . . .
>
> A modern use of territory is based most of all upon a sufficient political authority of power to match the dynamics of capitalism: to help repeatedly move, mold, and control human spatial organization at vast scales . . . Territory becomes conceptually and even actually emptiable and this presents space as both a real and emptiable surface or stage on which events occur.   (Sack 1986: 78, 87)

This modern capitalist territorial construction of space as abstract and emptiable underlies the structural spatiality of capitalism identified by the spatial dialectics theorists. The cycles of disinvestment and investment in the built environment identified by Harvey (1978, 1982) are, in effect, cycles of "emptying" and "filling" space, and are premised upon a territorial construction of space that facilitates the free movement of investments across a grid of coordinates (Johnston 1989; Steinberg 1994b; Vandergeest and Peluso 1995).[12]

The centering of this narrative around the concept of territoriality allows for a political history that steers clear of the "territorial trap," in which the world is seen as naturally divided into pre-existing, territorially defined nation-states and in which political relations at a scale larger than that of the state implicitly are defined as the sum of interactions among these territorially defined states (Agnew 1994; see also Murphy 1996; Taylor 1993, 1995). The "territorial trap" reinforces the presumed normalcy of realist geopolitics and limits the possibilities for envisioning or encouraging alternative conceptions of community, whether on a local or global scale (Shapiro 1997; Walker and Mendlovitz 1990). It also reduces extra-state spaces such as the ocean to a secondary status beyond the essential state-territories in which "society" occurs (Steinberg and McDowell 2000).

The history of marine governance presents one of the clearest pieces of evidence undermining the "territorial trap" and its liberal myth of state formation. The Dutch jurist Hugo Grotius is generally considered to have founded not only modern ocean law but modern international law with his 1608 treatise *Mare liberum* (*The Freedom of the Seas*) (Grotius 1916).[13] Yet this work appeared forty years prior to the Treaty of Westphalia (1648), which consolidated the modern political system of multiple, sovereign, territorially defined states. If global politics and law simply are the rules that emerge from anarchic interactions

---

[12] Sack himself does not explore this relationship between his theorization of the uses of territoriality under capitalism and others' theorizations of capitalist spatiality. Spatial dialectics theorists are referred to only in a footnote following the statement, "The history of territoriality is closely bound to the history of space, time, and social organization" (Sack 1986: 52).

[13] One noted international law scholar, for instance, has written, "[Grotius'] treatise achieved such an international reputation that before the end of the seventeenth century it was generally considered embodying the rules of international law and he, therefore, deserves the title 'Father of the Law of Nations,' by which he is usually styled" (Colombos 1967: 8).

among pre-defined state-actors, "international" law could not have been conceptualized prior to the formalization of the states that allegedly are the essential units of the system.

Territoriality is not an absolute variable. Social actors, including states, have varied the nature and intensity of their territorial practices over time, reflecting variation in their interests and available resources (Mann 1984; Johnston 1989). Nor is state territoriality practiced solely within state borders. A number of scholars have complemented the observation that sovereignty's ideal of absolute territorial control within state borders is never realized with a deconstruction of the myth that there is no territorial power beyond a state's designated space (Gottman 1973; Kratochwil 1986; Ruggie 1993). The very act of drawing boundaries reflects and constitutes identities and power differentials inside *and* outside the bounded area (Paasi 1996). Although not explicitly employing theories of territoriality, Thomson (1994) suggests that the development of state sovereignty within the modern state system cannot be understood without simultaneously studying the development of state authority within the non-state space of the sea. Actors have utilized various territorial mechanisms on land and at sea to manufacture specific social constructions. These social constructions have created certain spatial patternings which, during the modern era, have been linked with the logic of capitalist production, and these social considerations have conditioned further the manner in which social actors have reconstructed themselves and their environment.

Representations of ocean-space: discourse

The third pillar of the territorial political economy perspective is representation, the process by which social meaning (including the social meaning of spaces) is transmitted among individuals through literary creations, visual images, and other media. The history that follows makes frequent reference to representations in art, law, cartography, literature, public policy, and advertising. Each of these media is generated in a social context and serves as a means by which ideas are communicated and diffused throughout the general public, inscribed into the images and assumptions that guide the everyday thoughts and behaviors of individuals. The significance of representation lies in its role in the perpetuation and contestation of discourses, "frameworks . . . [that] constitute the limits within which ideas and practices are considered to be natural; that is, [that] set the bounds on what questions are considered relevant or even intelligent" (Barnes and Duncan 1992: 8). Mobilized by policy makers, discourses are used to establish "common-sense" parameters for problems and solutions (Roe 1994).

While discourses are utilized by policy makers, their reach is deeper than policy-making elites, and their truth-claims are more resilient than that of elite-generated ideologies. Unlike an ideology, a discourse does not *mis*represent the power relations underlying material reality. Rather, discourses enable, reproduce, and, perhaps most importantly, diffuse these relations throughout society. By reproducing the hegemonic discourse – something that individuals do unwittingly as they act, speak, and think within existing social conventions, definitions, and categories – individuals reproduce their own domination. Conversely, the conscious creation of alternative discourses can play a central role in the imagination, promotion, and implementation of strategies for social change (Foucault 1977; Marcuse 1969).

Because the sea so often is referred to in literary and artistic creations, there is a substantial literature on marine representation and its meaning within broader social discourse (see, for instance, Connery 1996). Interpretations of modernity's obsession with the sea have ranged from its being the embodiment of the desire of "Modern Man" to return to the womb, to His desire to deny His corporeality, to His search for new material conquests. To look at these (and other) marine representations within their social contexts, this book focuses on the emergence of marine representations within three discourses: development, geopolitics, and law.

The discourse of development is built around an absolute definition of progress, an assumption that the more developed can lead the less developed along this path to progress, and the belief that this progress can be achieved by applying scientific rationality to development "problems" (Sachs 1992; Watts 1993). The development discourse is rooted in Enlightenment concepts of science and reason: The world is knowable and individuals can shape it to serve themselves if only they utilize science to find the proper formula. It follows that both society and space are amenable to development. Space is perceived as an abstract field in which individuals can embed and redistribute social relations and structures in an attempt to better their lives. By establishing a grid (graphically expressed in the system of latitude and longitude lines), the location of every space in relation to every other space is made generalizable, a key prerequisite for scientific inquiry and the formation of scientific laws. An abstract element susceptible to manipulation (or, to use Sack's terminology, "emptying" and "filling"), space is represented as a canvas on which planners and engineers may test and apply their insights and work toward human progress (Harvey 1989; Lefebvre 1991; Smith 1990).

The modern construction of ocean-space is in some senses the antithesis of this land-space territorial construction. The sea largely has been constructed as a "non-territory," an untamable space that resists "filling" or "development." And yet, this construction of ocean-space as a "non-territory" or "other" in which rational planning *cannot* prevail also lies within the development discourse of scientific rationality and space-oriented planning. This discursive construction is possible only as a counterpoint to the paradigmatic modern construction of land-space as amenable to rational planning, and, as Said (1993) notes, antithetical counterpoints play a crucial role in producing discourses.

A second discourse frequently informing (and being reproduced by) the construction of ocean-space is the discourse of geopolitics, by which "intellectuals of statecraft 'spatialize' international politics in such a way as to present it as a 'world' characterized by particular places, peoples, and dramas" (Ó Tuathail and Agnew 1992: 192; see also Ó Tuathail 1996). In the modern era's geopolitical discourse, as in the era's development discourse, ocean-space typically is represented as a "special" space that lacks the paradigmatic attributes of "regular" space. For the development discourse, the key spatial unit is the manageable block of land that can be "filled" and "developed," and the ocean therefore is unique and an "other" because it is "undevelopable." For the geopolitical discourse, the key unit is the territorially defined state that interacts with the world's other states. As space outside state territory, the ocean is constructed within the geopolitical discourse as an empty "force-field" within which and across which states exercise their relative power over their competitors. This geopolitical counterpoint, like that of the development discourse, lies firmly within dominant ways of thinking: It reproduces the representation of space as a landscape of (developable and governable) terrestrial nation-states separated by an (undevelopable and anarchic) marine void.

A third discourse referred to here is that of law. Legal discourse theorists challenge the accepted perception of law as an autonomous set of rules and reasoning systems lying outside the structures and power relations of social life:

> Legal critics . . . insist that law . . . is not only deeply embedded in the messy and politicized contingencies of social life but [is] actually constitutive of social and political relations. (Blomley 1994: 7–8)

Like the other discourses discussed here, the legal discourse does more than operationalize and legitimize social relations. When one appeals to the legal discourse, one represents relations in a particular manner that serves to "naturalize" material reality as well as the autonomy of a seemingly distinct sphere of legal reasoning.

Critical legal geographers demonstrate how this scripting of social relations within a legal discourse serves to define places, their hierarchical order, and the scale and boundaries of social organization. The legal discourse historically has served both to reflect and construct social conceptions of space. Ideas about property and the relative mobility of privately held goods within the realm of one sovereign and among the realms of multiple sovereigns are at the foundation of legal thinking. The legal discourse plays a crucial role in reproducing the ideal of mutually exclusive sovereign nation-state territories that, taken as a whole and mapped next to each other serially across the surface of the earth, represent the rule of law and the space of society. As with the other discourses, the legal discourse implies that the sea is a "lawless," antithetical "other" lying outside the rational organization of the world, an external space to be feared, used, crossed, or conquered, but not a space *of* society.

All three of these discursive constructions – the development discourse's construction of the sea as a space devoid of potential for growth and civilization, the geopolitical discourse's construction of the sea as external to the territory of political society, and the legal discourse's construction of the sea as immune to social control and order – have been buttressed by cartographic representations of ocean-space. A map, while purportedly representing a pre-formed reality, has the effect also of *constituting* that reality, especially in places that are not encountered during the everyday lives of the map's viewers (Craib 2000; Harley 1988a, 1988b, 1989; Thongchai 1994; Turnbull 1989; Wood 1992). The unique power of maps from the era of European exploration and beyond lies not so much in their technical attributes that facilitate mapping of distant territories, but rather in the way in which techniques such as the grid (which may be found in many societies' cartographic conventions) are fused with a geometric concept of space in which all space is relative and generalizable. This allows for the societies that occupy these spaces to be represented as distant – but knowable (and conquerable) – "others" (Latour 1986; Law 1986; Mignolo 1995; Ryan 1996; Turnbull 1989).

As Said (1978, 1993) explains, the designation of a people (or a space) as an "other" implies a subtle blend of familiarity with an attitude of subordinate difference. In his writings about Europeans' representations of the peoples they encountered and dominated, Said notes that, on the one hand, the representation of a people as "foreign" names them as a "society" and thereby places their society within the dominant society's sphere of interest. On the other hand, the appellation "foreign" implies that their culture lacks some of the dominant society's paradigmatic characteristics. When combined with some justification of superiority (e.g. that one's own society is more "developed" or that one's people are superior biologically), the "foreign" designation discursively serves to construct the "foreigners" as suitable for domination. As a corollary, this definition of another people's "otherness" serves to reaffirm the identity of those doing the "othering," as the opposite of the people they are dominating. Systematic domination depends upon the construction of "contrapuntal ensembles, for it is the case that no identity can ever exist by itself and without an array of opposites, negatives, oppositions: Greeks always require barbarians, and Europeans Africans, Orientals, etc." (Said 1993: 52).

Implicit – and sometimes explicit – in Said's work is the *geographical* "othering" that underlies the representation of "other" peoples:

> Most cultural historians, and certainly all literary scholars, have failed to remark the *geographical* notation, the theoretical mapping and chart-ing of territory that underlies Western fiction, historical writing, and philosophical discourse of the time. There is first the authority of the European observer – traveller, merchant, scholar, historian, novelist. Then there is the hierarchy of spaces by which the metropolitan center and, gradually, the metropolitan economy are seen as dependent upon an overseas system of territorial control, economic exploitation, and a socio-cultural vision; without these stability and prosperity at home – "home" being a word with extremely potent resonances – would not be possible . . . The metropolis gets its authority to a considerable ex-tent from the devaluation as well as the exploitation of the outlying colonial possession.   (Said 1993: 58–59, emphasis in the original)

> What I find myself doing is really, in a certain sense, rethinking ge-ography. The emphasis on geography in *Culture and Imperialism* and

in *Orientalism* is extremely important. A kind of paradigm shift is occurring; we are perhaps now acceding to a new, invigorated sense of looking at the struggle over geography in interesting and imaginative ways. (Said 1994: 21)

The significance of marine "othering" is apparent in the history of shifts in the cartographic representation of ocean regions over the past two thousand years, from a depiction of the ocean as an indivisible whole, to the portrayal of large-area ocean basins, to the marking of continental regions defined by coastwise social interaction, and back to ocean basins. Lewis (1999) suggests that these shifts in the method of dividing the world-ocean reflect (and reproduce) differing views of the unity of the ocean's terrestrial antithesis: land-space.

While there are indeed parallels between the "othering" of people and the "othering" of space, spatial "othering" introduces new challenges. According to the Euclidian perspective, all space is, at one and the same time, unique yet comparable. Its "otherness" must therefore lie in its nature, and thus a narrative constructing a place's otherness must focus on its antithetical nature. This involves first constructing the space as empty of social processes (so that all focus may be directed to its nature, which then can be portrayed as essential to the space, and therefore constitutive of its "otherness"), and then using cartography, art, and literature to fill the space with an imaginary nature derived from the antithetical recesses of the European imagination. Ryan's (1996) description of the cartographic "othering" of Australia reveals some of the ways in which this construction of an "othered" space through designation of an "othered" nature is achieved:

> Representations of Australia as an upside-down blank are unavoidable given the founding assumptions of European cartography, and are best understood as part of the European process of "othering," whereby European self-identification can only proceed by the identification of other places and cultures as "different." This difference is produced by the creation of a semiotic *tabula rasa* and subsequently projecting upon it fantasies of difference that emerge from the European imaginative archive. Africa, Asia, and America have all been subject to this process. The maps created them as semiotic voids, which are immediately filled by exotica. So immediate is this projection that the blanks of these continents are rarely seen; what is forgotten amongst the elephants, trees, skiapods, and imaginary cities, is the fact that the creation of "Africa" or "America" was initiated by the construction of an empty space, subsequently filled. Australia in this regard is unique. It is formed as a blank and is filled occasionally by fantasy, but one

of these projections is blankness itself. Thus, Australia is semiotically "filled in" by projections of blankness – both cartographically and in explorers' aesthetic descriptions.   (Ryan 1996: 105)

As Ryan notes, the construction of Australia as a "semiotic *tabula rasa*" was achieved through frequent marine metaphors, and indeed the history of marine representation related here shows that during the same era when Ryan's explorers were applying a trope of "blankness" to Australia others were applying a similar trope to the ocean. The question of why Australia was not immediately "filled in" with imaginary nature is beyond the scope of this work. However, in the case of the ocean, it bears remembering that the ocean was being constructed not as a place *within* which social power was to be exerted (through naming, colonizing, and "filling") but rather as space *across* which power was to be projected and that therefore ideally would remain perpetually "empty." Just as modern mapping conventions have played a key role in constructing "other" alien natures and places, they have played a key role in facilitating the conceptualization of space as general and relative and therefore amenable to the projection of power across space. The portrayal of the ocean as "empty" of social relations has facilitated the trans-continental projection of power characteristic of the modern era (Latour 1986; Law 1986; Mignolo 1995; Turnbull 1989).[14]

Through the construction of distinct subordinate *places* within which power can be applied and through the construction of empty subordinate *space* across which power can be projected, modern society has developed an unprecedented ability to construct "distributions," hierarchical divisions of space into which people and social activities are placed so as to serve specific social functions (Foucault 1977). These representations have varied over time, as is detailed in the chapters that follow, but throughout modernity they have served to support and constitute a system of power/knowledge that has maintained the systematic colonization, exploitation, and domination of lands lying beyond the ocean's vast expanse.

---

[14] The modern construction of the ocean as "empty" has made it particularly difficult for planners operating under Western conventions to incorporate indigenous conceptions in which the ocean is anything but "empty" of social relations (Jackson 1995).

2   Ocean-space in non-modern societies

Beyond "freedom" vs. "enclosure"

D. P. O'Connell begins his history of the law of the sea with a paragraph typical of many works summarizing the politics of competing ocean governance systems:

> The history of the law of the sea has been dominated by a central and persistent theme: the competition between the exercise of governmental authority over the sea and the idea of the freedom of the seas . . . When one or two great commercial powers have been dominant or have achieved parity of power, the emphasis in practice has lain upon the liberty of navigation and the immunity of shipping from local control . . . When, on the other hand, great powers have been in decline or have been unable to impose their wills upon smaller states, or when an equilibrium of power has been attained between a multiplicity of states, the emphasis has lain upon the protection and reservation of maritime resources, and consequently upon the assertion of local authority over the sea.   (O'Connell 1982: 1)

O'Connell portrays the modern history of ocean governance as a seesaw between the concepts of free seas (Grotius' system of *mare liberum*) and enclosed seas (Selden's system of *mare clausum*). When there is a strong hegemon, a free seas regime prevails; when there is competition in the world polity, each state attempts to seize as much of the ocean as possible for itself. The two constructions of the sea are presented as polar opposites. The independent variable (relative strength of hegemon) determines which pole is dominant in a given era's ocean governance system.

O'Connell's characterization is factually accurate, but, like the coastal sea–deep sea and private law–public law distinctions discussed in the previous chapter, O'Connell's binary classification depends upon an ahistoric staticization of legal principles and ocean management strategies that obscures what actually has been a fluid and dynamic history. O'Connell's ahistoricism is exemplified in the final sentence of his opening paragraph:

> In the context of history, the absolute freedom of the seas was relatively short-lived, and coexistent with the naval supremacy of Great Britain. It was not formally established until the era of the suppression of the slave trade. (O'Connell 1982: 1)

The event that O'Connell identifies as heralding the institutionalization of a "free" seas regime – the suppression of the slave trade – was in fact an instance of Britain imposing its domestic legislation upon all other parties. It was a certain, historically specific "freedom of the seas" that Britain sought to institute in the nineteenth century, one that was favored only because of a number of historical, contextual aspects of nineteenth-century social organization and uses of the sea. Indeed, as Cafruny (1987) has demonstrated, Britain exercised its nineteenth-century maritime hegemony in a manner very different from that exercised by the United States in the twentieth century.

This example suggests that the binary categories of "freedom" and "enclosure" employed by most historians of modern marine governance might not be as absolute as they first appear. It also suggests that the construction of a "freedom-enclosure" dichotomy itself may lie within a specifically Western organization of space and society. To place the progression of Western ocean-space constructions in context, this history must be compared with examples from other societies, for it is only by appreciating non-Western ocean-space constructions that one may understand both the historical context and the inherent limits of the modern construction as it has developed over time.

To this end, this chapter first presents two historical examples of nonmodern ocean-space constructions, both of which differ greatly from each other and from the modern regime that followed. The construction prevailing in the Indian Ocean from approximately 500 B.C. to A.D. 1500 is discussed as an example of one in which the deep sea was a *non*-territory located entirely outside society. By contrast, the construction traditionally governing the waters of Micronesia is discussed as an instance wherein ocean-space was akin to land-space and thus subject to a high degree of social incorporation and territorial control. Following these examples, the Mediterranean construction of Greek and Roman times is used to illustrate an instance in which a limited degree of territoriality was mobilized to (re)produce hierarchy, domination, and uneven social power. This Mediterranean construction established a norm of marine stewardship that lies somewhere between the Indian Ocean and Micronesian constructions, and which has served as a foundation for modern ocean-space constructions through the present (Table 4).

The Indian Ocean: the ocean as distance

Of the three historical regions considered in this chapter, the Indian Ocean is the most diverse and least amenable to generalization. In the time period considered – roughly 500 B.C. to A.D. 1500 – and the geographical area considered – the east coast of Africa to the islands of Indonesia to the southern coast of China – there existed a broad range of societal forms. These ranged from land-based empires (e.g., China), to island-spanning empires (e.g., the Malacca Strait-based Sri Vijaya empire, from the seventh to the twelfth centuries A.D.), to numerous independent and semi-independent sultanates and city-states.[1] This variety among Indian Ocean societies notwithstanding, there is ample evidence of a coherent ocean-space construction that governed the region until disrupted by the Europeans at the end of the fifteenth century.[2]

The extent of trans-Indian Ocean trade and communication

Historians have determined that the entire Indian Ocean region had extensive sea links for thousands of years prior to the arrival of Vasco da Gama in 1498. This high level of trans-Indian Ocean trade was due in part to fortuitous geography:

> We are talking here of the tropical region where visibility is good, fogs do not exist, currents are not too strong, and the direction of the winds

---

[1] There is no consensus as to the geographical extent of the Indian Ocean, particularly its eastern limits. While the definition proposed here is more inclusive than many, the actual delineation of the boundaries of the Indian Ocean has little effect on the discussion below.
[2] Many Indian Ocean historians would extend the "pre-European" (or "pre-capitalist") era in the Indian Ocean to the early nineteenth century, arguing that during the first three centuries of European mercantilist activity the Europeans simply were the latest strong player in Indian Ocean trade, but that they were not disruptive of the overall system. Other historians, however, disagree with this assessment. For contributions to this debate – which, in turn, is linked with a number of debates concerning the origin of capitalism, the nature of mercantilism, and the role of trade in the capitalist world-system – see chapters in Bose (1990) and Chandra (1987a). To steer clear of this debate, the examples presented in this section all pre-date the arrival of state-supported European conquerors and traders, the first of whom was the Portuguese Vasco da Gama in 1498.

Table 4. *A typology of ocean-space constructions*

Non-modern society	Overall conception of ocean-space	Uses of ocean-space	Regulations of ocean-space	Representations of ocean-space	Society with analogous organization of land-space (after Sack 1986; see Chapter 1)
Indian Ocean (*circa* 500 B.C.– A.D. 1500)	Great void; separating space; space of distance to be crossed / annihilated; non-territory immune from state power	Extensively used for transporting goods long-distance, but not used intensively in everyday social life	Immune to assertions of power by land-based entities; power exerted only to ensure that ocean-space remained free for all to cross	Asocial "other" space outside society that presents opportunity for use as transport-space if one can cope with its hostile nature	------
Micronesia (throughout known history, until very recent times)	Land-like; provides essential resource of "connection" for everyday life; suitable for territorial claims and other exertions of power by states and other land-based entities;	Intensively used for transportation between islands providing resource of "connection"; space of everyday life;	Fully capable of being claimed and appropriated by land-based social units, although with customary provisions	Land-like space of distinct places (including routes), each of which offers distinct resources	Classless– primitive societies (territoriality differentiates access)

Mediterranean (circa 1000 B.C.–A.D. 500 especially Roman era (circa 300 B.C.–A.D. 500)	value of sea lies in specific resources it provides, not as abstract field for contesting social power; Placeless force-field; arena of competition among societies wherein units vie for power and control to enable stewardship but not ownership	secondarily used for extractable resources; Connection-space outside society but within the social system, used for transporting troops and goods to and from dominated lands	for free transit through areas distant from land; Not claimable, but suitable for individual societies to exert military force and access restrictions in order to express their will over other societies and prevent challenges to domination of neighboring land-space	Asocial space that resists most normal social processes and therefore is not claimable like land-space, but broadly within the social system and therefore a legitimate arena for competition among competing social units	Pre-modern civilizations (territoriality differentiates access *and* reproduces hierarchy, domination, and uneven social power)

> is regular in its alternate direction. This permits navigation by more
> fragile vessels in comparison to those which are essential for the Pacific
> or the Atlantic... Thanks to the clear skies of this region, the fishermen
> and the boatmen have known the regular movement of the stars, the
> direction of the winds, the changes of seasons.   (Verlinden 1987: 42)

As early as 3000 B.C., there was long-distance trade of heavy goods
across the western Indian Ocean, between Egypt, Arabia, and the west
coast of India. Most of this commerce apparently was conducted by
Indian traders (Nambiar 1975; Verlinden 1987). By around 300 B.C.,
Buddhist missionaries were traveling on merchant ships that regularly
plied between India and the Far East, some large enough to carry 800 passengers. By the fifth or sixth century A.D., Indian sailors had established
colonies in places as distant as Manila and possibly even the west coast
of South America. Other peoples of the Indian Ocean also were highly involved in maritime trade. Indonesian mariners were traveling throughout the eastern Indian Ocean before 1000 B.C. and were regularly traveling to the east coast of Africa by 200 B.C. Rome, too, entered the Indian
Ocean trade, being one of the main players there from about 200 B.C.
to A.D. 200. Latecomers to the Indian Ocean included the Arabs and
Persians in the west and the Chinese in the east. Both groups of traders
became heavily involved in Indian Ocean trade around the sixth or seventh centuries A.D. By the ninth century, Arab traders had traveled as
far as Korea and Japan. From the eighth to the fifteenth centuries, trade
in the eastern Indian Ocean was dominated by the Chinese (for the first
few centuries of that era in cooperation with the Indonesian–Malaysian-
based Sri Vijaya Empire), while trade in the western Indian Ocean during this later era was dominated by the Arabs (with the cooperation of
merchants from Gujarat and Calicut on the west coast of India). Thus,
when Vasco da Gama sailed into the Indian Ocean in 1498 he was entering an integrated commercial arena that had been in existence for some
1,500 to 2,000 years (Anand 1983; Hourani 1963; Nambiar 1975; Pineo
1985).

Before turning to a description and analysis of the Indian Ocean's
social construction, the relative *insignificance* of the deep sea for the societies of the region must be stressed. On the one hand, Chaudhuri (1985)
argues that the Indian Ocean provided the binding thread for a long-
standing and well-integrated pre-capitalist civilization, much as Braudel
(1972) argues for the Mediterranean in sixteenth-century Europe. Yet it
also must be noted that the Indian Ocean played a relatively minor role
in the daily workings of the majority of its social systems, making only

small contributions to the organization of political or economic power within these societies.

Paradoxically, some of the same physical geographic features that encouraged highly *extensive* trade among the Indian Ocean societies also served to discourage the *intensification* of that trade:

> The area . . . from the east coast of Africa to the Strait of Malacca was re-stricted by the annual rhythm of the monsoons. Naval domination over long distances was exceedingly difficult to maintain, as the Portuguese were to discover, and the practical impossibility of making more than one round trip a year on any long-distance sailing-route was a major obstacle to regular trade in bulk commodities . . .
>
> There can be no doubt about the seaworthiness of Indian Ocean shipping, the technical capability of the seafarers and the sophistica-tion of the merchants of the Indian Ocean before the arrival of the Portuguese. The point I want to make is that long-distance trade still remained marginal to the economies and empires round the Indian Ocean at the opening of the early modern period. The true concentra-tions of wealth and power lay not by the sea, but in the inland, by the rivers, and in those areas where a large agricultural surplus was easily available, and therefore, made possible a concentration of population and corresponding division of labour.   (Steensgaard 1987: 127–129)

While the sea was a presence in Indian Ocean social life, it was con-structed as a special space of trade, external to society and social processes.

Danger and distance: the construction of ocean-space as non-territory

Societies of the Indian Ocean viewed the sea as a source of imported goods, but the sea itself was perceived as a space apart from society, an untamable mystery. This paradoxical perspective is exemplified in the portrayal of Vishnu in Hindu folklore. Rising from the ocean, Vishnu brings forth nectar and other precious articles, but in the ocean he is a source of turmoil and strife (Chandra 1987b).

In some cases, this perspective resulted in outright fear of the sea. As the seventh-century Arabian caliph ʿUmar ibn al-Khattab instructed:

> The sea is a boundless expanse, whereon great ships look tiny specks; nought but the heavens above and waters beneath; when calm, the sailor's heart is broken; when tempestuous, his senses reel. Trust it little, fear it much. Man at sea is an insect on a splinter, now engulfed, now scared to death . . . How should I trust my people on its accursed

bosom? Remember al-ʿAlaʾ. Nay, my friend, the safety of my people
is dearer to me than all the treasures of Greece.

> (cited in Hourani 1963: 54–55)

At about the same time, talmudic scholars in Babylonia (Iraq) expressed
a similar fear of the sea when they identified four instances in which
one is required to say a prayer of thanksgiving after surviving an inor-
dinately stressful ordeal:

> There are four [classes of people] who have to offer thanksgiving: those
> who have crossed the sea, those who have traversed the wilderness,
> one who has recovered from an illness, and a prisoner who has been
> set free. (Epstein 1948: Berakoth 54b)

These reservations notwithstanding, most Indian Ocean societies did
engage the sea, but as a space to be crossed as quickly as possible so
that goods could circulate. The ocean was viewed as non-territory, a
space not suitable for control or even influence, but rather one that existed solely as a transport surface. The sea was a source of diversionary
consumer goods, but not a source of social power (Chaudhuri 1985;
Nambiar 1975). It follows from this perspective that the sea should
be rendered as invisible as possible, since any feature – political or
physical – on its vast expanse would serve only to impede the free
flow of goods. The sea was perceived not as territory but as a space
of distance, and the duty of the merchant sailor was to annihilate that
distance to the best of his[3] abilities.

If Indian Ocean merchants were to identify the space of trade, they
probably would identify not the ocean but rather the bustling ports.
Ports were especially large and busy around the Indian Ocean because
the seasonal monsoons necessitated frequent stayovers, and this led
to the emergence of ports as important transshipment, resupply, and
market centers. Tariffs generally were low, and many Asian ports had
strict rules guaranteeing equal treatment for all traders, even if they came
from a country with which the host country was at war. Host countries
often provided infrastructural support as well as standardized systems
of weights and measures, while expatriate trading communities were
permitted to establish semi-autonomous governments with authority to
adjudicate disputes so long as they did not impinge on the port state's

---

[3] In all three of the social systems discussed in this chapter the sea was almost exclusively
the preserve of men. Hence, the male pronoun is used when referring to mariners. This is
not to say that the sea – as a particularly all-male space – was not the site of intense and
complex gender construction (see Chapter 6).

national interest. Although some states, most notably China, went to great effort to ensure that all goods were purchased at the port by a state-sponsored monopoly, none attempted to control inter-state trade before goods came into port (Alexandrowicz 1967; Anand 1983; Chaudhuri 1985; Hourani 1963). Trade was an activity of the ports, and political and economic power was garnered through landward expansion and domination. The sea was merely the space across which goods came.

The aversion to sea power or possession of the sea

Since the ocean was constructed as "different" from social space, few if any attempts were made to use ocean-space for projecting power. Indian Ocean societies did not seek to claim or organize the sea as a means for generating economic wealth. Indeed, "[the policy] of combining trade with seeking to establish monopolies, and of dominating the ocean as a means to it" was uniquely European (Chandra 1987b: 26). Thus, while India established colonies throughout Indonesia, Cambodia, and Thailand, spreading Hinduism and Indian culture, "the connection between India and the 'Indianized' states of Southeast Asia was religious and cultural, but not political" (Anand 1983: 17). With no political interest in colonizing distant lands, Indian rulers saw little to gain by devoting resources to naval power (Chaudhuri 1985). Indeed, the demilitarized character of the Indian Ocean facilitated Portuguese conquests and monopolistic control of trade routes there in the sixteenth century. Because sea battles had been a rarity in the Indian Ocean, transpiring only occasionally and then as extensions of land-based military encounters, regional rulers were unprepared when the Portuguese engaged their ships at sea (Anand 1983; Braudel 1984).

Similarly, while China had been facilitating trade by merchants from around the Indian Ocean in entrepôts such as Canton (Guangzhou) from the fifth or sixth century A.D., if not earlier, it did not establish a standing navy until the twelfth century. At this point, China began projecting power overseas to construct formal tributary relations with lands extending from Java to southern Sumatra. However, China made a sharp distinction between the waters around these territories – the Eastern Sea – and the waters of the Indian Ocean west of Sumatra – the Western Sea. The Chinese even used different words for "sea" when referring to the two bodies of water. The Chinese word for "sea" in the place-name "Western Sea" (but not in "Eastern Sea") literally means "sea-route." The word implies not a discrete place or set of places but rather a placeless void, a connecting space across which merchants from distant, sovereign lands travel to exchange their wares. These distant lands across the "Western Sea-Route," while formally making token tribute payments, generally were perceived by the Chinese as equals, in sharp distinction to the subservient foreign lands within the inner "Eastern Sea" (Ray 1987).

China's lack of interest in achieving political domination through the projection of naval power is most clear in its decision not to seek a trans-oceanic empire when, in the mid-fifteenth century, such an empire seemingly was within its grasp. In 1405, China sent an armada of sixty-three warships with 27,870 men as far west as the southwest coast of India (Calicut). Over the next twenty-five years, six more expeditions were launched, some venturing as far as Aden and the east coast of Africa (Levathes 1994). Yet the Chinese chose not to capitalize upon this naval supremacy. China established relations of political fealty and economic tribute with its land-bordered neighbors and with the islands of the Eastern Sea, but it treated the conquered lands across the Western Sea as amicable trading partners.

Historians debate whether China's withdrawal from these trans-oceanic military adventures was due to their economic cost (Chaudhuri 1985) or domestic political considerations (Ray 1987); however, these two explanations are linked. The armadas were extremely expensive, and continued domination of distant overseas colonies would have proved even more costly. Such a military investment could be made to pay for itself only through formation of exclusive (and exploitative) trade relationships that would mirror the political–military relationships. But establishment of exclusive trading relationships across the ocean would require at least a partial claim of authority in the ocean itself (and a burden to enforce that claim). Although it may have had the capacity to exercise this authority in the sea, there is no evidence that China ever considered claiming such rights. To quote Chandra once again, "[the policy] of combining trade with seeking to establish monopolies, and of dominating the ocean as a means to it" was a uniquely European project (Chandra 1987b: 26).

The distinction between European and Indian Ocean attitudes toward possession of the sea was summed up by the ruler of Macassar, when opposing Dutch attempts in the early seventeenth century to monopolize trade with the Spice Islands: "God has made the earth and the sea, has divided the earth among mankind and given the sea in common. It is a thing unheard of that anyone should be forbidden to sail the seas" (cited in Anand 1983: 83). Or, as Chaudhuri explains, "The reason for this failure to exploit the sea for trade and empire is not easily found unless we remember that the Spanish and Portuguese claims to the exclusive domination of the Atlantic and the Indian Ocean were as unique as the new geographical discoveries" (Chaudhuri 1985: 14–15).

The ocean as "other"/ the sailor as outcast

Following from this conception of the sea as an ungovernable, undifferentiated void to be crossed as one travels from one place to another, the societies of the Indian Ocean constructed the sea in a manner similar to their construction of the desert. Indeed, in Arabic the same verb is used for "riding" a ship and "riding" a camel (Hourani 1963). The sea was merely distance and not a *place*, and therefore social rules were not needed for the sea itself (although they were needed for social life on board ships, as is discussed below). Thus, as in the Arabian desert, there was a widespread practice of raiding and piracy. While strong states with an interest in high levels of trade made efforts to control piracy on the approach routes to their harbors, pirates remained an ever-present danger on the open sea (Anand 1983; Chaudhuri 1985; Howarth 1977).

The construction of the ocean as a shapeless void also is evidenced in the cartography of the era. Portuguese sailors arriving in the Indian Ocean found that Indian and Arab navigators were using nautical charts of a sort. Landmarks along the coastline were meticulously drawn on the charts, to aid the navigator in making landfall. But the ocean itself – an abstract space to be crossed – was not drawn to scale (Arunchalam 1987).

Ironically, while the sea generally was conceived within Indian Ocean societies (and even within the formal science of navigation) as an abstract, formless space, the navigational techniques utilized by Indian Ocean sailors were informed by a conception of the sea as a highly differentiated space of discrete places:

> Ibn Majid [Vasco da Gama's guide] was [not] a scientific navigator: he was a man of experience in those seas and he knew things the Portuguese did not know – the set of currents, the behaviour of the wind, the colour of the sea, how much northing he must make to clear the dangers of Seychelles, how high in the sky the pole star should be before he ran east for Calicut.   (Howarth 1977: 126)

The construction of the ocean held by Indian Ocean navigators is further elucidated by Ibn Majid, as he discusses the skills of his predecessors:

> In describing the Boddhisattva as a perfect pilot, [the Jatakamala of Arya Sura (first century A.D.)] states, he "possessed every quality

49

> desired in such a one. Knowing the course of the celestial luminar-
> ies he was never at a loss with respect to the regions of the ship, being
> perfectly acquainted with the different prognostics, the permanent, the
> occasional and the miraculous ones, he was skilled in the establishment
> of a given time as proper or improper, by means of manifold marks,
> observing the fishes, the colour of the water, the species of the ground
> birds, rocks etc. he knew how to ascertain rightly the parts of the sea."
>
> (Majid al-Sadi 1971: 1–2)

In Micronesia, as discussed below, navigators possessed a similar "sense of place." However, while the Micronesian navigator, with his expert knowledge of the surface that provided so many of society's critical resources, was accorded high social status, the Indian Ocean navigator was not so honored. As we have seen, the ocean was peripheral to the individual societies of the Indian Ocean; the sea was a necessary space to be crossed, but mastery of its intricacies was not a route to wealth and status. Navigators were respected as curious experts who could interface between society and the capricious "other" of the sea, but generally they were not granted much status in their society's social hierarchy (Chaudhuri 1985; Hourani 1963). The sea and the sailors who crossed the sea served important functions *for* land-based society, but, at least while at sea, they were not constructed as being *of* society.

The Code of Malacca

The Code of Malacca, adopted by the Kingdom of Malacca in the late thirteenth century, is perhaps the most complete statement of Indian Ocean law surviving from pre-European times.[4] Similar codes were adopted throughout the region in that era, with many specific provisions borrowed from Indian law. The code is not a law of the sea; it is a work of maritime law, a law of ships and shipping. Nevertheless, the code reveals much about the status of ocean-space in the societies bordering the Indian Ocean.[5]

The code presents a strong concept of the high seas:

> The reading of these codes brings to our attention the peculiar position
> of a ship on the high seas beyond the reach of any territorial jurisdic-
> tion. She is treated by maritime custom as a piece of quasi-territory
> sailing in the legally undefined vastness of the sea, which is beyond

---

[4] The analysis here is based upon the 1879 translation by Sir Stanford Raffles.
[5] As has been noted in Chapter 1, the very distinction between maritime law and the law of the sea presupposes a perspective where the sea is a placeless void and the ship is the "territory" of seaborne society.

> any Sovereign's control except for the captain's powers on board ship
> determined by her "nationality." (Alexandrowicz 1967: 64)

Since the ocean is non-territory and has no social system binding its governance, jurisdiction reverts to the ship, which, in turn, is treated as a territorial annex of its home state.

The bulk of the code spells out a civil regime for governing the ship as state-like territory. Explicit analogies liken the ship to a kind of floating state:

> It is the law, that in all *Prahus* [ships] of every description the *Nakhoda* [captain] shall be as the Raja. That the *Juromudi* or Steer-man shall be as the *Bendahara*, or Prime Minister; and the *Jurobatus* [foreman of crew] as *Tememggong* or chief Peace officer; and it shall be the duty of those to superintend every one, and to negotiate right and wrong within the *Prahu*. (Raffles 1879: 65)

Further duties of men on board are spelled out, as are rights and obligations in case of shipwreck, encounter with hostile vessels, and so on. Much of the code is devoted to listing crimes that might be committed aboard the *Prahu* and the penalties that these offenses merit (these center around ship-specific crimes such as mutiny, since most other crimes are to be treated according to the laws of the *Prahu*'s home state).

Strikingly absent from the code is an extended discussion of the sea itself or of the relationship between ship and sea. To the twenty-first-century scholar, for instance, it appears that practically the entire code could be applied without revision if a society guided by the ethics of thirteenth-century Islam were to launch a spaceship. In fact, this omission of ocean-specific laws appears quite logical once one accepts the Indian Ocean construction of the sea as a vast, formless non-territory existing solely as a space of distance between places. As in modern maritime law, the territory to be governed is the ship, and the universe is one of ships on the ocean. The ocean environment itself is significant only as a source of danger, a grid of relative locations, and a materialization of distance.

There is one section dealing with the ship–ocean relationship: the section discussing the role of the *Malim* (navigator) (Raffles 1879: 67). The discussion of the *Malim*'s duties is conspicuously separated from the section delineating positions and responsibilities of other crew members. While these other crew members have positions analogous to roles they might have in land-based society, the *Malim* has an all together different job. The *Malim* is the one member of the crew who interfaces between the society on the boat and the "other" of the ocean, the void through which the boat is traveling. The *Malim* is given almost absolute authority on board: The *Nakhoda* (captain) must follow his recommendations and relay his instructions to the crew. The *Nakhoda* may be "as the Raja," but in the hostile marine environment, the Raja has a responsibility to listen to, and obey, the one man on board who can interpret that environment.

With this authority comes awesome responsibility: "If the *Malim* forgets the course he is to steer, and through his ignorance, the *Prahu* is wrecked, he shall suffer death; for such is the Law" (Raffles 1879: 67). By contrast, no other crew member faces nearly so severe a punishment for dereliction of duties. Additionally, "If every thing is not at sea as the *Malim* wishes it, and the sails are taken aback let him, on his return to Port, give alms to the poor, as an acknowledgement for his escape" (Raffles 1879: 67). The ocean is an inherently dangerous environment, and a safe return from an imperfectly executed voyage occurs only by the grace of Allah, and appropriate thanks are required.

In summary, in Malacca and throughout the Indian Ocean, the sea was viewed as a vast and dangerous expanse across which ships traveled to transport goods. The ocean was not perceived as a territory in the sense that a territory may be bounded, differentiated, and governed. Societies – or social space – clearly ended at the coastal waters (with an exception made for the ships themselves when they were on the high seas), and so the sea could not be conceived of as a space for exercising imperial domination. The ocean was perceived as distance, not territory.

Micronesia: the ocean as road map

The societies of Micronesia,[6] unlike those of the Indian Ocean, traditionally have constructed the ocean as territory. For the Micronesians,

---

[6] Micronesia generally is defined as consisting of four island groups – the Caroline, Mariana, Marshall, and Gilbert Islands – and the isolated island of Nauru. Because of their separate recent histories, however, contemporary accounts tend to omit the Gilbert Islands (presently one component of the Republic of Kiribati) and Nauru. The remaining portions of Micronesia – the Marshalls, Carolines, and Marianas – all have a history of administration by the United States. Presently, these three island groups are divided into three independent republics – the Republic of the Marshall Islands, the Republic of Palau, and the Federated States of Micronesia – and two US possessions – the Commonwealth of the Northern Mariana Islands, and the Unincorporated Territory of Guam. Together, the three island groups span a portion of ocean-space approximately the size of the continental United States, but with a land-area of just over 900 square miles (2,330 square kilometers) (Leibowitz 1989).

the ocean is[7] seen primarily as a resource provider, divided into distinct places, much as continental residents view their land-space. The sea provides food, transportation, communication, and even shelter during extreme storms when island homes must be evacuated:

> Nearly every aspect of life in Micronesia is significantly influenced or controlled by the sea . . . Though essential, the land is tiny and relatively barren. It provides people with protection from the elements and a place to eat and sleep in comfort. But the real focus of life is on the sea. The sea provides food and tools and the medium to transport an islander from one cluster of humanity to another. As compared to the power and moods of the sea, the land is insignificant, humble, dull. The rhythm of life is dictated by the sea.
> (Nakayama and Ramp 1974: 102–103)

> Micronesians are a people of the shoreline. Even on high islands with roomy interiors, like Truk, Kosrae, and Ponape, the villages tend to cluster along the water . . . They like the ready access to those salty pastures of reef, and proximity to that ocean highway their ancestors traveled here.
> (Brower 1981: 17)

While Indian Ocean societies constructed the ocean as a featureless space of distance, for Micronesians the sea is anything but "empty" (Jackson 1995).

Navigation along the "ocean highways"

Brower's reference to an "ocean highway" in the above quotation is particularly apt, for the ocean plays a crucial role as connecting-space in Micronesian society. "For tobacco, or for sea turtles, or just to see new faces, the small-islanders throughout history have had to jump in their canoes and set off" (Brower 1981: 29). Gladwin's (1970) description of the Micronesian attitude toward the canoe resonates with the American attitude toward the automobile. Two-to-three-week island-hopping trips covering hundreds of miles of ocean-space are common. Islands have excess canoes, so one will always be available. Groups of men often make journeys on the flimsiest of pretexts; often the actual reason seems a desire to "hit the road." Expert navigators are revered as relaxed and self-assured folk heroes who calmly – yet intently – utilize their expert knowledge to do what needs to be done,

---

[7] Unlike the other two ocean management models discussed here, elements of the Micronesian system continue, especially on the smaller islands of the region. Hence, the Micronesian model is discussed in the present tense.

an image more akin to a modern truck driver or commercial airplane pilot than the Magellans or Columbuses of Western marine navigation folklore.

Crucial to an understanding of the Micronesian perspective on the sea is an understanding of their dead reckoning navigation system in which one constantly monitors the direction and distance traveled from the last known point in ocean-space. An entire spatial perspective on the ocean and on the relationship between ocean-space and land-space is associated with the dead reckoning system. Like the Western highway traveler, the Micronesian navigator notes previous routes traveled, present points of reference, and future landmarks ahead. He uses a comprehensive set of directions and routes memorized since childhood. He might, for instance, know that his destination island lies under Star A. Because of the specific ocean currents prevailing at this time of the year, he should aim for Star B. However, if, when Star C is at a certain point in the sky, he sees a reef on his right and he feels a leeward ocean current on his boat,[8] he will know that he has drifted off course and that he should aim for Star D to compensate. But as long as he is over the reef, he may want to drop a line, because this "rest area" is known to be particularly abundant in a prized variety of fish.

The Micronesian conception of ocean-space, in short, is rife with a "sense of place." Since the primary resource provided by the deep sea is "connection," the primary "places" that are "sensed" are routes. Again, an analogy can be made with the Western highway traveler who sees a landscape of roads and landmarks that, while serving the purpose of connecting two points, also are places themselves.

This conception differs markedly from the Western conception of ocean-space. The classic image of a Western marine navigator is one who voyages across a vast and formless plane to get from Point A to Point B. Hence, the Western navigation system is based upon finding one's coordinates on an abstract grid whose utility lies in the fact that it is entirely *devoid* of place-specificity. The navigator, in the Western cognitive-navigational system, constructs himself in a "non-place," a space above the ocean from which he maintains an all-knowing gaze over the ocean beneath him (Hutchins 1995).

After extensive interviews with navigators on the tiny Micronesian island of Puluwat, Gladwin described the Micronesian conception of

---

[8] Micronesian navigators feel ocean currents, natural phenomena rarely noticed and never used by Western navigators (Gladwin 1970).

ocean-space as follows:

> What lies beyond [Puluwat] is a world of little islands, some inhabited and some not, but each with its own special shape and nature, and each in its own assigned place upon the vast surface of the sea. As one thinks of these islands, one over there, another there to the north, a third over here closer, Truk rising high from the sea off in the east, and many more among and beyond these, with reefs trenched between, the sea itself is transformed. No longer is it simply a great body of water which, encountering Puluwat, shoves around it and reforms on the other side to flow on to an empty eternity. Instead the ocean becomes a thoroughfare over which one can think of oneself moving, other islands left behind to right and left, toward a particular island of destination which as one comes up upon it will be waiting, as it always waits, right where it is supposed to be. When a Puluwatan speaks of the ocean the words he uses refer not to an amorphous expanse of water but rather to the assemblage of seaways which lie between the various islands. Together these seaways constitute the ocean he knows and understands. Seen in this way Puluwat ceases to be a solitary spot of dry land; it takes its place in a familiar constellation of islands linked together by pathways on the ocean . . .
>
> The Puluwatan pictures himself and his island in his part of the ocean much as we might locate ourselves upon a road map. On a road map places, mostly communities, appear as locations with names, linked by lines of travel. (Gladwin 1970: 33–34)

For the Micronesian, every rock, every reef, is a significant "road sign" on the highways of the sea.

The parallels between the modern conception of the highway and the Micronesian conception of the ocean-route are extensive. Both the Western highway and the Micronesian ocean provide the crucial everyday resource of connection. Each highway and each ocean-route is constructed as a "place" in its own right, even though its ostensible function is to connect other places. Micronesians see the world as a web of ocean pathways, connecting places and eventually connecting the whole world, so that distant places are referenced based on their location in this great web. A similar conception of the terrestrial highway is revealed in Jack Kerouac's 1955 novel *On the Road*:

> We flashed past the mysterious white signs in the night somewhere in New Jersey that say SOUTH (with an arrow) and WEST (with an arrow) and took the south one. New Orleans! It burned in our brains . . .

> Yes! You and I, Sal, we'd dig the whole world with a car like this because, man, the road must eventually lead to the whole world. Ain't nowhere else it can go – right? . . .
>
> The road is life. (Kerouac 1976: 134, 230, 211)

A reversal of elements occurs between the Micronesian navigators and Kerouac's itinerant travelers. For the Micronesians, land appears at the end of place-specific water-routes. For Kerouac, shapeless water and generic port cities lie at the end of place-specific land-routes:

> I stopped, frozen with ecstasy on the sidewalk. I looked down [San Francisco's] Market Street. I didn't know whether it was that or Canal Street in New Orleans: it led to water, ambiguous, universal water, just as 42nd Street, New York, leads to water, and you never know where you are. (Kerouac 1976: 172)

For the Micronesians as for Kerouac, everyday life is characterized by movement, and so connecting-space is the space that matters. Destination places and their characteristic element (water for Kerouac, land for the Micronesians) are merely incidental.[9]

When one perceives oneself as totally immersed in the landmark-differentiated channels of one's environment, one's entire perspective on movement changes. Abstract movement through abstract space ceases to be the focus of one's attentions; rather one focuses on the places that mark – and constitute – the channels of movement. Gladwin, during his investigations on Puluwat, remained baffled by the local navigation system until he grasped the mental framework within which navigators operate: the canoe is represented as fixed in space while the islands, the stars, and the sea itself pass by in the reverse direction. Kerouac's Sal Paradise, in a passage that – interestingly – relies on marine metaphors, evokes a similar mental construct to describe navigation through twentieth-century road-space:

> As a seaman I used to think of the waves rushing beneath the shell of the ship and the bottomless deeps thereunder – now I could feel the road some twenty inches beneath me, unfurling and flying and hissing at incredible speeds across the groaning continent with that mad Ahab at the wheel. When I closed my eyes all I could see was the road unwinding into me. When I opened them I saw flashing shadows of trees vibrating on the floor of the car. (Kerouac 1976: 234)

[9] Women in Micronesia, like the women in *On the Road*, predominantly are home-bound. They probably would have a very different interpretation of the significance of the destination points that constitute their "homes" vis-à-vis the spaces of connection that men use to assert a masculine identity (Cresswell 1996; McDowell 1996).

Kerouac's reference to the ocean notwithstanding, the modern Western perception and representation of the ocean generally has differed sharply from that of the Micronesians (or from that of Westerners toward the road). Particularly striking in contrast is how Western explorers, statespersons, and planners have viewed the very same islands and oceans that are traversed by the Micronesian navigators. From the Western perspective the landmarks on the seascape that provide the basis for Micronesian navigation are nuisance barriers on an otherwise uniform surface that must be crossed and obliterated as one makes one's voyage. Discussing sixteenth-century Spaniards who explored the area, Hezel writes:

> And what of those tiny islands that so often happened to lie in the path of the early Spanish captains? Barbudos, Arrecifes, San Bartolomé, Los Reyes, Matelotes – all found their way onto Spanish sea charts and were promptly forgotten. They had no spices or gold to attract the interest of the Spanish, and the souls that there may have been to convert to the true faith were few indeed. The Spanish shipping lane lay at about thirteen degrees north latitude, too high for vessels to happen on any of the Carolines or Marshalls. These islands, with their treacherous shoals and reefs, came to be regarded as nothing more than navigational hazards that were best avoided.   (Hezel 1983: 34)

Four hundred years later, American military planners found these islands to be worthy of attention, but they still were conceived of as nonplaces – "nothing but sandspits . . . of very little economic value" and "spots on that great ocean surface," according to General Eisenhower (cited in Leibowitz 1989: 487). These placeless landforms were of concern only because they ruined the perceived uniformity of the vast sea that separated West from East and upon whose formlessness military plans were dependent. As in Indian Ocean societies, contemporary military planners have perceived the ocean as a placeless void of distance, and so the role of naval forces has been to facilitate the annihilation of that distance by troop- carrying ships and the merchant marine. As such, the islands of Micronesia, during World War II, had to be "reduced or bypassed and rendered innocuous by air and naval attack" and, in the postwar era, they had to be controlled by the United States so that no other state could utilize the islands as strategic barriers preventing free transit between economically significant "places" (Austin 1985: 481).

The territorial delineation of ocean-space

Just as the Micronesian conception of ocean-space differs sharply from that of the West, so too does Micronesian ocean territoriality. On land, Micronesian societies use territoriality extensively to affirm membership in society and, on the larger islands, to signify and reproduce hierarchy within society.[10] Yet historically the Micronesians have not viewed territory on land as a good in itself. Eighteenth-century English soldiers who assisted one chief on Palau in a battle against his rival were surprised to find that their ally made no effort to seize territory in the aftermath of his complete rout of the enemy (Hezel 1983).

Since the ocean, like land, is viewed as a set of places containing specific resources, it follows that the ocean, like land in Micronesian society, is subject to "ownership" so long as it serves a purpose. There is no Micronesian concept of a high seas zone beyond possession. The area of ocean-space "owned" by one island extends until it borders the ocean-space of another island. At the same time, however, as on land, abstract possession is not a goal and territory is valued only for its functionality. Claims to specific fishing grounds are abandoned when, because of exhaustion of resources or discovery of more attractive alternatives, this territory is perceived as no longer being a significant resource provider (Gladwin 1970).

Additionally, because territoriality is driven by function, the exclusivity of resource-use rights associated with ocean ownership is variable. Exclusive transit rights in particular fade quickly as one ventures outward from inhabited islands. While the seas are "owned," exclusive usage restrictions are developed only in instances in which user conflicts are deemed likely to occur. Since use of the ocean's "connection" resource does not lessen its value for others (and since it would be difficult to use territorial means to restrict access to the hundreds of known

---

[10] There is, of course, considerable variation in the traditional societies spread out over such a large area. In general, the smaller islands and atolls traditionally have had fairly egalitarian clan-based matrilineal systems, in which producer goods (e.g., tools and boats), land, and consumables (e.g., fish) are controlled by the household, clan, or voluntary association. The larger Caroline Islands, as well as the Marshalls, more often are likely to have had a feudal hierarchy of chiefs who controlled all land and other property (including women) and distributed them at their own discretion to commoners (Hezel 1983).

On small and large islands alike, land was (and remains) a precious good, generally inalienable to outsiders. "Land is the rarest of commodities in Micronesia, and its ownership is at the heart of Micronesia's lineage and ranking systems. It is nearly impossible to alienate land in the islands, as numerous foreign administrators have found out. Land is owned by lineage, clan, or municipality and it is difficult to get it away from them" (Brower 1981: 21).

transit channels among Micronesian islands anyway), access to transit resources has been regulated not through direct territorial restrictions but rather through an elaborate system by which navigational knowledge is privatized and kept secret among the navigator elite (Gladwin 1970; Nakayama and Ramp 1974). By restricting access to knowledge, the Micronesians restrict not only one's ability to utilize ocean resources but even one's ability to recognize the ocean's "places."[11]

Micronesia and sea power

Some Micronesian islands historically had tributary relations with each other, and to this extent the ocean was a space across which power was projected. Yet, with Micronesia's low population density, vast distances, and numerous uninhabited islands, these relationships tended not to play a major role in island economies or island life. For instance, in the Yap empire, the most extensively documented of Micronesian multi-island empires, every two to three years a fleet of canoes would visit the empire's outer islands, collecting tribute for the nobility on Yap. The empire, however, played a relatively minor role in the day-to-day lives of outer-island inhabitants and the resource extraction largely was symbolic. The empire existed less as a means for dominating and extracting wealth from the outer islands and more as a mutual-aid system of contact and communications mobilized during emergencies such as typhoons and droughts (Gorenflo 1993).

Not only have the Micronesians traditionally eschewed using the ocean for projecting power to distant islands, but they also – like the peoples of the Indian Ocean – failed to develop the concept of the sea battle. The nineteenth-century Russian explorer Kotzebue attempted to aid one Marshall Island chief in his attack against another chief by providing him with grappling hooks and lances, under the impression that the battles were to take place at sea. Upon his return eight years later, Kotzebue found that the chief had ignored the marine warfare tools, but he had adapted Kotzebue's hatchets to land battle by tying them to poles (Hezel 1983).

To conclude, the Micronesians, in contrast to the peoples of the Indian Ocean, view the deep sea as territory. The ocean is seen as a resource-providing space, characterized by numerous specific places.

---

[11] This construction of territoriality as embedded within rules limiting access to knowledge is consistent with Sack's point that territorial restrictions generally are effective only when implemented in concert with non-territorial regulations (Sack 1986: 16).

The primary resource provided by this space is "connection," and therefore the "places" of the ocean are routes, much like in a modern highway system. Micronesians have not had the capacity to restrict physical access to this "connection-space," but they have been able to restrict knowledge of its secrets, and through this mechanism they have implemented a territorial regime akin to that identified by Sack as typical of "classless–primitive societies."

The contrast with Indian Ocean societies is extreme. The Indian Ocean societies viewed the ocean as a special trading space *outside* society and therefore immune to societal, land-like territorial control. In contrast, for the Micronesians the sea *is* the space of society. The Micronesians govern the sea much as they govern land: as a set of discrete places to be demarcated and controlled according to the general organizing principles of territoriality in Micronesian society.

The Mediterranean Sea: the ocean as space of stewardship

The Mediterranean frequently is hailed by Western scholars as the birthplace of modern Europe. Its political systems, including its norms for governing ocean-space, have attracted the attention of countless legal and political historians as well as classical scholars. Semple, for instance, identifies the heritage of 4,500 years of navigation in the Mediterranean by Phoenician, Greek, and Roman seamen as one of the key bases for the rise of the Renaissance-era Italian city-states and, ultimately, European world-dominance in the modern era (Semple 1931). Grotius' *Mare Liberum*, generally considered the first work of modern international law, relies heavily on Roman marine law and on statements made by Roman jurists, leading one early twentieth-century legal scholar to proclaim, "We should hardly err in terming [the Roman law of the sea and the Mediterranean antecedents on which it was based] the earliest international law" (Lobingier 1935: 32).

Despite near-universal agreement on the significance of Roman sea law, scholars and lawmakers disagree on the substantive content of the Roman legacy.[12] Some, noting Rome's behavior in the Mediterranean, credit Rome with bestowing to modern Europe the principle of freedom of the high seas (Fenn 1925; Gormley 1963; Grotius 1916). Anand (1983)

---

[12] While this analysis covers various pre-Roman Mediterranean powers, the policies of Rome are by far the best documented, and therefore much of this study focuses on the Roman Empire, although some attention is given to its antecedents.

goes so far as to equate the Roman Mediterranean with the extreme high seas norm of the Indian Ocean, and he notes that the two constructions historically were linked as well. He argues that it was only after the fall of the Roman Empire, after which there was a sharp decline in maritime trade between Europe and Asia, that a unique ocean-space construction not founded on high seas principles developed in the Mediterranean.

In contrast to these scholars, others point to Rome's Mediterranean policy as an early example of a state enclosing a large body of water and proclaiming it as national territory (Mollat du Jourdin 1993; Semple 1911, 1931). Indeed, Mussolini referred to the ancient Roman Empire's claims to what it called *Mare Nostrum* ("our sea") as justification for including the Mediterranean as integral territory within *his* Roman Empire (Gambi 1994; Mack Smith 1976, 1982).

A close look at the behavior of Rome and earlier civilizations in the Mediterranean reveals that neither interpretation is entirely correct. While Mediterranean societies did not construct ocean-space as a claimable set of places or as an extension of land (the Micronesian model), neither did they construct ocean-space as an extra-social space immune from state power (the Indian Ocean model). Rather, the peoples of the Mediterranean constructed the sea as a non-possessible space, but one in which and across which state power legitimately could be asserted in the interest of stewarding its bounty. State power routinely was mobilized to manage, conserve, or hoard its resources (including the ephemeral resource of "connection") and to bind peripheral lands to the metropole, but it never was extended to imply actual possession of the sea as land-like territory.

Physical geography and the domination of ocean-space

Practically every student of Mediterranean history notes that at some point – whether before, during, or after Roman times – the Mediterranean gave birth to the principle that distant portions of the sea could in some manner and to some degree be claimed as the exclusive domain of a land-based state. Semple (1931), citing evidence provided by Thucydides, traces the origin of this Mediterranean ocean-space construction back to Minoan Crete (*circa* 2000 B.C.). Minoan Crete was, according to Semple, a thalassocracy – a regime based upon maritime supremacy. Beyond this era, she notes:

> The Greek excluded the Phoenician from the Aegean and made it an Hellenic sea. Carthage and Tarentum tried to draw the dead line for

> Roman merchantmen at the Lacinian Cape, the doorway into the Ionian
> Sea, and thereby involved themselves in the famous Punic Wars. The
> whole Mediterranean became a Roman sea, the *Mare Nostrum*.
>
> (Semple 1911: 314)

Others have noted that "[during the Greek era] we observe the first
stirrings of territorial aspirations in the law of the sea" (Gold 1981: 7)
and that "there is . . . little doubt that almost all the states in antiquity
claimed a certain amount of sovereignty over the sea" (Gold 1981: 9).
Athens, Venice, Genoa, Marseille, and Barcelona all have been termed
"thalassocracies" (Mollat du Jourdin 1993: 28). According to Semple,
this European tendency toward domination of the sea failed to extend
further with the rise of European world-dominance only because of the
immense size of the world-ocean (Semple 1911).

While Mollat du Jourdin (1993: 28) argues that this tendency toward
domination of the ocean is "natural" and hence might be expected wher-
ever people set sail, the preceding review of other societies' ocean-space
constructions suggests that this is not the case. Semple argues that the
tendency among Mediterranean nations to dominate the ocean has its
roots in the region's particular physical geography. She notes that the
Mediterranean consists of numerous gulfs and basins, as well as narrow
straits of entrance and egress, and that "these choice sites as bases for
control, reinforced by the small area of the sub-basin, early gave rise to
the political idea of the *mare clausum* or monopolized sea, over which
exclusive trading rights were exercised by a single state" (Semple 1931:
63). Semple continues by explaining how this phenomenon of extensive
maritime traffic being channeled into narrow trade routes, coupled with
the Mediterranean's numerous coves, provided an ideal environment
for pirates. The prevalence of piracy further encouraged coastal societies
to implement territorial control of the sea as a means toward guaranteeing safety for maritime traffic (Semple 1931; see also Chaudhuri 1985).

The limits of ocean enclosure

Although compelling, Semple's thesis falls short on a number of counts.
Semple omits from her narrative several pieces of evidence, known already in her time, that contradict the claim that Rome (or previous states
in the region) exerted a territorial claim to the Mediterranean. Foremost
is Rome's reliance on the Rhodian Code (developed *circa* 900 B.C. by
the Greek island-state of Rhodes, then a major trading center), which
mandates freedom of the sea, as well as various well-known statements

by Roman statesmen affirming Rome's position that the sea belongs to all (Lobingier 1935). Additionally, she fails to consider evidence indicating that Rome and also many Greek states, including Athens, generally practiced a policy of encouraging free trade. They implemented simplified, "trader-friendly" port regulations, low tariffs, and customs clearing procedures more akin to the Indian Ocean regime of the time than to that of the European mercantilist empires of the early modern era with which Semple equates the Roman regime (Fenn 1925; Gormley 1963; Lobingier 1935; Phillipson 1911).[13]

Semple notes that not only the Mediterranean's numerous coves, but also its climate and topography, favored frequent, albeit seasonal, navigation:

> The long summer of cloudless days and starry nights, of steady winds and fogless atmosphere provided a favorable season for sailing, when the strong diurnal breezes favored the out-going and home-coming ships, and the countless promontories and mountainous islands, visible in the lucid air, furnished points to steer by before the invention of the compass . . .
>
> The entire sailing season, when the northeast trade winds prevailed, lasted from March 10th to November 10th. During this period merchant ships might venture out for the sake of profit; but war vessels with their precious cargo of human lives were restricted to the sailing season *par excellence* between May 26th and September 14th . . . Winter voyages were made rarely and only under stress of circumstances.
>
> (Semple 1931: 579–580)

She goes on to note that the vast majority of voyages hugged the coast, rarely venturing into the center of the sea. Others confirm that, due to primitive shipbuilding and navigational technologies as well as climatic considerations, long-distance travel in the Mediterranean was basically a coastal affair (Stevens and Westcott 1942).[14]

In other words, physical geographic conditions in the Mediterranean bear a strong resemblance to those found in the Indian Ocean. There,

---

[13] Semple does note that several of the Greek states adopted free trade policies, but she does not use this evidence to reassess her identification of a Mediterranean–European tendency toward the enclosure of ocean-space and the monopolization of trade.

[14] As is discussed in Chapter 3, Mediterranean maritime societies continued their aversion to long-distance voyages into the modern era. "Even in the seventeenth century seamen kept as close to the coast as possible. Tomé Cano, whose book appeared in Seville in 1611, says of the Italians: 'They are not sailors of the high seas.' To Mediterranean sailors, who went from one seaport tavern to the next, taking the plunge meant at most going from Rhodes to Alexandria (four days in the open sea, out of sight of land, if all went well)" (Braudel 1981: 409; see also Pryor 1988).

as we have seen, climatic conditions also made travel frequent and relatively easy during certain seasons, but dangerous if not impossible during the rest of the year. As has been discussed, territorial claims to the Indian Ocean necessarily were limited, for one would be unable to occupy one's "territory" for half the year, and even during the sailing seasons the deep sea was avoided where possible as sailors favored navigating by terrestrial landmarks (Arunchalam 1987; Steensgaard 1987; Verlinden 1987).

These similarities between the physical geography and navigational techniques in the Mediterranean and the Indian Ocean do not mandate a wholesale rejection of Semple's environmental determinist thesis. There are considerable differences in the size and shape of the two seas, and these differences in fact may explain much of the difference between the two regions' constructions of ocean-space. However, the analysis of the Mediterranean presented by Semple at the very least requires considerable revision. As we have seen, she omits evidence about the exact nature of Mediterranean states' marine behavior and she fails to consider certain regional environmental factors that, according to her own theory as well as the experience of Indian Ocean societies, one might think would have led the Mediterranean states to have adopted marine policies quite different from those she identifies. To assess Semple's thesis thoroughly and to establish an understanding of the Mediterranean ocean-space construction that will permit comparison with those of the Indian Ocean and Micronesia, one must specify further the *social* relationship between land-based society and the sea in the Mediterranean.

Imperium *and* dominium *in* Mare Nostrum

Much of the confusion surrounding Rome's Mediterranean ocean-space construction is hampered by a failure to specify just what is meant by "domination" of the oceans. Clearly, Rome claimed some kind of authority within the Mediterranean, as exemplified by the name given to the sea, *Mare Nostrum*. And yet even Gold, a legal scholar who goes to great lengths to reject the claim by Grotius and later jurists that Rome practiced freedom of the seas, acknowledges:

> It appears that expansionist Rome, which absorbed all the conquered territories surrounding the Mediterranean, did not actually claim exclusive jurisdiction over that sea. (Gold 1981: 13)

To unravel this paradox, one must distinguish between the Roman concepts of *imperium* and *dominium*. The Romans claimed *imperium* – the

64

right to command – in the Mediterranean, but they did not claim *dominium* – the power to own, use, enjoy, and dispose of property. Grotius himself noted:

> Now those who say that a certain sea belonged to the Roman people explain their statement to mean that the right of the Romans did not extend beyond protection and jurisdiction; this right they distinguish from ownership. (Grotius 1916: 35)

More recent legal scholars concur with this finding:

> The sea was held to be free to the common use of all men . . . There were claims to the right to exercise jurisdiction over some part of the sea, or to possess the *imperium*: yet this claim was not expanded into a claim involving any sort of property right in the sea itself, that is, the claim to *imperium* was not developed into a claim to *dominium*.
> (Fenn 1925: 717)

> The Roman interest always controlled, though it was never extended so as to include exclusive sovereignty over the seas.
> (Gormley 1963: 585)

The Romans constructed the Mediterranean as a space within their sphere of influence, but they never deigned actually to claim it as the territory of the state. Indeed, they emphasized this distinction by governing the sea according to *jus gentium* (common law, or the law of all peoples) as opposed to Roman civil law, which applied only in the land-space of the empire. As Emperor Antoninus Pius (A.D. 138–61) stated:

> I, indeed, am lord of the world; but let the law of the sea be applied according to the maritime law of the Rhodians, if no law of ours is opposed. (cited in Lobingier 1935: 12)

The question then arises: On what basis did Rome claim any degree of influence in the Mediterranean if indeed it were the common space of all? Rome based its claim on its role as regional hegemon. For several hundred years, beginning in 31 B.C., *all* of the lands bordering the Mediterranean lay within the boundaries of the Roman Empire. Modern legal scholars have concluded that Rome constructed for itself a doctrine of *stewardship* for this unclaimable space that lay in the middle of its realm:

> The conclusion would seem to be that the Roman jurists, postulating a legal person which is created in agreement with the most recent juristic philosophy, regarded the coasts as being protected and guarded by the Roman people as "a sacred trust of civilization." (Fenn 1925: 724)

> The Romans exercised definite guardianship over the seas under their
> concept of *populi Romani esse* and they regarded this guardianship as a
> sacred trust on behalf of the general welfare.   (Gold 1981: 30)

As the region's hegemon, Rome claimed the Mediterranean as lying
within its "sphere of influence," but it did not claim the sea as the *territory*
of the state.

The Mediterranean as militarized space

Having established a "guardianship," or "stewardship," over the sea,
Rome intervened frequently:

> Under the *jus gentium*, the sea was open to the legitimate use of every-
> one; still the oceans were not in a state of anarchy or beyond effective
> control. Moreover, the national interest of the Roman State always pre-
> dominated and was the basic point of determination relative to any
> dispute, legal or political that might arise concerning the status or uses
> of the high seas . . .
> In evaluating the Roman concept of the freedom of the seas, one
> must not lose sight of the fact that they were the dominant naval and
> military power and, as such, had a free hand in legislating and acting
> *as they alone saw fit* . . .
> [The Romans] never hesitated to utilize their military power in a
> completely ruthless and inhumane manner once they determined that
> such action was "desirable."
> (Gormley 1963: 562, 572, 585, emphasis in original)

In effect, Rome constructed the Mediterranean as a "force-field," a placeless surface that belonged to no one but upon which powerful states
could intervene so as to steward its resources for the national interest. Since the sea primarily was used as a surface for the movement of
troops and goods, interventions in this space centered on ridding the
space of pirates and other oppositional forces that could impede the
flow of goods and people. In developing this policy, Rome drew upon
an extensive legacy of Mediterranean sea powers, dating back to the
Cretans and Phoenicians (Stevens and Westcott 1942). Some of these
powers intervened in the sea so as to enforce trade monopolies, while
others intervened so as to keep the sea and its ports open to traders of all
nations. Whatever the national trade policy, the ocean was constructed
as a space unclaimable as territory but a legitimate surface for the expression of national force and aggression. The quest for commercial power
was linked with the imperative to exert a degree of influence in the
space across which commercial goods traveled. In the Mediterranean,

ocean-space was constructed as a non-possessible arena wherein competitive states, acting as resource stewards, asserted linked objectives of naval and commercial strength.

In summary, the Mediterranean construction of ocean-space falls somewhere between that of the Indian Ocean and Micronesia. In contrast to the Indian Ocean, Mediterranean powers, whether committed to free trade or protectionism, constructed the sea as a crucial space *within* the social system, not an insignificant space *between* societies. As such, the sea was a legitimate site for power projection. Even Athens, well known for its free-trade policy, on several occasions embargoed and attacked the ships of countries with which it was at war. Frequently even third parties' neutral vessels were attacked during wartime (Phillipson 1911; Semple 1931). By contrast, in the Indian Ocean and its ports, friendly commerce and interactions continued among traders whose governments were at war with each other.

On the other hand, Mediterranean societies stopped short of the Micronesian model wherein ocean-space is defined as a component of the space *of* society. While Mediterranean powers used the sea as a site for expressing social power, they nonetheless perceived the polity as constituted solely by its land-space. The sea was an element that needed to be controlled if one were to maintain hegemon status, but it was not the paradigmatic space of society. As in the Indian Ocean societies, individual Romans obtained honor and wealth solely through terrestrial pursuits (Phillipson 1911).

Rome viewed the sea as a space amenable to social influence but not to incorporation within the territory of individual states. The Micronesian-style construction of the ocean – as an extension of land to be governed through land-like territorial means – was as foreign to Mediterranean powers as was the Indian Ocean construction of the sea as a special trading space insulated from the power struggles of land-based societies. Rather, the Mediterranean was constructed as a placeless "force-field" upon which states exercised their military might so as to steward its resources, a construction that had a major influence on the constructions of ocean-space that have characterized the modern era.

3   Ocean-space and merchant capitalism

Ocean-space in pre-modern Europe

The merchant capitalist – or mercantilist – era was a transitional period in which European society developed the technologies, forms of social organization, and thought systems that were to characterize the industrial capitalist era that followed. Concurrently, the era had its own distinctive social organization: an economy based on state-sponsored trading companies and monopolized commerce. This chapter examines the dynamics of mercantilism: its social organization, political–economic processes, and constructions of space and, in particular, ocean-space.

Although the mercantilist-era ocean-space construction was related to the spatiality of merchant capitalism, it also was an outgrowth of European ocean-space constructions that pre-dated the rise of capitalism. Prior to the modern era, Europe was characterized by two distinct maritime spheres – north and south – each with its own set of attitudes, rules, and practices. Regular maritime interaction between the two regions of Europe began in the mid-thirteenth century, and by the mid-fifteenth century ships originating in the North Sea and the Baltic were frequently found in the Mediterranean, and vice versa (Mollat du Jourdin 1993). Thus, the mercantilist ocean-space construction, while developed as a component of the socio-spatial processes of merchant capitalism, was built upon a foundation created from the merging of two pre-capitalist European constructions.

Southern Europe

The norms and perceptions governing the Mediterranean during the late Middle Ages are of special interest because in many ways they served as prototypes for the mercantilist era. Additionally, strong connections can be found between the Mediterranean of the late Middle Ages and the Roman-era construction of the Mediterranean discussed in Chapter 2. As during the Roman era, extensive coastal navigation (during certain parts of the year) was relatively simple. With fairly regular trade over a space characterized by narrow, controllable inlets, the Mediterranean was constructed during the late Middle Ages much as it had been under the Roman Empire: as a space where adjacent states exercised and claimed *imperium* and practiced stewardship, but where they did not assert actual sovereignty. Chaudhuri, in particular, identifies a common "force-field" construction of ocean-space in the Mediterranean that remained constant from the Roman era through the Middle Ages and into the mercantilist era:

> In the Mediterranean . . . from Graeco-Roman times and perhaps even earlier periods of history, it was essential to exercise control over the vital sea-routes in order to control both economic resources and political settlements . . . When the Iberians developed long-distance armed merchant shipping, floating fortresses and warehouses, it became possible to extend the area of oceanic control from the home bases and to establish new bases in remote places.   (Chaudhuri 1985: 14)

Both Chaudhuri and Semple (1931) attribute this peculiarly Mediterranean construction to a unique "combination of [physical] geography, politics, economic factors, and historical experience" (Chaudhuri 1985: 14).

Of all Mediterranean states, Venice perhaps most clearly foreshadowed the maritime policies of the mercantilist states that followed. Venice, which became a Mediterranean power around 1200 and remained a strong state to the seventeenth century, consistently projected its military might in and across the sea. But its ultimate objective was neither possession of the sea nor possession of distant lands. Ocean power was used for these ends, but these ends themselves were means to a still higher goal – control of trade ("Commercial and fiscal policy" 1904; Lane 1973). For Venice, as for Rome, the sea was an important connecting space to be dominated as a means for controlling trade. The sea was an arena for collecting and projecting social power but it was not treated as a space of value (a *place*) in its own right.

Northern Europe

The waters of northern Europe have a physical character significantly different from those of the south, and these differences are reflected in

their historic social constructions. Where the Mediterranean is characterized by a relatively long season of easy coastwise navigation, no such
season exists in the North Sea or Baltic. The waters of the north are beset by fogs and storms, making extensive navigation difficult even for
coast-hugging ships. On the other hand, the waters of the north provide
excellent fishing grounds. Thus, while pre-modern southern Europeans
exerted power (but not sovereignty) over large swaths of ocean-space,
northern European households, feudal estates, and states carefully extended their domains to small patches of well-charted, intensively exploited, adjacent marine regions that, to a greater or lesser extent, were
constructed as annexes to terrestrial territories.

With its high degree of territoriality, the Renaissance-era construction
of northern European seas may have borne closer resemblance to the
Micronesian ideal-type than to that of the Roman (or Renaissance-era)
Mediterranean. Like the Micronesians, the northern Europeans lacked a
concept of the high seas across which individuals could navigate freely
and/or exercise their power. In northern Europe, the waters that mattered (those that one could navigate safely) were claimed as exclusive
fishing sites, while the remaining waters were so unattainable that they
were not even worthy of consideration. While the southern Europeans
constructed a regime based on the ability to move from place to place
across a formless ocean, the northern European perspective, like that of
the Micronesians, was riven with a "sense of place." While the southern Europeans navigated using rhumb lines, coordinating their position
relative to that of sited coastal land (and thereby downplaying the importance of the ocean environment within which their ships sailed), the
ships of the north navigated by lead lines and depth charts whose use
was dependent upon site-specific local knowledge of the ocean itself
(Law 1986; Mollat du Jourdin 1993).

The similarity between the northern Europeans and the Micronesians
should not be taken too far. While the northern Europeans did not have
a concept of the high seas, they did construct the deep sea as a kind of
"no-man's-land" or *res nullius* (unclaimed space that is susceptible to
possession). The Micronesians had no complementary concept of the
distant sea as an unclaimed but claimable void. Perhaps the most striking difference is in the level of fear that the northern Europeans had
for the sea. Throughout Nordic mythology, the sea was represented
as evil, endless, mysterious, and threatening (often punctuated by distant, Eden-like islands). Indeed, fishermen of Brittany still were fishing
exclusively on foot in the fourteenth century, so fearful were they of

the sea (Mollat du Jourdin 1993). Nonetheless, northern European and Micronesian constructions share a sense of place-rootedness that stands in contrast to the southern European constructions of either the Roman era or the late Middle Ages.

These differences between the maritime outlooks of northern and southern Europe continued into the early years of the mercantilist era. In the late fifteenth century, as discussed below, southern European powers began to expand their projection of sea power out of the Mediterranean and into the Atlantic and Indian oceans. Spain, Portugal, and – to a lesser extent – the Italian city-states competed to claim rights to trade routes and distant lands. At the same time, the sea powers of the north maintained a distinctly provincial attitude, centered not on the projection of power across the sea to distant lands as a means to channel trade, but rather on asserting control of "their" local waters.[1]

The spatiality of mercantilism

Just as these two European maritime cultures were beginning to interact with each other, Europe was being transformed by a new socioeconomic system with its own distinct spatiality, on land and at sea: mercantilism. Although mercantilist-era individuals and states invested in production facilities and pursued overseas territorial expansion, these activities were derived from a higher goal: the accumulation of precious metals within the territory of the state. To achieve this goal, states attempted to minimize imports (which would have to be paid for with specie) and maximize exports (or at least achieve autarchy). It was to this end that each mercantilist state developed a set of policies built around the control of trade. And because trade was primarily a marine affair, mercantilist states put a high premium on exercising social power at sea.

Economic and political activity under mercantilism

The era of merchant capitalism generally is characterized by the leading role of merchant – as opposed to industrial – capital. In fact, some of the capital generated through mercantile activities was invested in

---

[1] In the early sixteenth century, for instance, England "renewed her former claims to the possession of the 'British Seas,' which she now interpreted to mean the right to claim the salute to the British flag as a recognition of her sovereignty there; the right to prohibit every act of hostility or naval manifestation of power by other states and the right to prevent all foreigners from fishing in those waters without 'having regularly demanded and obtained a licence from the King'" (Colombos 1967: 51).

production. But even then, little attention was devoted to increasing the productivity of labor or capital. Although merchant capitalists co-ordinated "putting out" networks of rural producers (often part-time peasants),

> in so far as the production process itself was not controlled and modified, [this system] was associated with a tendency to preserve and retain the old methods of production based upon handicraft techniques as its precondition, and in the end it often stood in the way of the overthrow and transformation of the old mode of production.
>
> (Dunford and Perrons 1983: 169–170)

In fact, industrial agglomerations, either in cities or in rural mill villages, almost were unheard of until the Industrial Revolution of the eighteenth century. The requirements of water power made for few attractive industrial sites in pre-existing cities, and the costs of recruiting workers and building supportive infrastructure at remote, "green-field" sites in most instances far outweighed the productivity that could be gained by installing large-scale production machinery at these rural locations. "Until well into the nineteenth century in England and *a fortiori* on the European mainland, more value was created and more people were employed in small workshops than in centralised and mechanised production units" (Dunford and Perrons 1983: 193–194). While London's population is believed to have quintupled between 1560 and 1689, this increase was due almost entirely to its emergence as a seaport, not as a manufacturing center. Davis (1962) estimates that in 1700 more than one-quarter of London's population was involved directly in the shipping industry, and that the bulk of the remainder was providing support services for that population.

Just as productivity-enhancing investment was not the driving force of mercantilism, neither was the thirst for overseas possessions. As was the case with productive investment, overseas expansionist adventures were engaged in, but only as a means toward controlling trade. English efforts at territorial expansion, although justified by calls for the reclamation of "lost" ancestral homelands, generally were abandoned if they were found to interfere with commercial interests (Andrews 1984). The Dutch pursued a policy of depopulating some of the Spice Islands and establishing settler-run plantations. But they did this not so much as a means toward controlling overseas territory or rationalizing production but rather as a low-cost means of controlling trade. By controlling the supply of spices, the Dutch could establish a few coastal military bases near the plantations, a much more cost-efficient security program than one based on hundreds of ships patrolling the seas and attempting to interdict smugglers trading with independent producers (Chaudhuri 1985; Nijman 1994).

Finally, it must be stressed that trade, although extensive during the mercantilist period, was not a self-contained, profit-making industry. At a time when capital markets still were exceedingly small and there was relatively little non-agricultural capital available for investment, shipping was exceedingly expensive:

> The risks and the cost price relative to the cargoes transported were so great in long-distance shipping that they made transporting as a simple freight industry virtually unthinkable. Normally, long-distance transport was organized within the context of a trading operation in which it represented one heading among others of the merchant's expenditure and risks. (Braudel 1982: 371–372; see also Davis 1962)

At first glance, the Dutch stand out as an exception to this generalization. The Dutch were famous as traders, and they are known for having advocated a free-trade policy. The Dutch advocacy of free trade, however, was restricted solely to the intra-European arena, and there only because the nation happened to be in a relatively strong economic position and a relatively weak political–military position. When trading with the rest of the world, the Dutch acted much like the other mercantilist powers (Nijman 1994).

Mercantilism as channeled circulation

The spatiality that emerges from this picture of mercantilism is one of incessant circulation, whether among the network of marginally capitalized "putting out" producers who dotted the countryside or among colonial plantations, trading posts, and European port cities. Individual places did not have the significance they were to develop in later years, as production sites, consumption sites, or colonial areas to be dominated. Because there were few opportunities for profitable investment either in spatially fixed production sites or in the activity of trade itself, the mercantilist system of circulation that emerged was very different from the flexible "free trade" advocated at the end of the era by classical economists. Rather, the mercantilist economy was based upon closed, channeled paths of circulation.

Capitalists and sovereigns were not overly concerned with the actual process of production, but they were extremely concerned with ensuring that the entire product of a region found its way into their ships, that these ships found their way to their designated destination, and that distribution within the land of destination also remained under their control. National policy supported these closed networks as means toward minimizing the export of precious metals. Indeed, the genius of the strongest mercantilist powers lay in their ability to triangulate this trade in such a way as to generate a net importation of precious metals (Braudel 1982). Control of trade was critical to cement the links between exclusive producers and exclusive consumers.

It follows that in a system in which economic power was based upon controlling discrete channels of trade, the surface upon which trade was carried out (the ocean) would emerge as a site for exercising power. The control of trade routes rapidly became conflated with political domination and military might, and the deep sea became constructed as a "force-field" for exercising power over distant lands and controlling trade networks:

> Unable to occupy the great landmasses of the Far East, [the Portuguese] found it a simple matter to control the seas, the medium of transport and communications. This was what mattered after all: "If you are strong in ships," Francisco de Almeida wrote to the King in Lisbon, "the commerce of the Indies is yours." (Braudel 1984: 493)

> The leading fidalgos [of the Portuguese court] were all motivated by an economic ideology that did not see long-distance trade as contemporary merchants would have seen it but rather as a legitimate medium for extracting political tribute through the exercise of military means. It is certainly true that the aggressive attitude adopted by the Portuguese and their Islamic adversaries in the Indian Ocean was a fixation that did not take into account that co-existence or peaceful trading might be more profitable than waging perpetual war by land and sea. (Chaudhuri 1985: 69)

In summary, actual possession of the ocean and its incorporation within the territory of European states (i.e., the Micronesian model) was not on the agenda of mercantilist-era sea power advocates. Indeed, it is debatable whether the mercantilist powers possessed such an agenda for non-European *land*-space; certainly no such ambitious expansionist scheme was envisioned for the sea, which generally still was perceived as dangerous and inhospitable. Nor was the ocean constructed as an asocial void between the distinct social places of land-space (i.e., the Indian Ocean model). Rather, as in the non-modern Mediterranean (and similar to the land-space territoriality exercised by Sack's "pre-modern civilizations"), the mercantilist-era ocean was constructed as a special space within the social system, where territorial control was exercised as a means toward exercising social power. Ocean-space was constructed as an arena wherein states competed to contain, control, and steward the essential social interaction of trade.

Constructing mercantilist ocean-space

The mercantilist ocean-space construction did not simply emerge in the manner that it did because the structures of merchant capitalism "required" it. Rather, it developed from a series of political conflicts and rivalries among states and individual jurists, in the context of the political history of the era. By the mid-fifteenth century, according to Mollat du Jourdin (1993), all Europe had embraced the concept of sea power as a necessary route toward achieving economic and political power and as part of the state-ideal. Around this time, the maritime states of Europe universally adopted protectionist policies including tariffs on imports, taxes on foreign ships passing through territorial waters, and fiscal policies favoring goods carried on national ships. Nonetheless, regional and national differences persisted, and it was out of their interactions that the ocean-space construction characteristic of the era emerged.

1450–1495: early Iberian hegemony

For the first century of the modern era, from the mid-fifteenth to the mid-sixteenth centuries, long-distance trade, exploration, and conquest were dominated by two states: Spain and Portugal. As early as 1452, Portugal obtained a bull from Pope Nicholas V urging it to explore distant, non-Christian lands. This mission was clarified in several bulls issued over the next few decades as well as in a treaty with Spain (the 1479 Treaty of Alcaçovas) that granted Portugal exclusive rights to explore and claim lands in a vaguely demarcated region that covered the west African coast and other lands encountered as it forged an eastern sea route to India.[2] Following Columbus' 1492 voyage (during which he was ordered by the Spanish crown to stay far from the west African coast so as not to infringe on the region granted to Portugal under the Treaty of Alcaçovas) the papacy (now under Alexander VI) intervened again. Alexander VI

---

[2] Two of these bulls, as well as the Treaty of Alcaçovas, are transcribed and translated into English in Davenport (1917).

issued four bulls during 1493, the most famous of which gave Spain rights to all "islands and mainlands, found and to be found, discovered and to be discovered" lying "west and south" of a north–south line drawn from the Arctic Pole to the Antarctic Pole and passing 100 leagues west of the Azores and Cape Verde Islands, and which gave to Portugal exploration rights to all lands east of the line. The next year, Spanish and Portuguese temporal authorities signed the Treaty of Tordesillas, in which the line was moved to 370 leagues west of the Cape Verde Islands and in which Spain and Portugal agreed to prohibit their ships from entering each other's spheres (except as necessary to get to their own distant possessions).

The bulls and the treaty are frequently characterized as dividing the world-ocean between Spain and Portugal. Grotius, for instance, in his 1608 rebuttal of Portuguese claims (discussed in more detail below), writes:

> The Portuguese claim as their own the whole expanse of the sea which separates two parts of the world so far distant the one from the other, that in all the preceding centuries neither one has so much as heard of the other. Indeed, if we take into account the share of the Spaniards, whose claim is the same as that of the Portuguese, only a little less than the whole ocean is found to be subject to two nations, while all the rest of the peoples in the world are restricted to the narrow bounds of the northern seas.
> (Grotius 1916: 37–38)

In a classic early twentieth-century work on maritime law, Fulton writes:

> In the sixteenth century these powers, in virtue of Bulls of the Pope and the Treaty of Tordesillas, divided the great oceans between them . . . [making] preposterous pretensions to the dominion of the immense waters of the globe.
> (Fulton 1911: 4–5)

More recently, Gold has written:

> The waters of the world had been divided and allocated to two nations by papal decree, at that time the highest form of legal instrument.
> (Gold 1981: 35)

These assertions notwithstanding, there is little basis for the commonly held belief that these documents represent a parceling of foreign lands and even less basis for the belief that they represent a division of the world-ocean. The impetus for the bulls, the political objectives driving their promulgation, their precise dates and chronological order, and even the authenticity of the fourth bull, have all been questioned.

These questions, in turn, complicate the common interpretation that the pope claimed "sovereignty" over non-Christian lands and waters and that he proceeded to "donate" these spaces so that they could become the exclusive territories of the Spanish and Portuguese temporal sovereigns.[3]

The first bull, dated May 3, 1493, notes that Spain:

> ... for a long time had purposed to search and find some lands and islands remote and unknown, and hitherto not found by others in order to bring their natives and inhabitants to worship our Redeemer and to profess the Catholic faith.   (Gottschalk 1927: 21)[4]

In carrying out this mission,

> [Spain] appointed our beloved son Christopher Columbus with ships and men equipped for such purpose not without greatest labours and perils and expenses, to seek diligently such remote and unknown lands by seas, which had not been navigated before, who at last by the help of God, with utmost foresight, navigating through western parts in the Ocean, as it is said, toward the Indies, found certain far remote islands and also mainlands, which had not been discovered by others before, in which dwell very many tribes ... [that] seem sufficiently well fitted to embrace the Catholic faith.   (Gottschalk 1927: 21)

Following these statements, the pope grants to Spain "the aforesaid lands and islands in general in particular, unknown and up to this time discovered by your messengers and to be discovered in the future, which are not established under the actual temporal sovereignty of any Christian Sovereigns" (Gottschalk 1927: 23). In return, Spain is obligated "to instruct the aforenamed natives and inhabitants in the Catholic faith" (Gottschalk 1927: 23).

Additionally, the pope prohibits all persons from visiting these lands and islands that have been taken possession of by Spain "for getting goods or for any other purpose whatever without special license [from the Spanish crown]" under pain of excommunication (Gottschalk 1927: 23). Finally, the bull ends with a paragraph noting that this grant to Spain parallels several similar grants that previously had been made to Portugal "in regions of Africa, Guinea and the Gold Mine and elsewhere," and that all rights and obligations that previously had been

---

[3] For contributions to this debate, see Bourne (1904); Davies (1967); Dawson (1899); Derby (1671); Fiske (1892); Gottschalk (1927); Harrisse (1897); Nowell (1945); Nunn (1948); Ramos Perez (1974); Vander Linden (1916); Varela Marcos (1994, 1997); and Williams (1922).
[4] This quotation, and the quotations that follow from the four bulls of 1493 and the Treaty of Tordesillas, are taken from the translations that appear in Gottschalk (1927).

conferred upon Portugal in those lands similarly are conferred upon Spain in its new lands (Gottschalk 1927: 23).

Several points stand out in this bull. First, the purpose of the explorations, and the pope's authority to bestow rights upon exploring nations, clearly are based on the European sovereigns' mission of spreading Christianity. It follows from this point that the pope is not so much granting land to Spain as he is recognizing Spain's right to go forth and seize unclaimed (i.e. non-Christian) land. The distinction may have had little impact on those in the lands that Spain went on to subjugate, but, in contradistinction to those who have charged that the bulls indicate that the pope thought that the non-Christian world was his to "give away" (Derby 1671; Fiske 1892; Nunn 1948), the wording of the papal "donation" suggests that the pope merely was blessing the Spanish activities of spreading the Gospel and facilitating them by granting Spain exclusive rights to the lands discovered and to be discovered and promising excommunication for those Christians who interfered with Spain's efforts. At no point is any mention made of transferring parcels of land from the pope or a papal escrow to Spain; such gift would be impossible since the pope made no pretensions of being a temporal ruler. Rather, Spain is informed that if it engages in missionary activity in non-Christian lands it has the pope's blessing in asserting claim to these lands.

While there is little reason to believe that the pope is granting any land to Spain, there is even less reason to believe that he is granting any portion of the ocean. The ocean is referred to only as the surface that is crossed as Spain reaches these lands where it is being given exploration rights; since the purpose of the grant is to carry out missionary activities, a grant of the uninhabitable ocean would not serve any purpose.[5]

The second and third bulls – both dated the very next day, but, according to most scholars, probably backdated by a month or two – divide the previous bull into two distinct bulls, with a focus on clarifying the relationship between Spain and Portugal regarding their respective projects of exploration and conversion. The second bull largely is a revised version of the first bull, but all references to Portugal are dropped and the area in which Spain is to claim rights to all lands "discovered and to be discovered" is restricted to the region "west and south" of a line drawn 100 leagues west of the Azores and Cape Verde Islands. The third bull expands on the final paragraph of the first bull (in which Spain's rights

---

[5] None of the bulls, nor the treaty, considers the case of uninhabited islands or portions of the mainland. It is unclear whether Spain or Portugal legitimately could have used the authority bestowed by the bulls or treaty to claim these territories.

were equated to those previously bestowed upon Portugal), incorporating the 100-league line.

The easily apprehendible Line of Demarcation – a graphic representation of division – has probably led to the popular interpretation that with these bulls the pope divided the world, or, in a slightly more limited sense, divided the sea (Steinberg 1999b, 2000). However, a close reading reveals that the intent of these bulls is similar to that of the first one. To repeat a phrase used by both Dawson (1899) and Bourne (1904), by drawing the Line of Demarcation, Pope Alexander VI was merely denoting "spheres of influence" in which the two European powers were given monopolistic rights to carry out exploration, much as the papacy had arbitrated among competing monastic orders during the Crusades (see also Gottschalk (1927) and Harrisse (1897)). As Dawson notes,

> Nothing was awarded to Spain, but what she had discovered and what she might discover beyond a certain line . . . What the Pope really did was to confirm each power in what it actually had and to allot "spheres of influence" in which they might pursue their discoveries without quarrelling.   (Dawson 1899: 489)

Statements that the pope granted the western ocean to Spain and the eastern ocean to Portugal as their sovereign territories are particularly misguided. As in the first bull, these grants were solely grants of exploration rights, rather than donations of territory, and possession by the sovereigns could come about only through discovery (Dawson 1899). Furthermore, there is every reason to believe that the territory in question – that is, the space that potentially could be possessed by the sovereigns being granted exclusive exploration rights – is restricted to terrestrial territory. As in the first bull, the second bull states explicitly that the purpose of permitting possession of territories is to enable missionary activities (which are difficult to practice at sea), and the bull again refers exclusively to the sovereigns' rights to "islands and mainlands found and to be found, discovered and to be discovered" (Gottschalk 1927: 35). Even in the clause permitting the two sovereigns to exclude others who "presume to go to the islands and mainlands" (Gottschalk 1927: 37), the pope fails to grant the right to exclude each other (or representatives of other nations) from venturing into regional waters.

The third bull does include a reference to the ocean ("We, moreover, this day have given, conceded and assigned in general and in particular

The quotation from Dawson reprinted above alludes as well to a second curiosity of the papal bulls. Why, in the fourth bull, does the pope not deal with the problem of Spain reaching the East through a westward voyage simply by drawing a second line indicating the westward boundary of "The West" (which would also serve as the eastward boundary of "The East")? If the pope truly had the objective of parceling out the ocean (or claimed the authority to do so), he probably would have done so by drawing distinct boundaries. Instead, the ocean was constructed as a special transportation-space in which systemic social power could be exercised (hence the pope claimed the ability to draw lines and assign vectors of movement through ocean-space) but in which states were not permitted to practice sovereign territoriality. The ocean could be divided into spheres of influence that could serve to define the regions within which land-space was amenable to missionary activities by specific sovereigns, but the ocean itself was constructed as a transportation-space beyond possession, and its "division" could serve to divide only *movement*, not *territory*.

While the ocean *per se* rarely is mentioned in the four bulls, it is referred to much more explicitly in the Treaty of Tordesillas, and here the evidence is much greater that ocean-space was perceived as a legitimate arena for exercising social power. The very title of the treaty – noted below the signatures – is "Capitulation of the division of the Ocean-sea," and the treaty contains provisions such as:

> You can leave and do leave to the said King and Queen and to their Realms and successors, all the *seas*, islands and lands which shall be and might be within any boundary and demarcation which shall remain to the said King and Queen: and in the same manner we give you the said authority in order that in our name and the names of our successors and the heirs of all our Realms and Dominions, the subjects and natives thereof, you can, with the said King and Queen, or with their Representatives, accord, agree and receive and determine, that all the *seas*, islands and lands which shall be and might be within the limits and demarcation of coasts, *seas*, islands and lands, which shall remain for us and for our successors, shall be ours and for our dominion and conquest, and thus for our Realms and successors in them, with those limitations and exceptions of our islands, and with all the other clauses and declarations which shall appear well to you.
>
> (Gottschalk 1927: 61, emphasis added)

Similarly, while the exclusionary clauses of the first and second bulls refer only to "mainlands and islands" and the fourth bull to "regions," here

Spain and Portugal specifically are given the right to exclude each other from all ocean-space on their respective sides of the 370-league line (with the exception that Portugal must allow Spain to pass through Portuguese ocean-space as it travels westward to its American possessions).

Even in the treaty, however, while the sea is divided as a space in which social power is exercised, it is not claimed as territory. Regarding the title "Capitulation of the division of the Ocean-sea," Vander Linden (1916) notes that during this era the term "Ocean sea" referred not to the world-ocean but rather to the vast unknown region to the south, which lay across the known ocean and which contained both terrestrial elements (the "Southern Indies") and unknown waters. Indeed, the treaty refers to "that which up to the present is to be discovered in the Ocean-Sea" (Gottschalk 1927: 57) and "the Ocean-sea [and] the islands and mainland which shall be therein" (Gottschalk 1927: 61). Elsewhere, the treaty betrays a consistency with the tenor of the papal bulls, suggesting that while the ocean-sea as a whole (a primarily marine element) is to be demarcated so as to define where the two countries' ships may travel, it is the "mainlands and islands" *within* the ocean-sea that are to be possessed by the respective sovereigns as territories:

> it pleases us by the great love and friendship which there is between us, and for the seeking, procuring and preserving of greater peace and firmer concord and tranquility, that the sea in which the said islands are and shall be found, be divided and marked between us in some good, sure and restricted manner . . .   (Gottschalk 1927: 59)

Nowell (1945) proposes an intriguing scenario that suggests why the exercise of social power at sea is referred to only obliquely in the four bulls but much more explicitly in the treaty. He suggests that, despite the superficial resemblance between the 100-league Line of Demarcation drawn in the second bull of 1493 and the 370-league Line of Demarcation drawn in the Treaty of Tordesillas, the two are of entirely different origin. The bulls of 1493, as all historians agree, were promulgated by the pro-Spanish pope Alexander VI at the behest of Spain, which sought confirmation of the terrestrial discoveries of Columbus and which hoped to use these discoveries to leverage further rights of discovery in what previously had been a Portuguese monopoly. Nowell proposes that the Portuguese crown agreed to the bulls even though it was much stronger militarily, because it was aware that Portuguese sailors were on the verge of rounding Africa and finding the eastern route to India. Portugal was happy to encourage Spanish preoccupation with primitive lands to the

83

west that, the Portuguese had good reason to believe (correctly, as it turned out), were not even connected to the Asian mainland.

The Treaty of Tordesillas, on the other hand, according to Nowell, came about at Portugal's behest, and it followed a number of previous Portuguese diplomatic initiatives (both with papal and with Spanish authorities) carried out over the previous fifteen years. The primary concern of the Portuguese was to keep Spain away from the ocean surrounding Africa, because Lisbon had identified these waters as the route to India. Thus, the Treaty of Tordesillas, unlike the bulls, is replete with statements about exclusionary rights in ocean-space. But, even here, the value of the ocean is not as a territory of the sovereign state, but rather as a space of movement, amenable to exclusionary social power, but not to territorial incorporation. As evidence, Nowell argues that, as was the case with the bulls, no suggestion is made in the treaty that the Line of Demarcation should continue around the poles to the eastern hemisphere. Especially given the context of the loophole already uncovered by the fourth bull, the negotiators' failure to account for this eventuality is inexplicable *if* their goal were to divide the sea as sovereign territory. However, if their goal were to define maritime spheres of influence within which each country could carry out its exploratory activities (and make the land claims that had been sanctioned under the previous year's bulls), then the failure to draw a second Line of Demarcation is entirely logical.

The Line of Demarcation's lack of significance as a boundary line dividing sovereign space is evidenced in the cartography of the era. Several of the world maps that survive from the first decades following the treaty contain political notations (through text or, more frequently, flags and coats of arms) designating the European sovereign who rules over various regions of distant land-space, but on most maps the Line of Demarcation is absent. This absence is surprising, given that these maps highlight political relations over space and that they are almost all the products of Spanish or Portuguese cartographers, but it is suggestive of the interpretation that the line demarcates something less than a political division of the world. On the only known map from before 1519 that definitively contains the line, the 1502 Cantino map, the Line of Demarcation is accompanied by the text "Esta de omarco dantre castella y Portugall," but no coats of arms mark the two spheres of the planet (Figure 1). Portuguese and Spanish flags dot the land-space of the Atlantic islands, America, and Africa – indicating that points of land have been discovered and claimed as overseas territories of

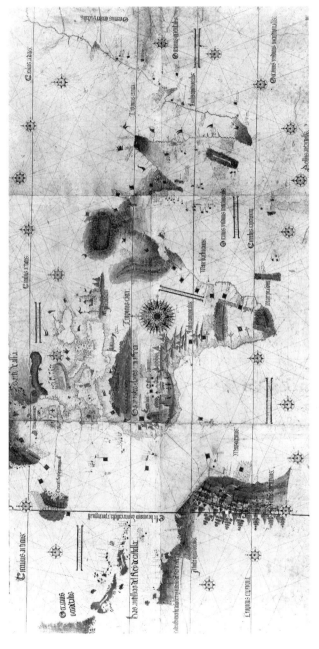

Figure 1. Map of the world by Alberto Cantino, 1502 (reproduced by permission of La Biblioteca Estense Universitaria, Modena).

European sovereigns – but there are no territorial markers whatsoever in the sea or denoting the two sides of the line generally (Steinberg 2000).[6]

In summary, the bulls contain little reference to ocean-space. Rather, they allocate the land-space within which European powers were to carry out missionary activities and make imperial claims. To the extent that the later bulls refer to the regions and seas around these distant land-spaces, they merely are specifying the spheres of influence within which these activities will be carried out and providing security zones around land-spaces so as to further enable colonizing missions. The treaty does, in a sense, "divide" the sea, but this can better be understood as an allocation of routes for movement and spheres for exploration rather than an allocation of boundable, claimable territory.

The construction of ocean-space implicit in both the bull and the treaty bears a strong resemblance to that of the non-modern Mediterranean. Just as Rome claimed a "sphere of influence" within *Mare Nostrum*, the Iberian powers claimed a similar set of exclusive rights within their portions of the world-ocean. Yet, as for Rome, these exclusive rights of stewardship did not imply any claim to possession of the sea. They merely implied that the sea was a "force-field" in which Spain and Portugal could legitimately exercise their power over other states (including each other) as they hoarded the ocean's resource of connection, control of which was crucial to the logic of mercantilism. The application of social power in ocean-space was accomplished through a geographically signified division of authority between Spain and Portugal: the Line of Demarcation. But such a division of space does not necessarily constitute a division of *territory*, in the modern, statist, sense of the concept; in this instance the line drawn through the ocean divided movement, not territory.

1495–1580: late Iberian hegemony

Following the treaty, the Spanish were fortunate that, in most cases, they had little trouble conquering indigenous cultures, whether by arms or pathogens, and they soon established a system of mines and, later, plantations. Spanish sea power was exercised so as to restrict trade to certain

---

[6] In the 1520s, following Magellan's circumnavigation, the Line of Demarcation began to appear more regularly, accompanied by signs indicating some degree of authority by the two sovereigns over their "halves" of the globe. At this point, however, the treaty was undergoing a wholesale reinterpretation as both countries were extending the line to the other side of the planet in an effort to claim authority over the Spice Islands (Steinberg 2000).

ports (in Spain as well as in the Americas) and to specially organized convoys. In part, this centralized control was established to protect shipping from pirates, but it also served to prevent the resources of the crown's territories from escaping into the hands of other European powers (or private Spanish merchants) who might be tempted to outbid the Spanish crown and negotiate their own deals with Creole settlers and miners. To ensure that the colonies served the purpose of generating specie for the crown, Creole settlers were prohibited from engaging in most processing or manufacturing activities. In the Mediterranean tradition, Spain constructed the Atlantic as a special space within which the crown exercised control of commerce and across which it projected power to distant lands. As a mercantilist power, Spain used this land and sea power to establish and maintain exclusive resource-extraction and trade relations, but it did not claim actual possession of ocean-space.

While Portugal was driven by considerations similar to those of Spain, it faced an entirely different situation in its sphere of influence. In the Indian Ocean, as was discussed in Chapter 2, there was a flourishing trading network, dominated, at that point in time, by Muslims. The geopolitical situation in Portugal's sphere of influence demanded a more outwardly aggressive stance as Portugal sought to utilize its authority to control connections with the Indian mainland and with the trade spanning across the Indian Ocean to east and southeast Asia. As Indian naval officer O. K. Nambiar notes,

> Vasco da Gama came to India a second time in 1502 with a fleet of twenty ships fully equipped for war. Formally proclaiming suzerainty over the Indian Ocean, he imposed a system of passes known as *Cartaz* on all shipping. Ships which did not carry the Portuguese pass were plundered and burnt. Indian and Arab ships were prohibited from carrying certain specified commodities of value. They had to confine their sailing only to authorised ports and never put in at Calicut.
> (Nambiar 1975: 51)

Nambiar's choice of words here is interesting. *Suzerainty* refers to a situation wherein one party asserts legitimate power over another without a goal of ultimate incorporation (*Black's* 1990). Again, although unilateral exercise of power within one's maritime sphere of influence was acceptable, physical incorporation of distant ocean-space within the territory of the state was not a legal norm of the mercantilist era.

The behavior of the Iberian powers in the world-ocean appears to validate Chaudhuri's (1985) thesis that the mercantilist ocean-space construction was an exportation of the militaristic system that had dominated the Mediterranean for the past 2,000 years: Ocean-space was viewed as a non-possessible "in-between" space that nonetheless served as a legitimate arena for expressing and enriching state power. Chaudhuri's thesis, however, needs to be tempered by the fact that Spain and Portugal were not the only active naval powers, even in this early period of mercantilism when they clearly were dominant. Northern European states increasingly became involved as mercantilist powers and, while they adopted much of the Mediterranean attitude toward ocean-space, they also contributed elements from their own waters which, as has been demonstrated, were characterized by a more place-oriented conception of ocean-space.

In the late fourteenth century, not long after southern Europeans invented (or, in some cases, rediscovered) navigational instruments, making possible long-distance navigation, Europe also discovered the technique of salting fish, making possible the exploitation of distant-water fisheries. In the fifteenth and sixteenth centuries, as the Iberian powers declared exclusive rights over the known routes to Asia and the Americas, northern Europeans began to explore northern waters, originally searching for routes to Asia but soon also looking for distant fishing grounds. By 1540, regular harvests of cod were being taken from the Grand Banks off the coast of Newfoundland. This long-distance fishing industry took on a pan-European character as a triangle trade developed between northern Europe, Newfoundland, and the saltworks and markets of Portugal and southern France. Thus the cod industry contributed to the maritime symbiosis of northern and southern Europe as it did to the incorporation of transatlantic traffic into European maritime life (Kurlansky 1997; Mollat du Jourdin 1993). There was no analogous custom of long-distance fishing among the nations of southern Europe. Indeed, southern European mariners had been so pampered by the coastwise routes of the Mediterranean that the states and merchants of southern Europe were forced to recruit sailors from the north for their long-distance military and commercial ventures (Braudel 1972).

Thus there was emerging during the early mercantilist period an ocean-space construction that fused elements of the pre-modern northern European construction with that of the pre-modern Mediterranean. On the one hand, as in the Mediterranean, ocean-space was a formless "force-field" within which competing states could assert their strength and claim powers of stewardship, using the sea to achieve and protect the exclusive trade and resource-extraction relations that lay at the heart of mercantilism. On the other hand, certain areas in distant and near-shore waters came to be constructed as resource-extraction sites, distinct places suitable for harvesting on an ongoing basis and potentially amenable to exclusionary territorial control.

1580–1650: the Battle of the Books

By the mid-sixteenth century the English and the Dutch began to challenge the Iberian trade monopoly in the southern oceans. This activity increased after the English defeat of the Spanish Armada in 1588, and by the end of the century the northern European powers had well-established trade routes to the East. Rejecting the papal bull of September 1493,[7] the English and Dutch launched a debate among international jurists commonly referred to as the "Battle of the Books." Besides discussing the status of the sea, this debate came to define some of the key principles guiding international law up to the present.

The opening salvo, the 1608 pamphlet *Mare liberum, sive de jure quod batavis competit ad indicana commercia dissertatio* (*The Freedom of the Seas, or the Right Which Belongs to the Dutch to Take Part in the East Indian Trade*), was written by the Dutch jurist Hugo Grotius on commission from the Dutch East India Company. The company had captured a Portuguese cargo ship in distant Asian waters, brought it back to the United Provinces (the Netherlands), and offered it for sale as a prize of war. Defending the right of the Dutch to claim the ship and its cargo, Grotius wrote a lengthy book, *De jure praedae* (*Commentary on the Law of Prize*), which argued that, because the seas historically had been free to all, the Portuguese had committed an act of war by claiming a portion of the sea as their exclusive domain. Hence the Dutch seizure and sale of the Portuguese ship was legitimate retaliation in the face of Portuguese belligerence. While the lengthy book remained unpublished, probably for political reasons, Grotius published the section in

---

[7] Shortly after the bull was promulgated, "the French King, Francis I, remarked that he refused to recognize the title of the claimants until they could produce the Will of Father Adam, making them universal heirs" (Gold 1981: 35). Foreshadowing some of the arguments put forward a short time later on behalf of the freedom of the seas, England's Queen Elizabeth I said "that she was unable to understand why her subjects and others should be barred from the 'Indies.' She could not recognize the prerogative of the 'Bishop of Rome' that 'he should bind princes who owe him no obedience.' Her subjects would continue to navigate 'that vast ocean,' since 'the use of the sea and air is common to all; neither can any title to the ocean belong to any people or private man, for as much as neither nature nor regard of the public use permitteth any possession thereof'" (Gold 1981: 41).

which he argued that the seas historically had been free for all to use as *Mare liberum* in 1608.[8]

In 1625, the Portuguese professor and monk Seraphim de Freitas wrote a response to Grotius, *De justo imperio luistanorum asiatico* (*The Imperial Right of the Portuguese in Asia*), in which he stated the bases upon which the Portuguese claimed exclusive rights to the waters of Asia. The third work considered here is *Mare clausum, seu de dominio maris libri duo* (*The Closed Sea, or Two Books Concerning the Rule Over the Sea*), written in 1617 or 1618 (but not published until 1635) by the English scholar John Selden at the request of the English crown, primarily to justify its claim to the waters surrounding England.[9] While these latter two books were written specifically to debate Grotius, they also stand as statements of their countries' maritime policies and of their authors' broad visions of the role of ocean-space in the emerging world order.[10]

Hugo Grotius

Grotius' argument can be reduced to six points:

1. Grotius begins his essay by considering whether Portugal might be able to defend its claim to Asian waters based on its possession of surrounding land. He concludes, however, that the Asian leaders are legitimate sovereigns and that therefore the Portuguese cannot use any claim built around possession of Asian land to support their claim to the sea:

> The Portuguese are not sovereigns of those parts of the East Indies to which the Dutch sail, that is to say, Java, Ceylon, and many of the Moluccas ... These islands of which we speak, now have and always have had their own kings, their own governments, their own laws, and their own legal systems ...
>
> Now these Indians of the East, on the arrival of the Portuguese, although some of them were idolators, and some Mohammedans, and therefore sunk in grievous sin, had none the less perfect public and private ownership of their goods and possessions, from which they could not be dispossessed without just cause.   (Grotius 1916: 11, 13)

[8] The complete manuscript of *De jure praedae* was discovered only in 1864 and first published in 1868.

[9] Grotius' work was translated into English in 1916 and may be found in both Latin and English in Grotius (1916). A 1652 English translation of Selden's work has been reprinted as Selden (1972). While Freitas' work has not been translated into English, it has been translated into French (Freitas 1882), Spanish (Freitas 1925), and Portuguese (Freitas 1959). English-language summaries of Freitas' work may be found in Anand (1983), Knight (1925), and, most extensively, Alexandrowicz (1967).

[10] There were several other contributions to the "Battle of the Books," but these three are representative of the range of views held.

Furthermore, Grotius asserts, there is no Christian doctrine of Just War that permits the seizure of private property. Thus, Grotius concludes this portion of his argument:

> Wherefore, since both possession and a title of possession are lacking, and since the property and the sovereignty of the East Indies ought not to be considered as if they had previously been *res nullius*, and since as they belong to the East Indians, they could not have been acquired legally by other persons, it follows that the East Indian nations in question are not the chattels of the Portuguese, but are free men and *sui juris*.   (Grotius 1916: 21)

While this first point does not directly address the question of the sea, it establishes the principle that the world is composed of equivalent, sovereign, territorial states. In asserting this, Grotius is anticipating the norms of international relations consolidated forty years later at Westphalia. Most significantly for the argument he makes later, Grotius, by asserting the existence of a community of sovereign, territorial states, establishes the necessary foundation for declaring that the space between these states is *res extra commercium*, a space that, because of its position and function within this community, is dissociated from the full package of rights to possession, exclusion, and alienation that normally may be claimed by holders of property.

2. Grotius then proposes that if the Portuguese cannot base their claim to a monopoly on trade in Asian waters on their possession of Asian land, perhaps they can base their claim on possession of the waters themselves. Grotius concludes, however, that the sea cannot be possessed. He states two reasons for this. First, because of its vastness and its unsuitability for permanent human habitation, the sea effectively cannot be occupied, a necessary precondition for possession. Secondly, Grotius asserts that because the two main uses of the deep sea – navigation and fishing – are inexhaustible, the sea lies within the realm of natural law and must remain open to all:

> The sea is common to all, because it is so limitless that it cannot become a possession of any one, and because it is adapted for the use of all, whether we consider it from the point of view of navigation or of fisheries.   (Grotius 1916: 28)

Grotius bases much of his argument on the vastness of ocean-space, this vastness being responsible both for its inability to be occupied effectively and also for the inexhaustibility of its fishing and navigational resources. In one passage in particular, Grotius waxes poetic on this point:

> The question at issue is the OUTER SEA, the OCEAN, that expanse of water which antiquity describes as the immense, the infinite, bounded only by the heavens, parent of all things; the ocean which the ancients believed was perpetually supplied with water not only by fountains, rivers, and seas, but by the clouds, and by the very stars of heaven themselves; the ocean which, although surrounding this earth, the home of the human race, with the ebb and flow of its tides, can be neither seized nor inclosed; nay, which rather possesses the earth than is by it possessed.
>
> (Grotius 1916: 37, emphasis in original English translation)

Again, Grotius is defining not just the status of the sea but also that of the land. Land – the territory of states – may be bounded and organized into discrete spaces. Indeed, the boundaries that divide terrestrial territories emerge naturally out of a place's characteristics. As a point of contrast, Grotius ridicules the lengths to which the Portuguese must go to propose such a construction for ocean-space:

> The [Portuguese] are so far from having [actually occupied the ocean] that when they divide up the world to the disadvantage of other nations, they cannot even defend their action by showing any boundaries either natural or artificial, but are compelled to fall back upon some imaginary line. (Grotius 1916: 39)

At the same time, nothing in Grotius' construction of the deep sea prohibits a Mediterranean-style construction within which certain states exercise power within those waters, spreading their power over the surface of the ocean so as to influence power relations on land. Grotius' only proviso is that these powerful states conserve the resources of the deep sea for all to use, a proviso that he believes requires little direct regulation given the ocean's vastness and its resources' inexhaustibility.

3. Having rejected the possibility that the Portuguese can claim possession of the ocean due to occupation, he raises the possibility of their claiming possession due to discovery. Grotius rejects this justification as well:

> Long before the [Portuguese] ever came, every single part of that ocean had been long since explored. For how possibly could the Moors, the Ethiopians, the Arabians, the Persians, the peoples of India, have

remained in ignorance of that part of the sea adjacent to their coasts! Therefore they lie, who today boast that they discovered that sea.

(Grotius 1916: 41)

This passage is particularly interesting because Grotius asserts that the sea definitely is not *res nullius*. Although it necessarily lies outside state territory, it lies within (and encompasses) the global community of nations.

4. As Grotius asserts that the deep sea is not *res nullius*, he also asserts that it is not *res communis humanitatis*, a commons to which all are guaranteed their fair share of resources. Users of the sea are bound to preserving *access* to the sea for all, since its major uses – navigation and fishing – are granted to all by natural law. Yet no user is under any obligation to share the fruits of the sea with the world community:

> In Athanaeus for instance the host is made to say that the sea is the common property of all, but that fish are the private property of him who catches them. And in Pautus' Rudens when the slave says: "The sea is certainly common to all persons," the fisherman agrees; but when the slave adds: "Then what is found in the common sea is common property," he rightly objects, saying: "But what my net and hooks have taken, is absolutely my own." (Grotius 1916: 29)

5. Grotius asserts that those who exert power within the sea have an affirmative duty to allow others to use the waters as well, because use of the sea is granted to all by natural law. Indeed, extensive users have an obligation to exploit the ocean in a manner promoting the conservation of ocean resources:

> All that which has been so constituted by nature that although serving some one person it still suffices for the common use of all other persons, is today and ought in perpetuity to remain in the same condition as when it was first created by nature. (Grotius 1916: 27)

Grotius thus clears the way for a fairly activist regulatory form of stewardship, and he also leaves open the possibility of the stewards being one or a few major users rather than the community of nations.

6. Finally, Grotius considers several cases in which the sea might actually be possessible. Here, he fully develops the principle of *res extra commercium*, asserting that in each of these cases use of the sea must remain open to all, since deep-sea uses have been granted to all humanity

by natural law:

> The sea can in no way become the private property of any one, be-
> cause nature not only allows but enjoins its common use. Neither can
> the shore become the private property of any one. The following quali-
> fication, however, must be made. If any part of these things is by nature
> susceptible of occupation, it may become the property of the one who
> occupies it only so far as such occupation does not affect its common
> use ...
>   There shall be no prejudice if any one shall by fencing off with stakes
> an inlet of the sea make a fish pond for himself, and so establish a
> private preserve ... Whatever has been occupied and can be occupied
> is no longer subject to the law of nations as the sea is ... But outside of
> an inlet this will not hold, for then the common use of the sea might
> be hindered ...
>   Even if a man were to have dominion over the sea, still he could not
> take away anything from its common use. (Grotius 1916: 30, 32–33, 43)

Grotius consistently holds that the principle of common property may be contravened but that the principle of common use is sacrosanct. While one may not implement exclusive use regimes within common property, one may implement a common use regime within privately held seas, should individuals or states develop the capacity actually to possess the sea or portions thereof. Indeed, Grotius acknowledges that "in a way it can be maintained that fish are exhaustible" (Grotius 1916: 43). He goes on to note, however, that even if one were to subscribe to this view (which evidently he does not) and even if one actually could possess the deep sea (which he also does not believe is possible), one still could not prevent others from navigating its waters since navigation is unquestionably an inexhaustible resource and, as such, it is granted to all by natural law.

Alexandrowicz (1967) and Anand (1983) stress the similarity between the regime favored by Grotius and that of the non-modern Indian Ocean, but there are substantial differences as well. As demonstrated in Chapter 2, the Indian Ocean construction posited that the deep sea was an empty, unclaimable non-territory outside society, a surface across which ships of various states traveled as they carried their goods to far-off lands. Grotius' vision is substantially different. There is nothing in Grotius' work defining the ocean as a space beyond the realm of states. Indeed, for Grotius, the ocean exists as an arena in which states interact. The ocean, theoretically, even could be claimed by a state, should one gain the capacity to possess it fully. The only proviso governing the behavior of states in the ocean is that they must not interfere with the access of other users to those resources which, by natural law, have been given to all humanity.

The Grotian ocean-space regime, in fact, is at least as similar to that of the non-modern Mediterranean as it is to that of the non-modern Indian Ocean. Grotius expands on the Mediterranean regime by defining the holder of *imperium* not as one state (e.g., the Roman Empire) but as the *community* of states. Like Rome in the Mediterranean, the community of states in Grotius' regime has a responsibility to steward the seas, allowing access and free transit by all across its surface. And yet, as stewards of a fundamentally social space, individual states may exercise social power within the ocean as a means toward bettering their status within the global society of competitive states.

Seraphim de Freitas

Seraphim de Freitas offered a semi-official Portuguese response to Grotius' challenge. As Alexandrowicz (1967) notes, Freitas concurs with several of Grotius' key points. Freitas agrees that the deep sea is *res extra commercium*, a special space not amenable to complete possession with all the associated rights of exclusion that normally are claimed by a sovereign. He also agrees with Grotius that the Asian rulers are legitimate sovereigns. However, Freitas differs from Grotius in that he holds that navigation is not a right given to all by natural law and that sovereigns may legitimately exercise their authority in adjacent waters in such a way that limits the complete freedoms of navigation and trade:

> *Prima facie* it may seem that [Freitas] envisages the possibility of a kind of limited sovereignty over the sea, but it is clear in the further text that what he has in mind is a *quasi navigandi possessio*, in other words only rights of control of navigation in parts of the sea which remain *res communis*.
> (Alexandrowicz 1967: 68)

Closely mirroring the rights to exercise power in ocean-space that Portugal and Spain had claimed for themselves in the Treaty of Tordesillas, Freitas states that Portugal has a right to police the sea (which, for him, includes restriction of navigation) in regions "adjacent" to Portuguese land-space. However, again paralleling the Treaty of Tordesillas, he makes no attempt to claim these seas as the space of the Portuguese state.

In effect, both Freitas and Grotius are attempting to adapt the Mediterranean ocean-space construction to the realities of an emerging multi-state system. Grotius adapts the monopolar Roman construction of ocean-space to the emerging multipolar world by arguing that although *imperium* or stewardship might hypothetically be asserted by individual states, it must be implemented on behalf of the community of states, because access to marine resources is guaranteed to all under natural law. Freitas takes a different tack, borrowing from the Treaty of Tordesillas (which assumed a world that was bipolar, but still not multipolar) to propose that rights of *imperium* to the deep sea be parceled among competent sovereigns, with each sovereign gaining exclusive usufruct rights, but not possession, over specific long-distance trade routes, those sites of channeled circulation that were the life-blood of mercantilist political economy.

John Selden

While Grotius and Freitas both can be seen as attempting to adapt the traditional Mediterranean/southern European construction to a changed world, the third contributor to the debate, the Englishman John Selden, works from a perspective rooted in the traditional customs of northern Europe.[11] The bulk of Selden's book is devoted to demonstrating how past civilizations in the ancient Mediterranean, contemporary European states, and England all have claimed their neighboring waters as the fully incorporated territory of the state.[12] Thus Selden appears to rebut Grotius directly by claiming that a state may possess ocean-space.

While this construction appears to be in complete opposition to that proposed by Grotius, there are in fact considerable similarities. C. J. Colombos notes:

> But whilst Selden disputed the arguments of Grotius and maintained the right of appropriation by the English Kings of the waters surrounding Great Britain, he admitted the principle that a State could not forbid

[11] One might expect that Grotius, as a Dutch national, would have found his groundings also in northern European, and not southern European, custom. It should be recalled, however, that the United Provinces had proclaimed its independence from Spain only twenty-seven years earlier, and Grotius appears, to at least some extent, to have considered himself a Spaniard. For instance, he writes, ". . . and although the common people among *our* own Spaniards seem to be of the same opinion, namely, that absolutely no one in the world except *us* Spaniards *ourselves* has the least right to navigate the great and immense sea which stretches to the regions of the Indies once subdued by *our* most powerful kings, as if that right has been *ours* alone by prescription . . ." (Grotius 1916: 54, emphasis added).

[12] In fact, many of the societies cited by Selden did not possess their neighboring seas but merely exercised power there (Anand 1983). Thus, Selden may have been among the first of modern scholars to confuse *imperium* with *dominium*.

the navigation of its seas by other people without being wanting in its duties to humanity. He was thus endeavouring to reconcile the British special claim to the sea with the general claims of the freedom of navigation. The same idea is found in one of Selden's most celebrated followers, Sir Philip Medows, who in his Observations concerning the dominion and sovereignty of the seas, published in 1689, fully supports the view that "the sea is the public property of the Crown of England," but at the same time declares that "as it is a way, it is common to the peacable traders of all nations." (Colombos 1967: 63)

Selden is arguing for a set of rules similar to that posited by Grotius for a situation where one effectively could possess a portion of the ocean. Grotius and Selden both propose systems wherein rights to private property are overlain with regulations forbidding usurpation of rights to common usage. These systems contrast with Freitas, who argues that the sea is common property but susceptible to private usufruct.

Selden writes little about the portions of the sea lying beyond nationally controlled waters. His definition of England's national waters is fairly expansive: the English Sea flows from the western coast of Ireland to the northern coast of Spain, northward to the limits of habitable space, and eastward only a short distance until it meets the German Sea. He justifies each of these borders by citing historical associations between particular regions of the sea and the people who live on the neighboring land. Thus Selden retains the provincial regional seas perspective of pre-modern northern Europe. In fact, Selden is not writing at all about the *deep* sea. He works through the implications of Grotius' statements for his nation's maritime policy and rebuts accordingly. But Selden offers little advice to an English monarch deciding, for instance, whether to interdict a Spanish ship laden with gold in the mid-Atlantic or whether to occupy and claim a trade monopoly with an island in southeast Asia. To the extent that he notes that *mare clausum* can go only so far as one can assert effective control and to the extent that he offers no alternative regime for the waters beyond this point, Selden, by default, is proposing a construction of the deep sea at least as "free" as that proposed by either Grotius or Freitas.

Behind the polemics of the "Battle of the Books," all three authors are proposing variations on the "Mediterranean" notion of stewardship. For all three authors, the sea is, at the most abstract level, a potential space of exclusion. However, claims to exclusive use or possession must be tempered because the ocean cannot be policed adequately and/or use

of its non-exhaustible resources is guaranteed for all by natural law. Beyond this consensus, each author envisions a different stewardship mechanism by which universal access and use rights are guaranteed in the space of the deep sea: Freitas envisions a world in which competing powers claim quasi-sovereignty over specific ocean routes and take on responsibility for policing these routes; Grotius implies that this quasi-sovereignty belongs to the community of nations; and Selden – by implication of omission – suggests a *laissez-faire* regime in which states may cooperate or compete freely, so long as they do not hinder navigation. In all three cases, the sea is a special space of commerce within global society. Freedom of the sea is preserved even as – in the Mediterranean tradition – society(s) and social actors exercise and gather power and, in the case of Freitas, make claims of quasi-possession.

1650–1760: post-Westphalian mercantilism

Despite an eventual resolution to the "Battle of the Books" that combined Grotian *mare liberum* in the deep sea with Seldenian *mare clausum* in coastal waters (see Chapter 4), the dominant construction for the duration of the mercantilist era was one that was closest to that advocated by Freitas. For the remainder of the seventeenth century, and well into the eighteenth century, states continued to make exclusive-use claims to portions of the sea (Colombos 1967). As in the Roman Mediterranean, states avoided claiming territorial appropriation of specific areas of ocean-space, but they continued to assert authority over specific sea-uses in specific locations. In particular, individual states claimed authority over the long-distance sea-routes that carried the channeled circulation of mercantilism.

To this end, even those nations most closely associated with advocating free trade and open seas – the Dutch and the English – continued restrictive practices begun by the Portuguese. As late as 1818, Britain passed a law requiring that merchants wishing to trade with overseas possessions employ a three-fourths British crew and trade only through ports that were under direct British control. The duty on a product landed at an Indian port was doubled if it had been transported in a non-British ship, regardless of the good's origin (Nambiar 1975). Thus, the sea remained throughout the mercantilist era a non-possessible space in which power politics was played out, all with the goal of achieving control of that most precious mercantilist good: channeled circulation.

Representing mercantilist ocean-space

Underlying this construction of the deep sea as beyond possession was a perception that the sea was wild, unruly, and untamable. The channeled circulation that characterized mercantilist capital mobility took place in a hostile environment: a dangerous and unpossessible sea. Power was needed not only for protection against other states, but also against the sea itself.

Figures 2 and 3, both from the mid-sixteenth century, portray the sea as a space of strife and struggle. Brave seamen do battle with fierce sea monsters, in sharp contrast to the happy, jolly landlubbers (and even, in Figure 2, land animals). These two figures also display a feature commonly found in maps of the era: the sea is portrayed as topographically more textured than the land, hardly an inviting environment for navigation. The sea monsters on these maps are not mere decorations; rather, they represent actual creatures thought to exist in the sea. The back of Figure 4, a map of Iceland from 1585, contains text describing the animals referred to by the reference letters on the front of the map.

> One, we are told (N), "sleepeth twelve houres together hanging by his two long teeth upon some rocke or cliffe"; another (M) "hath bene seene to stand a whole day together upright upon his taile . . . and greedily seeketh after mans flesh"; and a third (C) "hath his head bigger than all the body beside." (Campbell 1981: 88–89)

Other maps of the era distinctly portray the dichotomy between the sea, a space providing the resource of connection, and land, a civilizable space of distinct places that may be parceled into discrete territories. In Figure 5, directional vectors and topographic roughness stop when the sea reaches the coast of a civilized England characterized by grid-like farms, compact villages, and gentle pastures. A similar image is portrayed in Figure 6, although here the lines of connection pass through the tamed (and hence named) Europeanized coast to the interior of Java which, although not yet civilized (i.e. named), is amenable to civilization and territorialization.

Mercantilist-era literature similarly portrays the sea as a wild zone filled with untamed and untamable elements, animals, and people (Mollat du Jourdin 1993). States might assert their power in ocean-space – both to better themselves in competition with other states and to battle the sea's unruly nature – but in the end the sea resists outright control by state authorities. Shakespeare demonstrates the perceived impotence of land-based civil power when confronted by the ocean in

Figure 2. Map of Iceland by Hieronymus Gourmount, 1548.

Figure 3. Map of America by Diego Gutierrez, 1562.

The Tempest (*circa* 1610). In the opening scene, as the ship is going down, the king's counsellor, Gonzalo, attempts to help but instead gets in the way of the boatswain who frantically tries to save the ship. Finally, the boatswain admonishes Gonzalo:

> What care these roarers for the name of King? . . . You are a Counsellor: if you can command these Elements to silence and worke the peace of the present, wee will not hand a rope more: use your authoritie! If you cannot, give thankes you have liv'd so long, and make your selfe readie in your Cabine for the mischance of the houre, if it so happens.
>
> (*The Tempest*, Act 1 Scene 1)

The ocean was constructed as a space that resisted civil authority (and, hence, possession), even as land-based states attempted to harness the

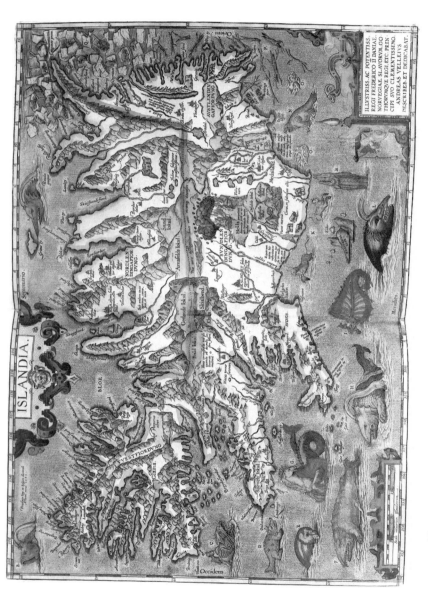

Figure 4. Map of Iceland by Abraham Ortelius, 1585 (reproduced by permission of the British Library, London, shelfmark Maps 9.8.108).

Figure 5. Map of the English coast from the Isle of Wight to Dover, from *De Spieghel der Zeevaerdt* by Lucas Janszoon Waghenaer, 1584 (reproduced courtesy of the James Ford Bell Library, University of Minnesota, Minneapolis).

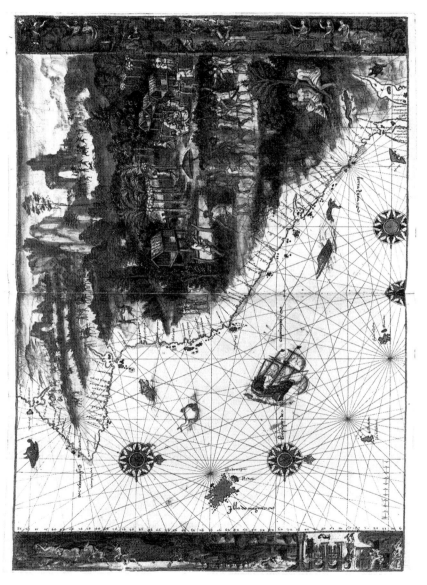

Figure 6. Map of Jave-le-Grand, from *The Vallard Atlas* by Nicolas Vallard, 1547 (reproduced by permission of the Henry E. Huntington Library, San Marino).

ocean's significant resource (transportation) for their own ends. The awe with which sailors of the era regarded the nature of the sea was expressed in 1493 by Christopher Columbus in his first letter written from the New World. Columbus notes that contrary to their appearance and his expectations, the natives "are of a very acute intelligence." The only evidence he gives to support this conclusion is that they "are men who navigate all those seas" (Columbus 1991: 31).

As the mercantilist era progressed into the seventeenth century, those who actually encountered the sea began to adjust their perspective. The sea remained a surface unsuitable for possession, but its character became considerably more benign. Increasingly, the sea shifted from being a space of mysterious danger to being a space without nature, unpossessible but also unremarkable. Captains' logs from the second half of the mercantilist era, while replete with poetic descriptions of far-off lands, fail to note any significant nature in the sea (Raban 1992).

By the early seventeenth century, maps featuring sea monsters representing marine nature and ships representing the social activity that transpired in the arena of ocean-space began to be replaced by maps portraying a grid over an essentially featureless ocean (Figures 7 and 8) (Whitfield 1996). Ships and a few gratuitous sea monsters, fish, and even humanoids still appear, but they strike the reader more as decoration than as a warning. Certainly these sea creatures, and the sea itself, appear much less ominous than in the earlier maps. By 1665, when the map in Figure 9 was drawn, the sea had become devoid of any substance whatsoever. Significantly, the only discernible topographical ocean feature on these figures, and one that appears on all three maps, is the Grand Banks off the coast of Newfoundland, a utilitarian and beneficial landmark.

In this shift from the ocean's representation as a terrifying wild wherein societies and nature interact to its representation as an empty space to be crossed by atomistic ships, one can see the beginnings of the ocean-space construction (and the scientific outlook) that was to predominate during the following centuries of industrial capitalism. Nonetheless, even as the mercantilist-era representation of the ocean shifted, its uses, regulations, and representations remained primarily within the Mediterranean "force-field" model, as the sea was constituted as a space – first terror-filled, then empty – that lay within the sphere of political–economic activity but beyond the possession of any one political–economic actor. The sea was the surface across which transpired much of the channeled circulation that characterized merchant

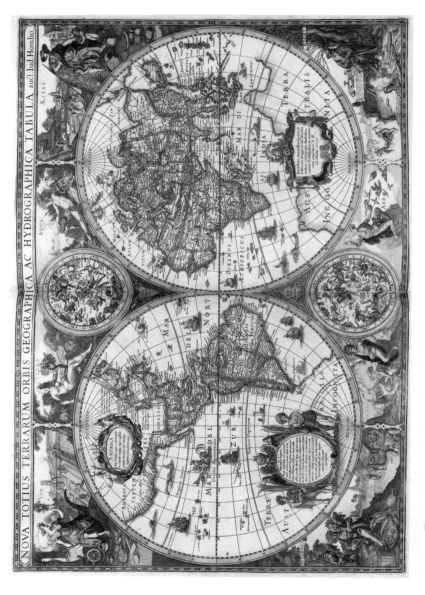

Figure 7. Map of the world by Jodocus Hondius, 1617 (reproduced by permission of the British Library, London, shelfmark Maps c.3.c.9v.1).

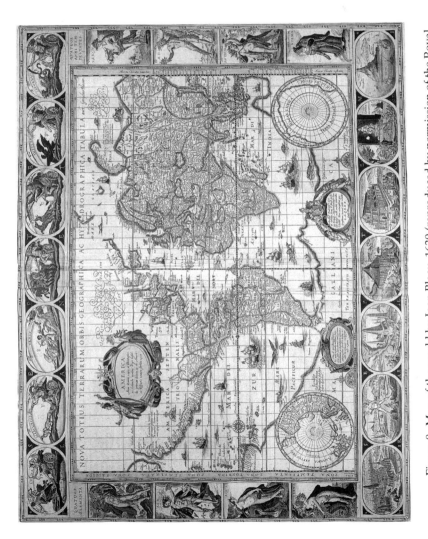

Figure 8. Map of the world by Joan Blaeu, 1630 (reproduced by permission of the Royal Geographical Society, London).

Figure 9. Map of the world by Frederick de Wit, 1665 (reproduced by permission of the British Library, London, shelfmark Maps C.K5.f2 (2/134)).

capitalism. It was a space in which state-actors exerted power and sought a degree of control, even though the territory of ocean-space per se elicited little interest. The sea was fought over not as a space to be possessed, but to be controlled, a special space within world-society but outside the territorial states that comprised its paradigmatic spatial structure.

4 Ocean-space and industrial capitalism

The spatiality of industrial capitalism

As the previous chapter demonstrated, the mercantilist era was characterized by a spatiality that revolved around control over channeled routes of circulation. Space – on land and at sea – mattered as points of access to these channels, and hence efforts were made to exert some degree of power across the surface of the world. As a major surface for movement, the sea was contested as circulation-space and it served as an arena for many of the political and economic contests of the fifteenth to eighteenth centuries. While the mercantilist-era sea was not perceived as a significant place (or set of places) in its own right, it was associated with the resource of connection, and hence perceived as an important arena in which individual states exercised social power and asserted their rights to stewardship.

The transition to industrial capitalism, beginning in the mid-eighteenth century, heralded a different spatial logic. The industrial era brought about the classic "capitalist" spatiality discussed in Chapter 1, one in which dual tendencies toward capital mobility and capital fixity were associated with capitalists alternately investing in (or "filling") and disinvesting in (or "emptying") discrete locations on the earth's surface. Although industrial capitalism progressed through several stages from around 1760 to 1970, it retained a common spatiality that was centered on a commitment to place.

During the early craft-production era (*circa* 1760–1840), the impact of industrialization on most sectors of production was limited. Transportation was revolutionized by the railroad and productivity improved dramatically in aspects of textile production. Yet there was little industrialization beyond these two sectors. Even in the textile and textile

110

machinery industries, crucial components of the production process remained nonindustrialized up to and including the mid-nineteenth century, in many cases limiting overall growth of the industry. For the most part, capitalists intervened in production not by investing in productive machinery, but rather by intensifying the coordinating functions they already had begun during the mercantilist era. Capitalists reorganized the division of labor within craft-production zones, often gathering the workers within a single factory building so as to rationalize further the production process as well as to ensure quality control, prevent embezzlement, and intensify the application of labor (Dunford and Perrons 1983). Thus, this era was characterized by a conception of the worker in (local) society as producer. Investments were made in the local society itself to maintain worker skills and productivity. Indeed, it is the commitment to people-in-place inherent in this model of industrial organization that has led Piore and Sabel (1984) to suggest it as a prototype for a new non-exploitative mode of capitalist development.

Following 1840, advances in the machine-tool and metallurgy industries were associated with increasing capital intensification, mechanized production, and the routinization and deskilling of the labor process that was elevated to a "science" by Frederick Taylor. Still, the commitment to place continued. The intense capital investments of this era were not easily mobile. The bulky commodities that frequently served as inputs for Taylorist production, the huge factories that facilitated supervision and rationalization, and the large production machines that most often were the products and tools of Taylorist production all limited location choice and mobility.

A further shift in industrial capitalist production systems occurred around 1920, with the rise of Fordism, as mass production became coupled with policies and wage scales encouraging mass consumption. Under Fordism, the primary producer remained the machine, supplemented by the contribution of the worker. At the same time, a new element was added to the economic equation: the worker and "his" family as consumer. Again, this system implied a commitment to place. Fixed capital investments remained high, and stable families were promoted as reliable consumers. When Fordism became linked with Keynesianism in the 1930s, the scale of both the producer and the consumer was expanded to that of the nation-society, but similar norms applied.

Thus, throughout the period of industrial capitalism there was a commitment to place unlike that of the mercantilist era. As Scott and Storper (1986) note, all instances of industrial capitalism are associated with spatial concentration, although the exact form of this concentration has varied across both time and space. The idea of investing in industrial production carries with it an idea of investing in a place. Once places become essentialized in this manner, space becomes abstract and conceptually separable from the social processes occurring in particular places (Lefebvre 1991). Capitalists idealize a world in which investments may be moved freely across space and places may be "developed" (or "filled") and "underdeveloped" (or "emptied") at will in pursuit of profit. Highly advanced forms of territoriality are implemented to facilitate the cycles of "emptying" and "filling" (Sack 1986; Steinberg 1994b).

As industrial capitalism took on a spatiality characterized by investment and disinvestment in discrete terrestrial places, the ocean, which had been a significant space during mercantilist times as a site of channeled circulation, came to be constructed, at least at the rhetorical level, as a space *outside* society. In the popular imagination, the space that *mattered* was the space of developable places, and most of the ocean did not present an environment for fixed capital investments. And yet, the sea clearly did matter, playing a crucial role in transcontinental empires and long-distance trade, two political–economic phenomena that remained important under industrial capitalism.[1]

In fact, the industrial capitalist era was characterized by a complex ocean-space construction that blended several tendencies, each reminiscent of one of the non-modern ideal-types presented in Chapter 2. The deep sea – the area distant from coastal lands – was idealized in a manner similar to the Indian Ocean, as a *great void* outside society and insulated from social forces. It was constructed as the wild antithesis of society (or place), the space of *anti-civilization*. As an unconquerable and uncivilizable space, the deep sea provided an ideal arena for Enlightenment society to test and affirm its own level of civilization, whether through annihilating the marine "other" or through scientifically analyzing it.

In reality, however, the deep sea was providing crucial resources (especially the resource of connection). This required active stewardship and governance. Thus, the Indian Ocean-style rhetoric toward the deep

---

[1] Between 1715 and 1787 the volume of England's overseas trade increased between 500 and 600 percent. Over the same years, France's imports from overseas increased 1,000 percent and its exports 700 to 800 percent (Anand 1983). The total value of world trade increased from US$1.5 billion in 1800 to $4 billion in 1850 to $24 billion in 1900. In other words, during the nineteenth century, as the world population increased three-fold, international commerce increased sixteen-fold (Stevens and Westcott 1942).

sea was accompanied by practical measures that more closely resembled the Mediterranean and mercantilist-era norms of stewardship. For the most part, this stewardship was practiced by the community of nations as a whole (the Grotian model) rather than through individual states projecting their power to discrete areas of ocean-space (the Freitian model, which had been dominant during the mercantilist era). Because these stewardship practices threatened to interfere with the construction of the ocean as a friction-free great void insulated from social intervention, the Grotian regulatory structures implemented tended to be fairly weak, in some instances empowering non-state actors rather than states so as to avoid any implication that the deep sea was suitable for extension of state territoriality. As the industrial era proceeded and ocean-space increasingly provided significant fish and mineral resources, a Seldenian element was added to the Grotian system of stewardship as individual states were granted limited stewardship rights and responsibilities in areas of the deep sea adjacent to territorial waters. Finally, the combination of Indian Ocean-style great void ideals and Mediterranean-style stewardship practices in the deep sea was complemented by a Micronesian-style construction of coastal waters as territorial extensions of land-space.

The "great void" idealization of the deep sea

During the industrial capitalist era, the ocean was idealized as the antithesis of land-space. Classical and neoclassical economic doctrines of the era held that nations should seek power not by controlling trade but by wisely investing in the resources for which they possessed a comparative advantage. If such nations were to trade freely with each other, all would rise to a maximum level of wealth and happiness. The implication of this economic doctrine was that the space between the nation-societies was a vast void, much as it had been constructed in the non-modern Indian Ocean. Little would be gained from exerting power or possession in this non-developable space; indeed, it was believed that mercantilist military missions and trade monopolies would hurt the entire community of nations (Kennedy 1976).

The ocean thus was idealized as an empty transportation surface, beyond the space of social relations, and projection of power in the deep sea was perceived as legitimate only when applied toward the end of destroying obstacles to free navigation. This is not to say that liberal, industrial capitalist ideology constructed the sea as an *unimportant* space. Rather, the sea was constructed, like money or markets, as without social "roots" – beyond society, politics, or the other "artificial" social constructs that could interfere with the "natural" free flow of capital. Gold concisely summarizes the view toward maritime commerce held at the 1815 Congress of Vienna:

> For most European countries, commerce was no longer "fashionable" nor something on which great amounts of energy needed to be expended. Commerce was considered to be sufficiently self-motivated and self-perpetuating that whatever loose regulation it needed could be supplied by lesser government bodies. As long as commerce could provide a convenient tax base for government ambitions, necessary employment for the expanding population, and new markets for imports and exports, it was left to its own devices. Ocean transportation, as a part of the commercial structure, fitted well into this laissez-faire philosophy.
>
> (Gold 1981: 80)

The ocean discursively became constructed as outside society and the terrestrial places of progress, civilization, and development. Movement across spaces that resisted development, although necessary, rhetorically was defined as a subordinate activity beyond social regulation. Thus, the narrators of such books as Herman Melville's 1849 novel *Redburn* (Melville 1957) and Richard Henry Dana's 1840 autobiography *Two Years Before the Mast* (Dana 1964) describe their fellow sailors as semi-barbarian outcasts. An inverse relationship was perceived between one's closeness to the nature of the ocean and one's level of civilization. In Melville's 1851 novel *Moby Dick* (Melville 1988), the role of the harpoonist – the individual on a whaling ship who most intimately encounters the nature of the marine environment – is reserved for the three principal "savages" on board: Queequeg, a South Pacific islander, Tashtego, a Native American, and Dagoo, an African.[2]

The idealization of the deep sea as a great void between developable, terrestrial places of civilization was aided and reflected by representations in maps, art, and literature of the industrial capitalist era. In cartography, the sea slipped into the background. The sea, once represented on maps by colorful fish, terrifying monsters, dramatic swells, and valiant ships engaged in battle, now was drawn as a blue, formless expanse (Whitfield 1996). Taking this representation to its extreme

---

[2] Seamen of color were "othered" in other ways as well. On nineteenth-century U.S. ships, for instance, African-Americans frequently were relegated to traditionally female tasks, such as laundering and cooking (Bolster 1990, 1996; Horton 1986).

absurdity, Lewis Carroll penned the following verses to accompany the "Ocean-Chart" (Figure 10) in his 1876 poem *The Hunting of the Snark*:

> He had bought a large map representing the sea,
>   Without the least vestige of land:
> And the crew were much pleased when they found it to be
>   A map they could all understand.
> "What's the good of Mercator's North Poles and Equators,
>   Tropics, Zones, and Meridian Lines?"
> So the Bellman would cry: and the crew would reply
>   "They are merely conventional signs!
> Other maps are such shapes, with their islands and capes!
>   But we've got our brave Captain to thank"
> (So the crew would protest) "that he's bought us the best –
>   A perfect and absolute blank!"
>
>   (Lewis Carroll, *The Hunting of the Snark*)

Rationalists of the era saw the ocean as a space resistant to social progress, modernization, and development, and that therefore must be conquered or annihilated (or, short of annihilation, reserved for outcast sailors and non-Western harpoonists). This attitude is aptly demonstrated in James Barry's *Progress of Human Culture* (1777–1783), a mural that adorns the great hall of London's Royal Society of Arts and Manufactures. Throughout the mural's six panels, Barry utilizes classical techniques (one critic calls the mural "ultra-Michelangelesque") to create a "Sistine Chapel of the Enlightenment . . . [celebrating] the missionary cult of genius, the glorification of the human faculties, the ameliorist confidence, the encyclopedic approach to both history and knowledge, the patriotic pride alongside the assertion of the brotherhood of nations" (Burke 1976: 250). The first panel, "Orpheus Reclaiming Mankind from a Savage State," is a pointed attack on the romantic glorification of the noble savage. Contrasting this notion, the mural, according to its artist, seeks to demonstrate that "the obtaining of happiness as well individual or public, depends upon cultivating the human faculties" (cited in Burke 1976: 248–249). The fourth panel, "Navigation, or the Triumph of the Thames" (Figure 11, later titled "Commerce, or the Triumph of the Thames"), is notable in that there is almost no water in the foreground. This seems at first an odd way to represent navigation, unless one defines navigation as the process whereby science is used not to tame or interpret but to *annihilate* ocean-space; in that case the sight of gods, goddesses, statesmen, scientists, and philosophers

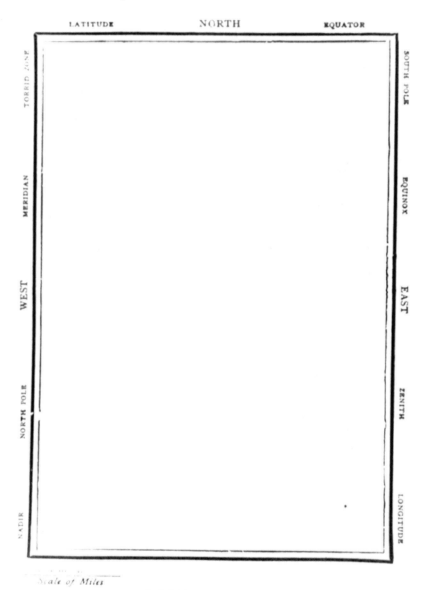

OCEAN-CHART

Figure 10. "Ocean-Chart," from *The Hunting of the Snark* by Lewis Carroll, 1876.

Figure 11. "Commerce, or the Triumph of the Thames" (originally titled "Navigation, or the Triumph of the Thames") by James Barry, 1777–1783, fourth panel in the mural *The Progress of Human Culture* at the Royal Society of Arts and Manufactures, London (reproduced by permission of the Bridgeman Art Library, London).

literally crowding out the vast expanses of the ocean is an appropriate celebration of the Age of Reason.[3]

Although writing in 1989, William Golding captures the spirit of the times in *Fire Down Below*, the third volume of his sea trilogy set in the early nineteenth century. After completing harrowing journeys from England to Australia, two British aristocrats carry on the following conversation while courting each other:

> "I did not know there was so much [sea], Mr Talbot, that is the fact of the matter. One sees maps and globes but it is different."
> "It is indeed different!"
> "Most of it you know, sir, is quite unnecessary."

---

[3] Apparently not all Londoners were enthused by Barry's congested representation of the glorious conquest of ocean-space. One dowager, on seeing the painting when it was first revealed, likened it to "a horse pond with a bevy of naked wenches" (cited in Burke 1976: 249).

"Quite, quite unnecessary! Away with it! There shall be no more sea!
Let us have a modest strip between one country and another – a kind
of canal –"
"The occasional ornamental lake in a prospect –"
"A fountain or two –" (Golding 1991: 730)

Although one of the two conversants, Talbot, had grown somewhat
attached to the sea during his voyage, once on land the sea has no place
in his aristocratic world-view. Clinging to pre-modern visions of delicate
upper-class English beauty as well as to the modern view that nature can
be transformed by applying science and reason to the task, the two spin a
scenario that effectively would eliminate the ocean as a barrier to a world
consisting of an endless succession of discrete, controllable places. The
elemental quality of water is retained in the aristocrats' vision, but the
canals, lakes, and fountains resulting from their imaginary landscaping
efforts are no longer things of nature.

This rationalist idealization of the ocean as empty and featureless was
complemented by romantics who praised the ocean for its wild nature
that resisted taming by the forces of modernity. Despite its contrast with
the rationalist attitude toward ocean-space, this romantic representation
also had its origins in the industrial era's construction of the sea as a
space beyond society. Romantics, like rationalists, identified the sea as a
wild "other," but they honored it as a space to be treasured and nurtured,
rather than vilified and annihilated.

In particular, romantics of the era celebrated the sea as the space of
the *sublime*. Raban (1992) identifies an early precursor to the nineteenth-
century view of the sea as sublime in a 1712 essay written by Joseph
Addison:

> Of all objects that I have ever seen, there is none which affects my imag-
> ination so much as the sea or ocean. I cannot see the heaving of this
> prodigious bulk of waters, even in a calm, without a very pleasing as-
> tonishment; but when it is worked up in a tempest, so that the Horizon
> on every side is nothing but foaming billows and floating mountains,
> it is impossible to describe the agreeable horrour that rises from such
> a prospect. A troubled ocean, to a man who sails upon it, is, I think,
> the biggest object that he can see in motion, and consequently gives his
> imagination one of the highest kinds of pleasure that can arise from
> greatness. (cited in Raban 1992: 8)

In his 1757 treatise, *A Philosophical Enquiry Into the Origin of Our Ideas of
the Sublime and Beautiful*, Edmund Burke (1958) identifies the ocean as
the paradigmatic space of the sublime because it combines a beautiful

vastness that attracts the viewer with a terror that repels. There are parallels between the "discovery" of the sublime ocean and that of the earth's subterranean regions, as both elements simultaneously were tantalizing and distressing to the authors of the early industrial capitalist era (Williams 1990). The underground and the sea were exciting frontier areas at a time when intellectual and geographic frontiers were being pushed to their limits, and yet they were inhospitable to the scientific, development-oriented control and spatially fixed investments characteristic of, respectively, Enlightenment thinking and industrial capitalism. Even as civilization expanded to encounter these new elements, the elements remained wild, untamable, and "pre-modern." Thus, the sea and the underground represented the points at which rationalism and industrialism – with all their social benefits and attendant evils – stopped, and where Nature – with an entirely different and grander set of beauties and evils – began. For romantics, the sea, untainted by the civilization people had built on land, provided an opportunity for individuals and groups to reclaim a more pure humanity (Corbin 1994; Lenček and Bosker 1998; Raban 1992).

Marine painting blossomed during the industrial capitalist era, especially in England, where there already was a tradition of marine art dating back to mercantilist times. Prior to the nineteenth century, marine paintings primarily were representations of actual ships and historical events, with the technical details of each ship often painted with astounding accuracy. The ship, like the noble, was an important actor in mercantilist society, and both "posed" for "portraits." Following 1800, there arose a new school of marine artists, led by the English painter J. M. W. Turner. In Turner's works, as in those of later artists such as the American Winslow Homer, the ship is often overshadowed by the ocean itself, portrayed in dazzling reds and oranges during calm sunsets and brooding dark greens during storms.[4] On maps, the sea, as the asocial space of distance and "anti-civilization," was portrayed as a great blue void. In artwork of the era it was portrayed as a different kind of asocial space: a sublime environment of Nature, beyond History, against which Man could test his physical strength and moral courage, far from the corrupting influence of land-based society (Cordingly 1973; Gaunt 1975).

This construction of the sea as moral testing ground extended beyond the visual arts to the literature of the era. For many nineteenth-century

---

[4] Barry's painting is an exception to this trend. He was not, however, generally a marine artist, but rather was using a marine representation in that one painting to make a broader statement about Enlightenment civilization.

novelists and poets, the sea was an arena untainted by modernity, wherein one was challenged to reclaim a pure, pre-modern humanity. In Samuel Coleridge's 1798 poem, "The Rime of the Ancient Mariner" (Coleridge 1961), the sea is a space of humanity in which Christian Love and the Glory of God are valued over the superficial creations of Man. For Coleridge, the vast, sublime nature of the sea is one of dazzling beauty, gruesome creatures ("a thousand thousand slimy things"), and tortuous hardships. Against this proving ground, the mariner suffers dearly for asserting his land-like civilized powers over the natural, God-like albatross. Redemption comes only when he appreciates that even the least pleasant aspects of the sea are worthy of his awe and respect. The allegory *could* have been set on land, but it would have been difficult to construct God's creations as so awesome, His punishment so severe, or His redemption so dramatic in a less sublime, more mundane and civilized environment.

While Coleridge's sea provides an opportunity for humanity to engage in pre-modern religious submission, other writers of the era, such as Rudyard Kipling and Joseph Conrad, constructed the sea as an environment in which the rigid hierarchical political order of bygone days still ruled, uncorrupted by the democratic weaknesses of land-based society:

> One cannot separate Conrad's writing about the sea from his far-right political beliefs: they are two sides of the same coin. The land was polluted beyond repair – by socialism and "radical reform." . . . For Conrad, the sea was the last untainted, venerable, and holy place left on the earth's surface, and that conviction fires his most brilliant writing, and gives his vision of the sea its incandescent quality.   (Raban 1992: 18)

This tradition is continued in the late twentieth-century submarine film. On the one hand the sea is presented as an untamed frontier and the ship is alone, frequently cut off from communication with civilization on land. Out of necessity, the captain must maintain something of a free-wheeling buccaneer spirit. On the other hand the ship itself – and the military organization of which it is a part – is run according to a strict hierarchy that has its leadership outside the vessel. In two recent films of this genre, *The Hunt for Red October* (1989) and *Crimson Tide* (1995), individuals with different mixes of these two contradictory tendencies are pitted against each other as they each face an impossible task: to build a viable society amidst the space of anti-civilization.

As some novelists – particularly those in Britain in the earlier part of the era – constructed the sea as an anti-civilization existing in opposition to land-based society, other authors – particularly Americans – constructed the sea as a different kind of "other" space. In this "American" construction, the sea, while awesome and worthy of fear, also was to be analyzed and understood. The American construction, while retaining the identity of the ocean as anti-civilization, nonetheless proceeded to apply Enlightenment-era science to the sea. As in Coleridge's "Ancient Mariner", characters in these American novels used the wildness of the sea to achieve liberation from the corruption and banality of land-based society, but they did this not through conquering the sea or submitting to the awesome powers that it represented. Rather, they achieved liberation by using science to become one with the sea.

Several authors, most notably Olson (1947), have connected this attitude toward the sea in American literature from the mid-nineteenth century onward with the American experience of successfully conquering a terrestrial frontier. From the lengthy scientific digressions permeating Herman Melville's 1851 novel *Moby Dick* (Melville 1988) and Jules Verne's 1870 classic *20,000 Leagues Under the Sea* (Verne 1962),[5] to the 1900 autobiographical travel narrative presented by Joshua Slocum in *Sailing Alone Around the World* (Slocum 1903) and the environmentalist writing of Rachel Carson in *The Sea Around Us* (Carson 1951), the sea is an "other" and, one could even say, an "anti-civilization." But it is an "other" to be appreciated, not loathed, conquered, feared, or annihilated, and it is through *understanding* and *analysis* that one can utilize one's encounter with the sea to move beyond the limits of mundane land-life.

Verne's *20,000 Leagues* merits special attention here. Besides serving as an excellent example of this "American" attitude toward the sea, it also foreshadows elements of the postmodern ocean-space construction discussed in the next chapter. Verne, in the tradition of Coleridge and Conrad, views the sea as a "pure" arena where individuals can escape the evils of land-based society. In *20,000 Leagues* and Verne's many other sea- and island-based stories,

> [the sea] is the negation and antithesis of the land with its police-ridden societies and its constraints. To borrow a word from the anarchist circles of the end of the nineteenth century, the sea is a "free medium" in the

---

[5] Although Verne was French, Bradbury (1962) identifies him as having an "American" style and, in particular, one that emerges from the same tradition as Melville. Chesneaux, in his study of Verne's novels, devotes an entire chapter to the special role of the United States in Verne's works. He notes, "It is not by chance that in twenty-three of his novels, out of a total of sixty-four, the action takes place on American soil, either wholly or in part, or that American characters play an important role" (Chesneaux 1972: 150).

> highest degree . . . [The sea and its islands (which are "of the sea")] pos-
> sess the essential characteristics of "free environments": wide horizons,
> freedom from governmental restraint, and the possibility of organizing
> social relationships with ease and flexibility.   (Chesneaux 1972: 88, 96)

There is a strong anarchistic element in Verne's conception of ocean-
space, a sentiment that in part may be attributed to his friendship with
the anarchist geographer Elisée Reclus.

Despite his links with Reclus, Verne's anarchism is tempered by a love
of classificatory science that more closely resembles the thoughts of another anarchist geographer of the era, Petr Kropotkin. In *20,000 Leagues*,
Captain Nemo seeks to encounter the sea and achieve liberation there,
but in doing so he engages science, a creature of the Enlightenment discourse and a paradigm that supports many of the world's evils. Captain
Nemo's attitude toward the sea is summarized aptly in an oft-quoted
passage from *20,000 Leagues*:

> "Yes, I love [the sea]! The sea is everything. It covers seven-tenths of
> the globe. Its breath is pure and healthy. It is an immense desert where
> a man is never alone, for he can feel life quivering all about him. The
> sea is only a receptacle for all the prodigious, supernatural things that
> exist inside it; it is only movement and love; it is the living infinite,
> as one of your poets has said. And in fact, Professor, it contains the
> three kingdoms of nature – mineral, vegetable and animal. This last is
> well represented by the four groups of zoophytes, by the three classes
> of articulata, by the five classes of mollusks, by the three classes of
> vertebrates, mammals and reptiles, and by those innumerable legions
> of fish, that infinite order of animals which includes more than thirteen
> thousand species, only one tenth of which live in fresh water. The sea
> is a vast reservoir of nature. The world, so to speak, began with the
> sea, and who knows but that it will also end in the sea! There lies
> supreme tranquility. The sea does not belong to tyrants. On its surface,
> they can still exercise their iniquitous rights, fighting, destroying one
> another and indulging in their other earthly horrors. But thirty feet
> below its surface their power ceases, their influence dies out and their
> domination disappears! Ah, Monsieur, one must live – live within the
> ocean! Only there can one be independent! Only there do I have no
> master! There I am free!"   (Verne 1962: 73–74)

This monologue is remarkable in that Nemo identifies three very
different reasons for his love of the sea. First, it is the world of the sublime ("an immense desert"); second, it is the world of Linnean science
("more than thirteen thousand species"); and third, it is the world of
anarchy ("Only there can one be independent"). Verne makes much of

these contradictory foundations underlying Nemo's behavior at sea. Distrust of nationalism, for instance, is a persistent theme throughout the book. Professor Aronnax, who never quite understands what drives Captain Nemo, is obsessed with nationalism, continually referring to the national characteristics of his Canadian and Belgian colleagues and repeatedly trying to figure out Captain Nemo's nationality. Nemo, the anarchist, keeps Aronnax (and the reader) guessing, proclaiming that he belongs to the "nation" of the world's oppressed (Verne 1962: 204), thereby asserting that the primary division in the world is between "haves" and "have-nots" and not between nation-states. And yet, Nemo remains committed to land-based national struggles; his chamber is decorated with portraits of nationalist leaders and it is revealed that he pillages sunken treasure ships and uses the money to fund national liberation movements. The paradox of Nemo's "anarchist nationalism" is particularly apparent when he begins to behave much like the despised warring land-based states: sinking vessels and taking prisoners.

Similarly, his ship's motto, *mobilis in mobile* (translated in the novel as "mobile in mobile element") is an explicit rejection of the spatial fixity that characterizes both the politics of the territorial nation-state and the economics of industrial capitalism. Yet, he explains to Aronnax:

> "What your d'Urveille did on the surface of the ocean, . . . I have done beneath the surface, and more easily and completely. Whereas the *Astrolabe* and the *Zélée* were at the mercy of the storms, the *Nautilus* is like a calm, stationary studio in the midst of the ocean!"
>
> (Verne 1962: 161)

To live amidst the anti-civilization of the ocean, Nemo is compelled to use the science of land-based society to establish land-like spatial fixity. In the process, he creates a society frighteningly similar to the land-based world he is attempting to escape. The irony of Nemo's politics is that its very success marks its very failure. True liberation is unachievable.[6]

Much of Nemo's politics and the eclectic way in which he uses science as a weapon against the civilization of land-space and, inadvertently, the anti-civilization of ocean-space, is elucidated in another Verne novel, *The Mysterious Island* (Verne 1959), which was published five years after *20,000 Leagues*. At the end of this novel, Captain Nemo makes a

---

[6] In his later, post-1879, novels, Verne becomes much more critical of science, associating it with the evils of greed, militarism, and territorial expansion (Chesneaux 1972).

cameo appearance and reveals his identity as Prince Dakkar, a wealthy, English-educated Indian noble. Prince Dakkar's politics, like those of Captain Nemo (and, indeed, Verne himself), are somewhat muddled. Like Nemo and Verne, Dakkar reveals an ambivalent relationship with the Enlightenment; he thirsts for knowledge, but he also has a romantic spirit that seeks out an inner sustenance unattainable through the application of reason and science. Succeeding in life, but still wandering aimlessly, he became a leader in the 1857 Indian Mutiny against British rule, driven, it appears, more by romantic ambition than by specific political grievances or a desire for personal power. Following the mutiny's failure, Prince Dakkar, "alone in the world, overcome by disappointment at the destruction of all his vain hopes, a prey to profound disgust for all human beings, filled with hatred of the civilized world," escaped into the ocean. "The warrior became the man of science" (Verne 1959: 526–528).[7]

The liberation one seeks in the "American" sea of Verne is more complex than that of Coleridge or Conrad, perhaps because it looks to the future instead of the past. Rather than turning away from the Enlightenment and industrial capitalism, Verne (and Melville, Slocum, and Carson as well) seek to use science to gain that liberation. Despite the differences in the various ocean-space representations discussed here, they are linked by a common idealization of the ocean as anti-civilization. How that anti-civilization is to be encountered and what kind of liberation is to come from that encounter differs greatly from author to author. For all, however, the ocean exists as a counterpoint to land. Taming the ocean and making it like land-space is out of the question; it lacks the essential spatial properties of industrial capitalist land-space. Instead, those encountering the industrial capitalist-era great void idealization of ocean-space are faced with three alternatives: to construct the sea as a great space to be crossed as quickly as possible (as in the featureless representation on maps or Carroll's "Ocean-Chart"); to wish it away (as in the Barry and Golding works); or to construct it as a sublime, non-modern "other," in opposition to Enlightenment reason, which, through dramatic encounter (perhaps combined with scientific inquiry), might lead one to transcend the banality of land-based civilization.

---

[7] Captain Nemo's politics are further elucidated if one accepts the theory that the character was inspired by Narcis Monturiol i Estarriol, a Catalán utopian socialist who, in the 1850s and 60s, was a pioneer in submarine technology (Hughes 1992).

Regulating anti-civilization: the ascendancy of Grotian stewardship

Despite the idealization of the industrial capitalist-era ocean as an empty void outside society, it *was* a space intensely used (and hence shaped) by society, and thus social regulations were required. The challenge was to develop a regulatory mechanism that complemented the great void idealization. Regulation, especially if coupled with territorial ac-quisition, ran the risk of evolving into a situation of state competition wherein states would interfere with the construction of the ocean as a friction-free transportation surface. To this end, policy makers during this era turned away from the Freitian model of stewardship – wherein individual states claimed a degree of territorial authority over specific ocean routes – and toward a more Grotian model – wherein the sea's resources were stewarded by the global community as a whole. As a further cautionary measure, these Grotian instruments generally were implemented in a rather "weak" form, for fear that stewardship by *any* entity (even the world community as a whole) might imply a degree of territoriality that could threaten the great void ideal. Likewise, pow-ers of stewardship often were given to non-state entities rather than states, under the assumption that they would be less likely than states to expand rights of stewardship to assertions of territorial enclosure.

This new attitude toward regulating ocean-space is particularly ev-ident in the approach of the era toward regulating ocean commerce, the industry that uses the ocean's all-important resource of "connec-tion." The great void idealization of the deep sea constructed the ocean as non-territory, upon which floated discrete territorial entities (ships). Paralleling the Code of Malacca, which was based upon a similar "great void" idealization of ocean-space, most legislation concerning ships and shipping during the industrial capitalist era related to behavior on board individual ships and fell within the municipal law of the ship's home state. During the nineteenth century, however, as the shipping industry grew, it became apparent that a certain degree of standardization was needed for the rules governing behavior on ships and between a ship and its home-country. Furthermore, a need arose to develop norms for the relationship between ships of different nationalities when they inter-acted on the high seas and also for the relationship between a ship and the foreign state in whose territorial waters or port it might be situated.

To this end, a host of calls for international conferences to codify rules of maritime traffic were made between 1850 and 1890. While support grew for a comprehensive conference to deal specifically with marine transport, there were a number of international conferences on related topics that began to regulate the behavior of ships on the high seas.[8] Finally, in 1889, the International Maritime Conference was convened in Washington. Although some preliminary progress was made on technical matters, the conference was for the most part a failure. Among the entities supporting standardization of maritime rules were the shipping industry and the strong maritime powers. But these entities were also interested in preserving the construction of the deep sea as non-territory, and feared that the conference, and in particular its mission to establish a permanent international maritime commission, might set a dangerous precedent by granting to an international organization territorial power to govern the deep sea (Gold 1981). Such a construction was anathema to these interests, whose survival depended on the construction of the sea as a non-territorial void upon which ships could act with total freedom so long as they respected the freedom of other ships.

Nonetheless, these actors, and also manufacturers and insurers, had a strong interest in seeing ships arrive at their destinations safely, with their cargo intact. The insurance industry, in particular, was an active promoter of shipping standardization and regulation. Already, in 1760, Lloyd's had begun publishing its Register of Shipping (reconstituted in 1834 as Lloyd's Register of British and Foreign Shipping), which classes each major cargo ship according to the construction standards by which it was built and the adequacy with which it has been maintained. Lloyd's also began operating lighthouses and signal stations around the world, forming an intelligence network still used by shipping companies and governments in assessing social and natural dangers to shipping (Colombos 1967). On the one hand, the shipping sector, led by the insurance industry, was faced with the task of creating standardized rules for the shipping industry. On the other hand, shipping interests and states whose power rested on maritime trade were reluctant to implement these rules within the context of the community of states. State power is exercised through territorial control, and rule by the community of states would imply a kind of global territorial regime. As Cafruny (1987) notes, the challenge facing global shipping countries was to assert *hegemony* without exercising *power*.

---

[8] Among the international agreements of this era that indirectly affected the behavior of ships on the high seas were conventions on war wounded (1864), telegraph standards (1865), postal standards (1875), railway traffic (1890), sanitary standards (1903), and radio broadcasting (1906) (Gold 1981).

It was in this context that shipping and insurance industries settled upon an alternate strategy for achieving international shipping regulations: the Comité Maritime International (CMI). The first meeting of the CMI took place in Brussels in 1897. The organization's purpose, according to its constitution, is:

> To promote by the establishment of national associations, by conferences, by publications, by any other activities or means, the unification of international maritime and commercial law and practice, whether by treaty or convention or by establishing uniformity of domestic laws, usages, customs or practices. (cited in Gold 1981: 129)

The CMI essentially is an association of national maritime-law associations, each of which, in turn, tends to reflect the interests of the various sectors of the shipping industry active in that country (e.g., shippers, importers–exporters, insurers, manufacturers, passenger line operators, etc.). Every few years the organization meets to discuss such issues as marine shipowners' liability, duty to tender assistance, salvage rights, mortgages and liens on ships, safety of navigation, immunity of state-owned ships, treatment of stowaways, status of ships in foreign ports, and registry rules.[9]

Although the CMI's purpose is to adopt rules as codes of conduct that may be implemented without state approval, the standards agreed to at CMI meetings sometimes require changes in national legislation. One route for achieving such changes in municipal law would be for each delegation, on returning from the meeting, to lobby its national government to adopt the legislation. However, this route would be slow and there would always be the risk that governments might amend the standards unilaterally as they approved the laws. As an alternative, the CMI developed a system whereby the Belgian government acts as a one-way conduit from the "private" world of the shipping industry to the "public" world of diplomacy. In instances where CMI standards require national legislation, it drafts the regulations in the form of a treaty which then is proposed by the Belgian government at an international intergovernmental conference. Following approval, participating governments need only to ratify the treaty instead of going through the difficult process of writing and approving national legislation. In 1972 the CMI revised its constitution, granting to the United Nations rather

---

[9] See Colombos (1967) for an account of many of the shipping and safety standards agreed to during this period, a large number of which were sponsored by the CMI.

than the Belgian government the responsibility of convening intergovernmental conferences to translate its regulations into international law. Aside from this change, however, the making of maritime law remains in the "private" domain, much as it has been for the past hundred years (Gold 1981). Throughout the entire process, the shipping and insurance industries clearly are in control, an arrangement that suits not only these industries but also states fearful of establishing a system of territorial governance that might interfere with their idealized construction of the ocean as a great void beyond social regulation and immune to socially imposed obstacles to shipping.

After serving as a medium for transport, the second most significant resource of the ocean during this period was its function as an arena for fishing. Like use of the deep sea for transport, deep-sea fishing greatly intensified during the era of industrial capitalism (especially during the twentieth century), and there soon emerged a consensus that regulation was needed for certain species and certain heavily fished areas. Early agreements tended to cover specific regions of ocean-space where only a few countries' vessels – generally those of the states bordering the region – fished extensively. Examples of these agreements include an English–French accord on fishing in the English Channel (1839) and a six-state North Sea convention (1882). These agreements, while certainly spatial, were only marginally territorial. The agreements affected certain actors' behavior through the mechanism of defining permitted activities in a bounded area, and, in some cases, each state's vessels were given the right to police the other signatory states' vessels to ensure compliance. Nonetheless, signatories were powerless to prohibit non-signatories' vessels from passing through or even fishing in these waters. Thus, these agreements failed to contain the exclusionary or enforcement provisions that Sack (1986) identifies as essential components of territorial control. The agreements were merely statements by each state to abide by certain harvesting quotas, size restrictions, and/or equipment limitations within a bounded area of ocean-space.

A second type of fishing convention emerged in the twentieth century in response to the overexploitation of highly migratory, deep-water species, a problem resulting from advanced deep-water fishing techniques. To cope with this overexploitation, a series of accords were signed covering the harvesting of specific species in very large areas (or the entirety) of the world-ocean. Examples here include a United States–Canada accord on North Pacific halibut (1923), a United

States–Canada accord on salmon (1930), an accord signed by eleven states on various fish species in the Atlantic and Arctic oceans (1943), and numerous whaling conventions (beginning in 1926) and tuna conventions (beginning in 1949) (Colombos 1967). Again, the signatory states claimed no right to control access to the sea or even behavior in the sea but merely acceded to self-regulation so as to promote the long-term preservation of fish stocks.

This Grotian attitude toward marine governance may be observed not just in industrial capitalism's regulation of positive uses of ocean-space (e.g. transportation and fishing) but also in its regulation of negative uses (e.g. piracy and privateering, slave transport, interference with undersea cables, and polluting activities). Piracy is defined in the 1982 United Nations Convention on the Law of the Sea (United Nations 1983) as:

> Any illegal acts of violence or detention, or any act of depredation, committed for private ends by the crew or the passengers of a private ship or a private aircraft, and directed: (i) on the high seas, against another ship or aircraft, or against persons or property on board such ship or aircraft; (ii) against a ship, aircraft, persons or property in a place outside the jurisdiction of any State. (Article 101)

Two crucial aspects of this definition are that (i) piracy occurs on the high seas; and (ii) piracy must involve an action by one ship against another ship. Marine robberies occurring in territorial waters or within one ship on the high seas are crimes occurring within the territory of one state and are punishable according to municipal legislation – regardless of the offender's citizenship – just as if the crime had occurred on land.[10] Privateering is an act of piracy or war carried out by a private ship acting under the commission of a sovereign state.

Eliminating privateering was fairly simple, once the will existed. Since privateering is, by definition, carried out under state sponsorship, an agreement acceded to by all sovereign states to end privateering effectively would illegalize and – presumably – end the practice. As Britain's navy grew during the nineteenth century, its need for privateers

---

[10] Thus, while the popular press decries the prevalence of piracy, noting, for instance, that "from 1989 to 1993 . . . 523 commercial vessels reported being attacked by pirates" ("Today's pirates pose double trouble" 1994: 16), practically all of these attacks actually occurred in territorial waters. Municipal laws frequently present broader definitions of piracy, and some scholars have argued that the international law definition similarly be broadened (Birnie 1987), but at present incidences of marine robbery in territorial waters are not, *sensu stricto*, acts of piracy.

diminished. Privateering, like state-sponsored terrorism today, was a poor country's means of asserting limited military power; wealthier states preferred more formal (and costly) military engagements in which they could be more certain of victory. At the same time as Britain sought the abolition of privateering, the world's other states, seeking to obtain some degree of insulation from Britain's overwhelming naval power, sought provisions that would grant their commercial fleets protection from British naval vessels. These two goals were achieved in the Declaration of Paris of 1856. Serving the British agenda, the declaration proclaimed that privateering was to be outlawed forever. At the same time, the declaration met other states' interests by holding that non-contraband goods shipped in a neutral flag's vessel were immune from seizure by ships of a warring state, even if the goods were destined for the warring state's opponent. This agreement effectively put an end to privateering (Thomson 1994).

Ending piracy was considerably more complex. Since piracy is defined as non-state-sponsored violence, an agreement by states to abandon the practice would be of only limited effectiveness. As Thomson (1994) notes, several anti-piracy strategies were available. One possibility would have been for individual states to claim sovereignty (or at least policing responsibilities) over broad portions of the deep sea. This strategy, however, besides imposing enormous expenses on the enforcing states if they were to carry out their duties effectively, would imply that all foreign vessels in the protected zone were potential pirates. This policy would make it difficult to distinguish "real" pirates from those merely using their right of free transit and would probably lead to an erosion of the great void idealization of ocean-space upon which the extensive trade of industrial capitalism depended. A second strategy, also territorial, would have been to grant policing authority over the deep sea to a superstate authority. Even today, however, neither the politics nor the economics of the multi-state system has permitted the formation of such a strong and costly superstate entity; certainly nothing of the kind was conceivable in the early nineteenth century.[11]

A third and *non-territorial* strategy would have been to hold the "home state" of the pirate vessel or the individual pirates responsible for the actions of its citizens on the high seas. This strategy would have been

[11] Thomson does not mention this strategy, since apparently it received no consideration in the historical debate. Nonetheless, it remains an additional, theoretically possible alternative and as such is mentioned here.

in keeping with the industrial capitalist construction of ocean-space, in which the deep sea was a non-territorial void of anti-civilization traversed by naval mini-societies – territorial extensions of land-based societies. Practically, however, this strategy posed several problems. Ships sailing under one state's flag often carried sailors from other states. Also, many pirate ships claimed allegiance to anarchic "pirate commonwealths" and had their land-bases in remote non-European ports that were *de facto* and sometimes *de jure* beyond the control of any recognized sovereign.

The strategy which was finally implemented expanded upon the third option presented above, eschewing any attempt to assert territoriality on the sea. Rather, the regime asserted more firmly than ever before that land-space was the space of territorial civilization and that the ocean, by contrast, was a space of anti-civilization. The anti-piracy strategy adopted by the European states in the early nineteenth century expanded the system of sovereign, territorial states to all land-space on the planet. Settler colonies were given more power to control shipping to and from their territory; in effect, it was affirmed that these colonies were legitimate territories within the "civilization" of territorial landspace. Other non-European lands were incorporated as places in which European state law could be applied. The land-bases of pirate commonwealths were taken by force and declared to be within the territorial domain of one or another European state.

With land-space throughout the world established as the territory of state civilization, the sea now could be constructed as its antithetical counterpoint: the space of anti-civilization. State-sponsored ships were the sole bastions of society on the ocean; they were accorded this status because they acceded to the territorial control exercised on land within the system of sovereign states. Ships *not* flying a national flag were *of the sea*, not *of the land*. Since civilization was equated with being bound within the rules (and the space) of a territorial state, ships not flying a flag sailed without the rights normally given to those who were *of civilization*. Vessels not sailing under a national flag, as well as national vessels that were acting in a piratical manner and thereby were forfeiting the protection of a home state, were identified with the anti-civilization of the sea. As such, they were constructed not just as the enemy of the state whose ship they attacked, but as the enemy of the entire state/civilizational system. Indeed, piracy, because it implies an attack not just against the individual or the state but against the *state system*, is defined in international law as a crime against *humanity*. As

Justice Moore wrote in the *Lotus* case (1927):

> Piracy by law of nations, in its jurisdictional aspects is *sui generis*.
> Though statutes may provide for its punishment, it is an offence against
> the law of nations; and as the scene of the pirate's operations is the high
> seas, which it is not the right or duty of any nation to police, he is de-
> nied the protection of the flag which he may carry, and is treated as an
> outlaw, as the enemy of mankind – *hostis humani generis* – whom any
> nation may in the interest of all capture and punish.
>
> (cited in O'Connell 1982: 967; see also Colombos 1967)

Thus, pirates were defined as legitimate prey for ships of all land-
based "civilized" nations. The axis of social power enabling regulation was scripted as a "free-for-all" between the forces of land-space
and ocean-space rather than a structured, intrasystemic competition
among land powers seeking riches from assertions of social power at
sea. Grotian norms of collective stewardship of marine resources were
affirmed.

Despite the world community's creation of a regulatory mechanism
that banned piracy without dividing the sea into national territories
(or even national spheres of influence), state leaders remained uncom-
fortable with the anti-piracy legislation's endorsement of states exerting
social power at sea. They resisted applying the mechanism to the regulation of other noxious ocean uses, including the slave trade and interference with undersea cables. The Congress of Vienna (1815) declared the
slave trade to be "repugnant" and urged participating nations "to cooperate to the most prompt and efficient [sic] of the universal suppression
of the trade by all the means at their disposal" (cited in Colombos 1967:
458). Nonetheless, trafficking in slaves was not – and still is not – defined
as a "crime against humanity" on the order of piracy. The slave trade is
not inherently an attack against the state system in the sense that piracy
is; theoretically it could be carried out among sovereign states and as
such is protected by all of the rights and privileges due to a sovereign
power. Not having the authority to exert territorial regulation in the
deep sea (e.g., by disallowing slave trading vessels access to the high
seas), early nineteenth-century Britain attempted to equate the slave
trade with piracy, and it adopted municipal legislation declaring that
the slave trade was a form of piracy. However, Britain was not able to
transfer this definition to international law. An English court in the case
of the ship *Le Louis* (1817) determined "that the slave trade was not piracy
or a crime by the law of nations, and that, apart from treaties, no British

warship had a right to visit and search the vessels of another state to see if they were engaged in such trade" (Colombos 1967: 457). Article 110 of the 1982 United Nations Convention on the Law of the Sea (United Nations 1983) lists suspicion that a ship is engaged in the slave trade as one of five conditions under which a vessel on the high seas rightfully may be boarded by a foreign warship.[12] If such a boarding results in the discovery that the ship is a pirate ship, the warship has the right to seize the foreign vessel (Article 105). However, no such right is conferred if the ship is found to be engaged in the slave trade, unless the state of the warship had previously obtained this right through a bilateral treaty.

A similar tack was taken with regard to the protection of submarine telegraph cables. The first such cable was laid across the English Channel in 1851 and the first transatlantic cable was laid in 1866. In 1869 the United States proposed that willful acts of destruction of undersea cables on the high seas be treated as acts of piracy, in which case ships of all states would have the right to stop and seize any ship found interfering with a cable. This proposal was rejected as the international community once again displayed its reluctance to adopt any regulation that might impinge on the construction of the state-sponsored ship as a sovereign piece of state territory – even if engaged in mischievous behavior – on the empty void of the high seas. Instead, the international community adopted the International Convention for the Protection of Submarine Telegraph Cables (1884), with enforcement provisions considerably weaker than those permitted in the case of piracy. Under the convention, which is similar to that established for suspected slavers, warships of all states are permitted to stop and verify the nationality of a merchant vessel suspected of violating the treaty regulations to leave cables untampered with. But "the competent Tribunals for the determination of any violation of the provisions contained in the Convention are exclusively the national Courts of the flag state of the infringing vessel" (Article 8, cited in Colombos 1967: 382). Neither the state that utilizes the cable nor the state whose ship ascertains the nationality of the offending vessel has any recourse should the home state of the vessel choose not to prosecute those who deliberately tampered with the cable. As is the case

[12] The other four grounds for a warship boarding a foreign vessel on the high seas are (i) reasonable suspicion that the ship is engaged in piracy; (ii) reasonable suspicion that the ship is engaged in unauthorized broadcasting; (iii) reasonable suspicion that the ship is without nationality; and (iv) reasonable suspicion that the ship, although flying a foreign flag or refusing to show its flag, is in reality of the same nationality as the warship (United Nations 1983: 35).

with the slave trade, states are encouraged to disallow such behavior in their municipal laws, but since the sea itself is not a territory that can be governed, the international community has no rights to enforce the international no-tampering norm in the great void of ocean-space.[13]

A final example of marine regulation from this era can be seen in the case of marine pollution. Unlike deep-sea fishing, ships from a large number of countries might at any time engage in marine pollution, quite possibly accidentally. And, unlike shipping, there is no industrial interest strongly committed to developing its own set of stringent regulations. More so than fishing or shipping, the issue of marine pollution requires regulation at the intergovernmental level rather than the industry level, because the industry most affected (the fishing industry) is unrelated to that which is capable of inflicting the greatest damage (the shipping and, especially, tanker industries). Also, while the shipping industry is the largest potential marine polluter it is not the only one, and so industry-generated self-regulation would remedy only part of the problem. Furthermore, marine pollution damages not just one use of the ocean but an *area* of the ocean in its *entirety*. Hence it would be logical for the regulatory regime to be built around the concept of protecting the ocean-space as territory.

The need for more general regulations notwithstanding, any claim by the world community to stewardship of the deep sea, with consequent penalties of prosecution for those who pollute either willfully or due to negligence, would imply the right of a world organ to *control* the sea as its *territory*. Such an ocean-space construction perhaps could be nested within Grotian norms. However, as the previous two examples of the slave trade and cable tampering regulation demonstrate, the international community has remained so wedded to an Indian Ocean-like ideal of ocean-space lying outside society that it has permitted "strong" applications of Grotianism only in what have been perceived as extreme cases, such as piracy. Thus, while the Convention on the High Seas (United Nations 1958c) that emerged from the First United Nations Conference on the Law of the Sea (discussed below) decrees that "every State shall draw up regulations to prevent pollution of the

---

[13] In more recent international legislation, foreign ships are given even less power to enforce the ban on interfering with cables than they were in the 1884 convention. In the United Nations-sponsored 1958 Convention on the High Seas and the 1982 Convention on the Law of the Sea, warships are given the right to stop and board ships suspected of carrying slaves, but no such right is given to stop and board ships suspected of interfering with cables.

seas by the discharge of oil from ships or pipelines . . ." (Article 24) and that "every State shall take measures to prevent pollution of the seas from the dumping of radio-active waste . . ." (Article 25), the international community assumes no enforcement powers with respect to these issues.

Likewise, although the 1982 Convention on the Law of the Sea (United Nations 1983) contains a lengthy section on the preservation of the marine environment (Part XII), enforcement of environmental regulations on the high seas remains solely the responsibility of the offending vessel's home state, which is urged to enforce standards agreed to at international conferences or enshrined in domestic law (Article 217). According to Gold (1981), industry standards of minimum insurance coverage in case of pollution – and in particular pollution by oil tankers – are woefully inadequate. Even in this most territorial of marine issues, the regulations emerging from the period of industrial capitalism remain non-territorial and voluntary and, in the case of marine pollution, relatively ineffective.

In summary, during the industrial capitalist era the idealization of ocean-space as an Indian Ocean-style, non-territorial transportation surface outside society was complemented by a series of regulations loosely derived from a Grotian model that transfers the Mediterranean notion of stewardship to the scale of the world community. However, because stewardship itself implies a degree of social interaction, and this implies a potential for territorialization that could interfere with the construction of a friction-free transportation surface, the Grotian model generally was applied in a weak manner that minimized the power of the community of states as global steward.

The designation and reclamation of the coastal sea

Complementing the industrial capitalist era's construction of the *deep* sea as the non-territory of free trade was a reclamation of the *coastal* sea as a component of the developable territory of the nation-state-society. Hence, as the deep sea was constructed as an asocial void reminiscent of the Indian Ocean model, tempered by a weak, Grotian form of Mediterranean-style stewardship, the coastal sea came to be constructed in a manner that more closely resembled the territorialized ocean-space of Micronesia. The coastal sea was constructed first as a legitimate arena for state power and possession and, later in the era, as part of the integral territory of the state.

The social construction of the ocean

In the period of transition to industrial capitalism, claims by coastal states to nearby waters generally were made on the grounds that the nearby ocean was space claimed by the state, much like an overseas territory. As in the writings of Grotius and Selden, coastal waters that could be controlled by a neighboring state rightfully could be claimed under the suzerainty of the state. Summarizing the legal norms of his time, the United States Secretary of State, Thomas Jefferson, wrote to the British Prime Minister in 1793:

> The greatest distance [of the outer boundary of territorial waters] to which any respectable assent among nations has at any time been given is the extent of human sight, estimated upwards of twenty miles, and the smallest distance, I believe, claimed by any nation whatever, is the utmost range of a cannon ball, usually stated at one sea league [three nautical miles]. (cited in Anand 1983: 139)

In the early years of the industrial capitalist era, the territorial sea was defined not by its existence as a *place* in its own right but rather by its ability to be controlled from land (with "control" being defined by visual range, cannon range, or some other measure). Up to the mid-nineteenth century, legal norms fell short of asserting that the coastal sea could be part of the integral territory of the nation-state, with the same status as the land-space of the nation. Rather, in the spirit of the "Battle of the Books" scholars (especially Selden), the territorial sea was such because it was *controllable* from the national territory of the land (O'Connell 1982).

This norm soon was to evolve, however, as the Industrial Revolution brought about a major change with respect to European countries' views of coastal waters and their abutting shorelines. Until the late eighteenth century, large parts of Europe's shoreline remained virtually uninhabited. The sea was an element to be feared, and so was the land facing out to the sea; this portion of land-space was subject to frequent storms and was not usually agriculturally productive. With the exception of port towns and cities, the shore, like the ocean, generally was avoided (Corbin 1994; Lenček and Bosker 1998; Mollat du Jourdin 1993).

Enlightenment ideals of controlling nature, the search for new locales for capital investment, improved transportation systems, and the increasing squalor of urban living conditions combined in the late eighteenth and early nineteenth centuries to give birth to the seaside resort. As with the deep sea, the coastal sea became an area of sublime attraction. Dangerous and indescribable in its vastness, the sea somehow was mystically appealing and relaxing. As the deep sea became impressed in the European imagination as "anti-civilization," the seaside resort was constructed as a safe locale from which this sublime spectacle could be viewed. Indeed, because the shoreline was the place where civilization met "anti-civilization," the seaside resort became a kind of "sin city." Staid London ladies and gentlemen literally and figuratively "let their hair down" as they approached the water, gambling and frolicking amidst the often risqué entertainment of the Brighton pier, while Britons of more modest means flocked to the summer community of Blackpool (Corbin 1994; Lenček and Bosker 1998; Urry 1990).

These changes in social perception of the coastal sea were reflected in the legal realm. Until 1840 the coastal sea was constructed as an uncivilized, placeless area, different from the deep sea only in that it could be controlled from land. After 1840, however, this construction began to give way to a stronger conception of the territorial sea as a unique place that was part of the sovereign territory of the nation-state. Between 1840 and 1900, both constructions of the coastal sea appeared in judicial proceedings and laws in which the status of coastal waters was debated. By 1900, this latter, stronger view was held almost universally, with the only remaining questions being the breadth of the territorial sea, the method to be used for measuring this breadth, and the extent to which coastal states were obliged to construct laws that allowed for innocent passage of foreign vessels through territorial waters (O'Connell 1982).

From the late nineteenth century onward, there was a general acceptance of a territorial sea at least three nautical miles wide. There also was a general acceptance that foreign ships were to be allowed innocent passage through these waters. Differences emerged, however, on the breadth of territorial waters beyond three miles, the method for calculating this distance,[14] and whether coastal states should be allowed to establish "contiguous zones" in the waters beyond their territorial sea

---

[14] Countries favoring a small territorial zone generally favored drawing the line parallel to the peninsulas and coves of the coast, with the border always a fixed number of nautical miles from the shoreline. Other countries, however, favored a system whereby a straight baseline would be drawn between the two outermost points on the country's coast, with the territorial waters' border demarcated a certain number of nautical miles from this straight baseline.

wherein they would be allowed to search incoming ships for contraband and diseases and/or retain rights to fish and minerals. When the world community met in 1930 at the League of Nations Conference for the Codification of International Law:

> Twenty countries were in favour of a three-mile territorial sea; but eight of them would accept this limit only on the condition that a contiguous zone of some kind should be recognized. Only Great Britain, supported by other Commonwealth countries (Australia, South Africa, Canada, India, and the Irish Free State) and Japan, supported the three-mile limit and expressed opposition to any contiguous zone. Twelve states demanded six miles, the Scandinavian states four miles, while some were in favour of not fixing a uniform distance for all purposes for all countries.
> (Anand 1983: 141)

The exact breadth of the territorial sea and/or its contiguous zones remained a matter of contention throughout the era and, in some cases, to the present. Nonetheless, the general principle of a coastal zone that is an integral part of the nation-state was established during the industrial capitalist era.

The industrial-era coastal sea regime was constructed as a counterpoint to that implemented in the deep sea. As capitalism came to be characterized by intensive investments and uses of discrete places on land, the deep sea was constructed as the asocial space between these societies, immune from regulation, social power, or territorial control that might hinder free trade. Regulations were implemented sparingly, and then with the agents of stewardship being the global community and/or non-state entities, so as to limit any creeping territoriality that might interfere with the idealization of the ocean as an asocial void. The coastal sea, however, came to have many of the properties of developable land-space, and it was thus constructed as amenable to the functions and technologies of territorial control applied to the space of terrestrial society under industrial capitalism.

Truman, UNCLOS, and the resurgence of Seldenian stewardship

After World War II, the ocean-space construction of the industrial capitalist era was presented with new challenges. For the first time, fishing technologies made the exhaustion of deep-sea fishstocks a real possibility. The 1930s witnessed a number of fishing disputes, in particular between the United States and Japan over North Atlantic salmon. Heavily capitalized distant-water fishing fleets threatened the combination of a minimalist "high seas" regime and non-binding multilateral production limitations that previously had governed deep-sea fishing.

Concurrently, in 1937, the Pure and Superior Oil Company sunk the first offshore oil well, in fifteen feet of water, one mile off the coast of Louisiana. Within a few years offshore drilling technology had advanced to the point where petroleum extraction could be undertaken in depths far greater than fifteen feet and in waters beyond the three-mile limit which at the time was accepted by most countries as the outer boundary of territorial waters. This opportunity for spatially fixed investments outside the narrow coastal zone posed an additional threat to the strict dichotomy between land-like territorial waters and a non-territorial deep sea that previously had characterized the industrial capitalist era (Anand 1983; Gold 1981; Watt 1979).

Faced with these challenges, the final decades of the industrial capitalist era were turbulent years for ocean policy. Between 1945 and 1982, there were a number of high-profile ocean-space governance negotiations. Nonetheless, at the end of the era, the overall construction informing ocean-space governance remained much the same as it had been when the negotiations began. Aside from the international seabed regime, which is considered in the next chapter, the substantial change in the industrial capitalist era ocean-space construction was the addition of a Seldenian element of state stewardship, applied to resource-rich areas of ocean-space located beyond areas susceptible to territorial control but still relatively proximate to state coasts. These zones were superimposed on the great void ideal and the weak Grotian regulatory framework, and they ultimately became established as exclusive economic zones (EEZs) in the Convention on the Law of the Sea that was signed at the Third United Nations Conference on the Law of the Sea (UNCLOS III) in 1982.

The Truman proclamations

On September 28, 1945, U.S. President Harry Truman responded to the emergence of new oil exploitation and fishing technologies by issuing two proclamations expanding US authority beyond territorial waters. The first proclamation asserted the right of the United States to establish "fisheries conservation zones" in areas of the high seas adjacent to US waters "wherein fishery activity had been or in the future may be developed and maintained on a substantial scale" (United States

1945a: 12303). In cases where only US vessels fished the zone, the United States claimed the unilateral right to establish a resource management regime. In areas where foreign vessels fished as well, the proclamation called for the United States to establish bilateral or multilateral agreements. By itself, this proclamation did little more than reaffirm the United States' commitment to the kinds of fishery management regimes that had become increasingly common during the industrial capitalist era.

More significant was the second proclamation, spurred on by difficulties the United States had experienced accessing foreign petroleum sources during World War II (Watt 1979). It stated, in part:

> The Government of the United States regards the natural resources of the subsoil and sea bed of the continental shelf beneath the high seas but contiguous to the coasts of the United States as appertaining to the United States, subject to its jurisdiction and control. In cases where the continental shelf extends to the shores of another State, or is shared with an adjacent State, the boundary shall be determined by the United States and the State concerned in accordance with equitable principles. The character as high seas of the waters above the continental shelf and the right to their free and unimpeded navigation are in no way thus affected. (United States 1945b: 12304)

Both proclamations were worded so as to avoid implying territorial expansion. The second proclamation in particular, which could have been interpreted as a statement of territorial expansion, noted that the continental shelf was to be "subject to [the United States'] jurisdiction and control" rather than claiming that the area was part of the sovereign territory of the United States. Additionally, the proclamation affirmed that this "jurisdiction and control" was to apply only to the seabed and not to the waters above it.

These precautions notwithstanding, elements within the US government feared that the proclamations would be misinterpreted. The State Department's Office of Economic Affairs, one of the leading agencies within the US government supporting trade liberalization and a key player at the 1944 Bretton Woods conference, warned the Executive Office and the Department of the Interior that the proclamations could be taken as statements of economic nationalism and might prompt retaliatory responses (Watt 1979). The two proclamations, especially when regarded as one unified policy statement, could be interpreted as a movement by the United States toward territorial enclosure of its adjacent seas out to the limits of the continental shelf.

The first significant response came one month after the proclamations, when Mexico issued a presidential declaration on its marine resources. While the fisheries portion of the Mexican presidential declaration closely mirrored that of the first Truman proclamation, the seabed component went slightly further, asserting that the Mexican portion of the shelf was "incorporated into the national property." This claim was somewhat stronger than that of the United States to "jurisdiction and control" over the *resources* of the shelf. As Extavour (1979) points out, however, this difference is relatively minor, and the Mexican declaration generally can be viewed as being in line with the Truman proclamations.

More radical were a series of national decrees and proclamations made over the next five years by the governments of Argentina, Brazil, Chile, Costa Rica, El Salvador, Guatemala, Honduras, Panama, and Peru, culminating in the 1952 Santiago Declaration signed by Chile, Ecuador, and Peru (Armas Pfirter 1995; Extavour 1979).[15]

> [These proclamations] broke new ground in claiming *sovereignty* over the continental – or insular – shelf "at whatever depth it lies and whatever its extent," *and also over the waters covering it* to a minimum distance of two hundred nautical miles measured from the appropriate baselines. These claims in general reserved the power to exercise such sovereignty ". . . within those limits necessary in order to reserve, protect, preserve and exploit the natural resources," especially fisheries. On the whole, the right of free navigation of vessels of all nations was, however, recognised. (Extavour 1979: 74, emphasis in original)

The Santiago Declaration and most of the national declarations did not use the term "territorial sea" to describe this zone of ocean-space (Extavour 1979), and many jurists have argued that even when this term was used the intention was not actually to add area to the national territory but to lay sovereign claim to the *resources* of the area above the continental shelf (Armas Pfirter 1995; Clingan 1993; Harlow 1985). The Latin American states were maintaining that the sea beyond the narrow strip of territorial water retained its character as "high seas" in the great void idealization. Nonetheless, they were reserving the unilateral right to proclaim resource management regimes in the portion of the high seas abutting their territorial waters. While some have argued that such an expansion of sovereign power is likely to lead to an extension of territorial control in the region in question (Ball 1996; Clingan 1993; Joyner

---

[15] Following the Santiago Declaration, Iceland and South Korea made similar proclamations (Extavour 1979).

and De Cola 1993; Zacher and McConnell 1990), the bulk of the Latin American declarations specifically eschewed any claim to incorporate these areas of the sea as the territory of the state; they specifically denied themselves the right to restrict access to space, a tendency of territoriality that states invariably claim in their sovereign, national territory. This is not to say that these regimes did not contain a small degree of territorial power, much like the spatial resource regimes discussed in the previous section of this chapter, but the declarations fell short of claiming adjacent waters as the territory of the state.

While the Latin American declarations did not attempt to incorporate adjacent areas of the high seas as national territory, even those who defend the limited nature of the Latin American claims acknowledge that they went beyond the original Truman proclamations (Armas Pfirter 1995). Whereas the United States called for bilateral resource management regimes in heavily fished areas above the continental shelf, the Latin American states claimed the right to implement unilateral regimes designed explicitly to benefit the abutting state. The United States reacted to these claims by writing disapproving notes to the Latin American states when they adopted their new maritime zones, and in 1950 the US State Department asserted that the Truman proclamations "did not represent a new concept in international law nor alter the pre-existing regime of the high seas" (cited in Watt 1979: 223). This position is maintained by the United States to this day. In 1985, for instance, an official of the US Department of Commerce's National Marine Fisheries Service wrote that the first Truman proclamation "is best forgotten" and that "neither Proclamation led directly to the 200-nautical-mile limit [of exclusive economic zones]," that being "used as a rationale only later as an excuse to justify political desires for greater jurisdiction" (Sullivan 1985: 86).

By 1958, when the First United Nations Conference on the Law of the Sea (UNCLOS I) was convened, only one (El Salvador) of seventy-three independent coastal states had unequivocally extended its territorial waters out to 200 miles.[16] Twenty-three other states had declared territorial waters in excess of the "traditional" three-mile limit, ranging

---

[16] Article 7 of the Salvadoran Constitution of 1950 reads: "The territory of the Republic within its present boundaries is irreductible. It includes the adjacent seas to a distance of 200 sea miles from low water line and the corresponding airspace, subsoil and continental shelf" (cited in Extavour 1979: 78).

from five to twelve nautical miles[17] and six had rejected the three-mile rule but had not specified their limits.[18] In addition, four states (Chile, Ecuador, South Korea, and Peru) claimed "sovereignty and jurisdiction" over areas of the high seas adjacent to territorial waters while five states (Argentina, Costa Rica, Honduras, Mexico, and Panama) claimed rights to living resources of the "epicontinental sea" or superjacent waters of the continental shelf (Anand 1983; Extavour 1979).

UNCLOS I and II

Amidst these unilateral efforts to transform the rights of coastal states in ocean-space, the United Nations convened the First United Nations Conference on the Law of the Sea (UNCLOS I) in Geneva in 1958. Although the conference generally is considered a failure because there was stalemate on the most difficult issue (the breadth of the territorial sea) and it failed to achieve universal ratification, it did succeed in codifying the bulk of the ocean-space construction that had characterized the industrial capitalist era. Particularly noteworthy are two of the four conventions emerging from the conference which respectively codify the "great void" principle of the deep sea and the "land extension" principle of coastal seas.

The Convention on the High Seas (United Nations 1958c) defines the "high seas" as "all parts of the sea that are not included in the territorial sea or in the internal waters of a State" (Article 1) and declares that "the high seas being open to all nations, no State may validly purport to subject any part of them to its sovereignty" (Article 2). Along with establishing the principle that the sea is a great void of non-territory, the convention establishes the territoriality of the ship traveling across its surface: "Ships shall sail under the flag of one State only and, save in exceptional cases expressly provided for in international treaties or in these articles,[19] shall be subject to its exclusive jurisdiction on the high seas" (Article 6).

---

[17] Of these states, one (Cambodia) claimed five miles; ten (Ceylon, Greece, Haiti, India, Iran, Israel, Italy, Libya, Spain, and Yugoslavia) claimed six miles; Mexico claimed nine miles; Albania ten miles; and ten (Bulgaria, Colombia, Ethiopia, Guatemala, Indonesia, Romania, Saudi Arabia, the Soviet Union, the United Arab Republic, and Venezuela) claimed twelve miles (Anand 1983).

[18] These states were Honduras, Lebanon, Portugal, Thailand, Uruguay, and Yemen (Anand 1983).

[19] See the discussion of piracy earlier in this chapter for an example of one such exception.

The Convention on the Territorial Sea and the Contiguous Zone (United Nations 1958d) similarly codifies the "land-like" construction of the coastal sea. It notes that "the sovereignty of a State extends, beyond its land territory and its internal waters, to a belt of sea adjacent to its coast, described as the territorial sea" (Article 1) and institutionalizes the provision that "ships of all States, whether coastal or not, shall enjoy the right of innocent passage through the territorial sea" (Article 14). Furthermore, each coastal state is given the right to establish a contiguous zone of not more than twelve nautical miles beyond the territorial sea in order to: "(a) prevent infringement of its customs, fiscal, immigration or sanitary regulations within its territory or territorial sea; [and] (b) punish infringement of the above regulations committed within its territory or territorial sea" (Article 24). The other two conventions – the Convention on the Continental Shelf (United Nations 1958a) and the Convention on Fishing and Conservation of the Living Resources of the High Seas (United Nations 1958b) – effectively internationalize the two Truman proclamations.

Despite these achievements, the overall impact of the conventions was limited. As late as 1980, when there were 169 sovereign states recognized by the United Nations, there were only fifty-six parties to the Convention on the High Seas, fifty-three parties to the Convention on the Continental Shelf, forty-five parties to the Convention on the Territorial Sea, and thirty-five parties to the Convention on Fishing (O'Connell 1982). In large part, the lack of enthusiasm for the treaties was a result of their failure to make new law. On the main topic in which state practice diverged widely – the breadth of territorial seas and/or zones of the high seas in which states claimed exclusive rights over resources – the conventions were silent. States attending the conference had strong and sharply divergent interests on this topic and compromise proved impossible. States with large long-distance fishing fleets – much of Western and Eastern Europe and Japan – favored narrow territorial seas and no exclusive resource zones so as to allow maximum access by their ships to distant fish stocks. Latin American and other Third World states with limited long-distance fishing capabilities but considerable resources off their coasts favored large areas (incorporated either as territorial waters or as exclusive resource zones), so that long-distance fleets would have to pay royalties to exploit "their" resources. The Soviet Union, still a relatively weak naval power and not yet heavily involved in long-distance fishing, favored a large territorial sea as a security buffer. The United States, although somewhat engaged in long-distance fishing, was primarily a coastal fishing state and therefore would have been thought to favor large exclusive resource zones. However, the United States, with its large "blue-water" navy and its strong interest in world trade, was extremely wary of any enclosure movement that might lead to an expansion of territorial waters. Such an enclosure movement potentially could erect obstacles to the free navigation of commercial and military ships across the asocial frictionless surface of the deep sea. The United States therefore argued for a three-mile territorial sea and an exclusive resource zone that would apply only to the seabed (Anand 1983; Gold 1981; Zacher and McConnell 1990).

The United Nations convened a second conference in 1960 (UNCLOS II) with the sole purpose of resolving the territorial sea/ exclusive resource zone issue. The United States and Canada proposed a six-plus-six formula: a six-mile territorial sea plus a six-mile zone in which a coastal state would have exclusive rights to living resources. The Soviet Union countered with a proposal whereby a state could claim up to twelve miles in a combination of territorial sea plus exclusive fishing zone. The Soviet proposal would have allowed a state to claim territorial waters of up to twelve miles, and this was steadfastly opposed by the United States. Of the world's international straits, 116 – including the Strait of Dover, the Bering Strait, the Bab el Mandeb, and the Strait of Hormuz – are under twenty-four miles wide. A twelve-mile-wide territorial sea would have placed these straits entirely within territorial waters, eliminating the high seas corridors that previously had run through their centers. Safeguards requiring the right of innocent passage through territorial waters notwithstanding, the United States found this enclosure of critical channels on the "free" surface of the deep sea to be unacceptable.[20] In the end, both the U.S.–Canadian and the Soviet proposals failed to receive the necessary votes, and UNCLOS II concluded without any progress being made (Anand 1983).

UNCLOS III

Seven years after UNCLOS II the United Nations revisited the law of the sea. This time the impetus was not fear of a global enclosure movement near territorial waters but rather the development of technologies that might someday enable commercial extraction of polymetallic manganese nodules from the seabed beyond the continental shelf. Third

---

[20] For an elaboration of the distinction between "right of innocent passage" and "freedom of the seas," see the discussion of UNCLOS III below.

World states sought wealth from this global resource, the United States sought to avert what now could become an *ocean-wide* enclosure movement as states staked out portions of the deep sea for exploitation, and potential mining states and companies sought a legal regime to guarantee the significant investments that they would have to make in discrete areas of the deep sea before commencing mining and generating profits. As such, there was unanimous support when, in 1967, Arvid Pardo, the Maltese permanent representative, addressed the United Nations General Assembly, calling for the establishment of a regime to govern the international seabed and to guarantee that its exploitation be consistent with its status as the "common heritage of mankind" (Pardo 1967).

The General Assembly's Committee on the Peaceful Uses of the Sea-Bed and the Ocean Floor Beyond the Limits of National Jurisdiction, formed in 1968, soon determined that this issue could be resolved only in the context of resolving other ocean law issues and so, in 1970, the General Assembly called for a Third United Nations Conference on the Law of the Sea. This conference – UNCLOS III – first met in Caracas in 1973 and eventually, in 1982, resulted in the signing of the United Nations Convention on the Law of the Sea, a mammoth 320-article "Constitution for the Oceans" (Koh 1983). The convention, which entered into force in 1994, is best known for its innovative and controversial Part XI, which establishes a regime to govern mining of the seabed beyond the continental shelf. The bulk of diplomatic energy and confrontation revolved around this section of the convention. Yet, as supporters of the treaty frequently point out, most of the convention deals with other aspects of the law of the sea, and in these areas it codifies, standardizes, and elaborates on customary practice as well as establishing avenues of recourse for states that assert that other states have violated the norms proclaimed in the convention (Galdorisi 1995b; Galdorisi and Stavridis 1993; Oxman 1985; Panel on the Law of Ocean Uses 1990, 1994; Stevenson and Oxman 1994).

Part XI indeed is significant and will be discussed in Chapter 5. Here, however, attention is focused on the other parts of the convention, many of which already were agreed to by the conclusion of the first substantive meeting in 1974. By the end of the first session there already was general agreement on a twelve-mile limit to the territorial sea, with a special provision guaranteeing free transit through international straits. By the early 1970s the Soviet Union had joined the United States in possessing a strong ocean-going fleet (for military, transport, and fishing activities) and both states were interested in preserving rights of free transit through international straits. While international law mandates that coastal states permit "innocent passage" through territorial waters, this provision was not strong enough for either superpower (Comptroller General of the United States 1975; Janis and Daniel 1974). Under the "innocent passage" provision, a coastal state retains the right to prohibit passage of submerged vessels, airplanes, or any surface vessel it chooses to interpret as having threatening or hostile intent. The principle of "free transit," by contrast, grants an irrevocable right of passage to all foreign vessels.

Leaders of the US navy, praising the convention's free transit guarantees, have remained staunch supporters of the convention even as other interest groups in the US diplomatic community have wavered in their support. As Rear Admiral William Schachte, a member of the US delegation to UNCLOS III, later noted:

> Even before the Third UN Law of the Sea Conference first convened in the early 1970s, the critical importance and unique nature of international straits were recognized. These choke points form the lifeline between the high seas areas. In order for the high seas freedoms of navigation and overflight to be preserved in international straits, which would be overlapped by 12-mile territorial sea claims (displacing the earlier recognized 3-mile territorial sea norm), the navigational regime in international straits would have to share similar basic characteristics with these high seas freedoms. General support existed in the Conference for a 12-mile territorial sea. Such support depended, however, on ensuring that in international straits less than 24 miles wide at their narrowest point, an adequate navigation regime be preserved to ensure essential elements of the right of freedom of navigation and overflight. The lesser navigational right of nonsuspendable innocent passage was simply not enough.
> (Schachte 1993: 181; see also Galdorisi 1995a; Galdorisi and Vienna 1997; Wedgwood 1995)

Even James Malone, President Ronald Reagan's Assistant Secretary of State for Oceans and International Environmental and Scientific Affairs, leader of the final US UNCLOS III delegation, and a staunch opponent of the convention, noted: "The United States is a leading maritime nation and unimpeded commercial navigation and military mobility are vital to our national interest" (Malone 1985: 555).

Along with the twelve-mile territorial sea (with special provisions for international straits under twenty-four miles wide), the convention allowed for an additional twelve-mile contiguous zone for coastal state enforcement of anti-smuggling and sanitary regulations (Article 33). This provision was a carry-over from the 1958 Convention on the Territorial Sea and the Contiguous Zone.

There also was general agreement from the start of UNCLOS III that coastal states should have exclusive rights to minerals found on and under the seabed, out to the limit of the continental shelf, a carry-over from the second Truman proclamation and the 1958 Convention on the Continental Shelf. However, there was disagreement about the status of seabed minerals in those instances where the continental shelf extends beyond 200 miles from shore (Comptroller General of the United States 1975). The eventual compromise reached by the convention was that coastal states would have exclusive rights to continental shelf minerals beyond 200 miles, but they were to contribute payments totaling 7 percent of the proceeds from such mining activities to a UN-administered fund to be distributed to developing and landlocked states (Article 82).

Besides the issue of the international seabed, the main topic still under debate after the first substantive session of UNCLOS III was that of exclusive fishing zones. There were three basic proposals on the table. One, favored by the distant-water fishing states, resonated with the Freitian notion of individual states projecting stewardship to distant points in space, as it called for regional management schemes to be directed by those who presently were fishing in an area's waters. A second scheme, favored by much of the Third World and generally in line with the Latin American exclusive fishing zones claimed during the 1950s, adopted a Seldenian perspective, putting regions of the high seas adjacent to territorial waters entirely within the management purview of the coastal state, with the coastal state being under no obligation to share the resources of that area with other countries' fleets. A third scheme, favored by the United States and generally in line with the first Truman proclamation and the 1958 Convention on Fishing and Conservation of the Living Resources of the High Seas, was closer to the Grotian perspective. Coastal states were to be empowered to establish conservation regimes in adjacent areas of the high seas, but with the provision that the coastal state must let others fish there so long as fish stocks were not in danger of exhaustion (Comptroller General of the United States 1975). In the end, the regime of the exclusive economic zone (EEZ) established by the convention most nearly resembled the Seldenian model favored by the Third World states. The EEZ was established as a distinct zone between the twelve-mile limit of territorial waters and the 200-mile start of the high seas. In this zone, coastal states have exclusive rights to living and non-living resources, but for all other purposes high-seas freedoms prevail.

Remaining items in the convention generally were consistent with those of the 1958 conventions; in many cases articles from the 1958 conventions were adopted without any revision. Some parts were entirely new, such as those on the marine environment and scientific research, but these tended to establish language for applying specialized resource regimes within the non-territorial high seas/land-like territorial seas division of ocean-space. As one member of the US delegation and active promoter of the convention noted,

> Except perhaps for the provisions on deep seabed mining and the settlement of disputes, the stipulations of the Convention are already regarded by some government and private experts as generally authoritative statements of existing customary international law applicable to all states. (Oxman 1985: 559)

Although President Reagan refused to sign the convention because of the regime it established for mining the international seabed, when rejecting the convention in 1983 he acknowledged, "The Convention also contains provisions with respect to *traditional* uses of the oceans which generally confirm existing maritime law and practice and fairly balance the interests of all States" (Reagan 1990: 227, emphasis added). Similarly, the US delegate to the final meeting of UNCLOS III, although refusing to sign the convention, declared:

> Those parts of the Convention dealing with navigation and overflight and most other provisions of the Convention . . . reflect prevailing international practice. They also demonstrate that the Conference believed that it was articulating rules in most areas that reflect the existing state of affairs – a state of affairs that we wished to preserve by enshrining these beneficial and desirable principles in treaty language.
> (Clingan 1986)

While the United Nations Convention on the Law of the Sea has been hailed for "irrevocably transform[ing]" international law and constituting "a fundamental revision of sometimes age-old institutions" (Pérez de Cuéllar 1983: xxix), it also can be interpreted as the codification and institutionalization of a multifaceted ocean-space construction developed over the previous 200 years of industrial capitalism. The key tenets of the industrial capitalist ocean-space construction were all clarified and affirmed: the idealization of the high seas as an Indian

Ocean-style asocial, friction-free transportation surface; the implementation of relatively weak Grotian measures to enable the community of states and non-state actors to steward the ocean's resources (including the resource of connection); the application of a Micronesian-style perspective to coastal waters as they were constructed as land-like, developable components of state territory; and, increasingly, the growth of a Seldenian regime for near-coastal waters in which individual coastal states claimed unilateral stewardship rights and responsibilities.

Sea power and industrial capitalism

No history of ocean-space during the era of industrial capitalism is complete without a discussion of military uses of the sea. The nineteenth century, after all, was the apogee of Pax Britannica, when "Britannia ruled the waves." And in the twentieth century, the United States' naval superiority played an important role in its Cold War victory over the Soviet Union. Nonetheless, despite these public manifestations of naval force, it is argued here that the importance of sea power during this era has been exaggerated and that the industrial capitalist naval powers, once they achieved greatness, frequently were left searching for a mission to justify the huge expenses incurred in military build-up.

As demonstrated in Chapter 3, sea power played an important role in the mercantilist era. Political–economic development was dependent on control of trade, which in turn was facilitated by exercising power over specific ocean routes. The sea was constructed as a "force-field" in which states, while not attempting to claim absolute possession of the deep sea, did seek dominance. With the rise of the industrial era, the prevailing economic doctrine and construction of ocean-space changed dramatically. The ocean was no longer a space to be "controlled," even in the sense of the Mediterranean-style *imperium* that characterized the mercantilist era. Rather, it was a great void in which exertions of social power were to be kept to a minimum, for fear that these social interventions might impose barriers to friction-free transport between the developable terrestrial places of "society."

But if the sea were no longer a space in which to exert social power and attempt control, then what could be the role for the world's navies? If the sea were merely a "great void" across which trading ships sailed as quickly as possible to get from one point to another, it is not clear what role a naval force would have except to transport troops to distant lands and escort trading vessels when they might be endangered by other nations' warships. Faced with these important but inglorious tasks, the sea powers of the nineteenth and twentieth centuries adapted their missions accordingly. But all the while they maintained the ideology of "command of the sea" that had defined the great navies of a bygone era.[21]

Already in the Napoleonic Wars (1793–1815), sea power played a relatively minor role. The British so clearly were dominant that their opponents did their best to avoid engaging them at sea, and so the major battles were fought mostly on land. Napoleon's strategy was one of "defeating the sea by the land" – challenging British sea power not directly in ocean-space but rather by closing the continental markets that sustained Britain's political and economic dominance at sea (Stevens and Westcott 1942). This aversion to constructing the ocean as a battlefield continued for the remainder of the nineteenth century: "From 1815 to 1898, naval power, though always an important factor in international relations, played in general a passive role" (Stevens and Westcott 1942: 245).

Considering Britain's overwhelming superiority at sea during this century, it is not surprising that other states avoided challenging its supremacy. More complex was Britain's reason for not using its superior forces to greater advantage. In the mercantilist era, a state with as overwhelming an advantage as that held by Britain in the nineteenth century would probably have attempted to clear the deep sea of foreign ships and claim exclusive rights to engage in military, shipping, and fishing activities. As an industrial capitalist power, however, Britain's interest lay only in ensuring that the great void idealization was maintained. Hence the British navy saw little purely military action during this period. This is not to say that the nineteenth-century British navy was without purpose, but its mission was redefined to revolve around projecting power to distant lands as opposed to fighting pitched battles for domination of the sea. Writing about the British navy in the period between 1815 and 1853, Bartlett notes:

> The Royal Navy was used for two main purposes during this period. In power politics, Britain strove to deny to her naval rivals, France, Russia and the United States, the acquisition of new naval bases, or the spread of their influence to strategically and economically important areas. Thus Belgium, Spain, Portugal, Italy, Greece, the Ottoman Empire, the North African coastline, Cuba, South America, China, Tahiti

---

[21] While this assertion appears to contradict Modelski and Thompson's (1988) finding of a close correlation between naval power and political–economic power during the modern era, they focus on naval *capabilities*, not the *use* of naval power.

and many lesser points were the objects of much British diplomatic activity, often reinforced by the British Navy. In addition, the Navy was on call to promote and protect British interests in those parts of the world where respect for a British citizen and his property was not automatic, where conceptions of justice differed from those of western Europe, or were not enforced with sufficient regularity and thoroughness. This period, indeed, witnessed a great expansion in such duties by the Navy, sometimes to the embarrassment of the naval and more purely [military] objectives of the fleet.   (Bartlett 1963: x–xi)

Although Britain eagerly used its navy to project power to distant lands, it shied away from further asserting its power within the ocean itself. Indeed, when Robert Fulton developed a prototype of a submarine in 1804 and requested British support for continuing his project, Britain paid him £15,000 *not* to proceed with development. The British had no need for a vessel that only would aid offensive maneuvers in the sea, and it had no desire to risk such a weapon being acquired by a potential enemy (Stevens and Westcott 1942).

In the late nineteenth century, as Britain's hegemony began to decline, the two major challengers – the United States and Germany – sought to mount challenges to Britain's "command" of the sea. Both states found justification for their expensive undertakings in *The Influence of Sea Power Upon History, 1660–1783*, in which Captain Alfred Mahan (1890) of the US navy asserted that sea power was essential for any state aspiring to world power status. Although late twentieth-century historians have critiqued Mahan's argument, questioning both the accuracy of his historical depictions and his assertions of these instances' typicality and generalizability to other eras (Kennedy 1976), his pronouncements were seized on by naval officers throughout Europe and the United States to justify a naval dimension to the tremendous military build-up of the early twentieth century.

Faced with a serious challenge from Germany, Britain reassessed its own naval mission and structure. Throughout the nineteenth century, even as its mission changed from the offensive goal of controlling the sea to the goal of defending commerce and land-space (in Britain and in the colonies), the British navy retained its glorious mercantilist-era ideology and expansive structure. The mismatch between the British navy's structure and its mission had not been a problem during the nineteenth century, when there were no serious challengers, but with the German (and American) naval build-up reforms were urgently needed. Admiral Sir John Fisher, First Sea Lord from 1904 to 1910, shocked the British establishment by restructuring the British navy to meet its industrial capitalist mission. Under Fisher, "the old policy of showing the flag all over the world was abandoned, 160 old ships were sent to the scrap heap as unable 'either to fight or to run away,' and eighty-eight percent of the fleet was concentrated at home" (Stevens and Westcott 1942: 307). Still more radical was Admiral Sir Percy Scott, a Fisher protégé, who "caused a minor furor by a letter to *The Times* of June 1914, in which he prophesied that submarines and aircraft would make the battleship worthless and pleaded instead for a naval policy based upon a large air force, a great fleet of submarines and many cruisers (for trade protection)" (Kennedy 1976: 199).

In spite of the early twentieth-century naval arms race, sea power was largely ineffectual during World War I. By concentrating its fleet in the English Channel and the northern reaches of the North Sea, the British were able to confine practically the entire German navy within the North and Baltic Seas.[22] At the same time, however, the presence of submarines in the shallow German coastal waters prevented the British from closing in and destroying the German fleet. The bulk of the two navies spent the entire war in this restless stalemate. In the end, "the vast pre-war expenditure upon the battle-fleets was made to look absurd, as was the Mahanite insistence upon the primacy of the capital ship and the decisive naval battle" (Kennedy 1976: 245).

In the industrial capitalist era, sea power revolved not around control of the sea but rather around efforts to maintain or disrupt the free trade across the great void of ocean-space that underpinned industrial capitalist states' power. Given this redefined mission, the submarine emerged as the perfect offensive weapon. Although the submarine was fairly ineffective as a means of combating one's opponent's naval forces and laying claim to marine territory, it proved well suited for the task of challenging the free flow of commerce, as Germany demonstrated in World War I (and again in World War II). Despite the acknowledged risk that submarine attacks on neutral shipping might draw the United States into the war, in 1915 the Germans sent U-boats beneath the British blockade, declared a large exclusion zone around the British Isles (and, later, the Atlantic coast of France and much of the Mediterranean as well), and began attacking vessels indiscriminately. As a "blockade,"

[22] At the start of the war, Germany had ten cruisers located outside its coastal ports. "Within six months' time, these, together with a few auxiliary cruisers fitted out abroad, were either destroyed or forced to intern in neutral ports" (Stevens and Westcott 1942: 315).

the U-boat strategy "was only in the slightest degree effective, causing a destruction each month of less than one percent of the traffic [to and from England]" (Stevens and Westcott 1942: 398). However, the U-boat strategy was not designed to mount a traditional blockade (which would have required achieving a degree of "control" in ocean-space). Rather, it was designed to attack the commerce that had freely traversed the high seas and that was both supported by and supportive of the allied powers' global economic vision of free trade. Given its particular objectives, the U-boat campaign was quite successful. Germany succeeded temporarily in redefining the sea as a frictioned surface wherein social power was exercised, conflict was played out, and obstacles were erected on what had been idealized as a seamless plane for trade and transport.[23]

Faced with a world in which mercantilist–Mahanian objectives of control of the sea no longer made sense, and confronted with the evidence from World War I, British and American naval strategists were faced with a dilemma. To acknowledge that Mahan was wrong (or outdated) would amount to a diminution in their own status, from grand warrior of naval battles to a service provider giving police protection to merchant ships and transportation to land troops seeking to attack distant lands. Although Law (1986) associates this use of ocean-space for the *projection* of power with the ultimate triumph of modernity, such a mission was perceived as degrading by naval institutions whose valor had been premised upon achieving territorial *control* and the conquest of enemies. Coping with these new and less glamorous missions, Vice-Admiral J. E. T. Harper of the Royal Navy went to great lengths to couch this new role within the trappings of mercantilist–Mahanian notions of "command of the sea":

> In time of war a nation which exists by the sea must be strong enough at sea to ensure the safe transport of its own ships, or it will cease to exist as a nation. The mere fact that for over four years our Navy maintained free communications by sea when faced by problems which were never foreseen, and could not have been foreseen, shows that

---

[23] The U-boat was a warship of industrial capitalism in another way as well. In an era when most warships still were designed individually and endowed with a "personality" in the tradition of craft production, the U-boat was produced according to Fordist mass-production techniques, and – in modernist fashion – was endowed not with a name but with a functional number. In 1918, by which time Germany was devoting its entire naval construction budget to submarines, 372 U-boats were built on German assembly lines (Stevens and Westcott 1942).

during the Great War we had command of the sea, although no opportunity occurred to actually destroy the main fleet of the enemy.

(Harper 1930: viii–ix)

The United States Navy also remained wedded to the Mahanian ideology, planning for war with Japan by adhering to War Plan Orange, a
pre-World War I document calling for defeat of the Japanese navy and
"control" of the Pacific by means of a pitched sea battle in the north
Pacific. And yet, even as the US navy remained true to War Plan Orange in its dealings with the State Department and Congress and in its
statements to the popular press, other military planners were developing a route for a Pacific Ocean "island-hopping" campaign that would
bypass the objective of ocean control and instead use the navy to deliver
forces to distant lands, thereby depriving the Japanese of forward military bases (Baer 1994). Like Napoleon at the beginning of the industrial
capitalist era, the United States was choosing not to wage a war for control of the sea, instead favoring a strategy based on "defeating the sea
by the land."[24]

When World War II broke out, there was, as in World War I, no great
struggle for control of the sea. Instead, the Atlantic naval war was almost
an exact replay of World War I. The German navy and its commander,
Grand Admiral Karl Dönitz, explicitly eschewed any strategy based on
attacking Allied warships for control of the sea. Dönitz' sole goal was to
destroy Allied tonnage. Even empty ships were considered good targets.
By destroying enemy shipping capacity and denying enemy ships the
free right to traverse the sea, the German navy sought to erect socially
generated friction barriers and undermine the great void idealization of
the sea that lay behind the world order favored by Britain and the United
States and that enabled the flow of goods between the Allied powers.
To his many critics within the German military hierarchy, "Dönitz' decision to attack shipping tonnage instead of targets of immediate military
value was a failure of strategic insight. His submarines paid no attention to conventional assessments of sea control" (Baer 1994: 192). After
the war, Dönitz acknowledged that "conventional assessments of sea
control" were never in his calculations, writing, "The strategic task of
the German Navy was to wage war on trade; its objective was therefore
to sink as many enemy merchant ships as it could. The *sinking of ships*

---

[24] There were, of course, substantial differences in the two strategies. Napoleon sought to
defeat the British by depriving them of land *markets*. The United States sought to defeat
the Japanese by depriving them of land *bases*.

155

was the only thing that mattered" (cited in Baer 1994: 192, emphasis in original).

The Allies, for their part, also adopted an Atlantic Ocean naval strategy reminiscent of World War I. Allied warships were devoted to two main tasks: guarding troop and material transports and hunting down submarines. Neither of these tasks implied a need, or even a desire for control of the sea. The Allies merely sought to maintain free travel across the ocean's surface. Meanwhile, in the Pacific, the islands of Micronesia served a purpose for Japan similar to that which submarines served for Germany: they were barriers standing in the way of unimpeded ocean transit. As such, the US navy adopted a strategy based on destroying these islands' potential as transit barriers, a strategy that necessitated forcible conquest and occupation of the islands but that was never based on challenging Japan for "control of the sea."

As World War II ended, the US navy again was left trying to adapt its Mahanian–mercantilist sea-control ideology to the industrial capitalist-era ocean-space construction. With the United States clearly hegemonic, rooted in industrial capitalism, and committed to free trade, and with no conceivable challengers to free transit across ocean-space, the navy had little choice but to let itself be downgraded once again to a small force with the dual missions of protecting merchant shipping and transporting troops and weapons to land-space battlefields. Even this downgraded mission was to lose some of its importance as aircraft took on a greater role in military transport. The navy received a boost with the development of nuclear ship-to-surface ballistic missiles; now the navy would have the role of delivering not only troops but also some of the military's most important ordnance to enemy land-space. Nonetheless, these new missions struck naval planners as a subsidiary diversion from the Mahanian goal of *control* of the sea that was ingrained in the navy's ideology.

The staying power of the Mahanian ideology became apparent during the Second Cold War of the late 1970s to the late 1980s. Beginning in 1977 with Vice Admiral William Crowe's statement that "sea control is the [US] Navy's preeminent function" (cited in Baer 1994: 395), the navy proposed that the United States prepare itself for a protracted series of ship-to-ship and submarine-to-submarine battles with the Soviet Union for sea control, thereby deflecting a future US–Soviet war from land where Soviet inter-continental ballistic missiles could endanger US security. The US military and political establishment ultimately rejected the navy's proposal because of the destabilizing effect it might have had on the "mutually assured destruction" deterrence doctrine that lay at the heart of US Cold War military planning (Baer 1994). Nonetheless, this most recent gasp of Mahanian doctrine shows that the mercantilist-era concept of sea power remained alive within the US navy, some 100 years after it was first articulated and some 200 years after its strategic exhortations fell out of synch with the ocean-space construction of the dominant political economy. The doctrine was formally abandoned only in 1992, when the US navy announced that its strategic thinking was undergoing "a fundamental shift from open-ocean warfighting *on* the sea toward joint operations conducted *from* the sea" (United States Navy 1992: 2, emphasis in original), a theme that also has been advocated by civilian proponents of a post-Cold War naval arms build-up (Will 1995).

The ideologies and uses of naval power during the industrial capitalist era provide an outlying postscript to this chapter's history and analysis of ocean-space in the era of industrial capitalism. While other marine user-groups, managers, and planners adjusted their perspective on the ocean to align themselves with (and reproduce) the distinct spatiality of industrial capitalism, naval planners retained a mercantilist-era vision of their role in the world. Other actors constructed the deep sea as a great void outside society, useful only as a transport surface between the land-based places that hosted the economic activity of industrial capitalism (investment and disinvestment in fixed locations). Social interactions in ocean-space were to be restricted to the minimal degree of community stewardship necessary to preserve access to its resources. But the navies of the world continued to view the sea as an important space within the social system, an arena in which social conflict was to be played out and social power exercised, as it had been under merchant capitalism.

The tenacity of naval planners demonstrates that although ocean-space constructions have historically been embedded in the spatiality of particular eras' political–economic systems, this correspondence is complicated both by structural tensions and by the needs and desires of individual and collective actors. Tensions surrounding the issue of adaptation to changing conditions existed in the world's navies, and at certain crucial times the navies did adapt (e.g., Fisher's pre-World War I reforms of the British navy and the US navy's decision to pursue an island-hopping campaign rather than sea control in the Pacific in World War II). But at other times, opponents of change won out.

The attitude of the British and US navies during this period was not merely an anachronism. It also was symptomatic of contradictions within modernity as various social actors attempted to construct ocean-space. As Lefebvre notes, the history of the construction of a space is more than the cumulative imprint of society's "spatial practices" over a series of eras. Because spaces (even the ocean) are simultaneously creations of social processes *and* arenas for everyday experiences, there is a constant negotiation between the "spaces of representation" implied and reproduced by users of the sea (e.g. the world's navies, as well as its fishers, refugees, sailors, etc.) and the "spatial practices" emanating from the structural imperatives of the world economy. The ocean is a repository of culture as well as a place of economic processes, and in this particular instance institutions with strong cultural attachments to the sea (the British and US navies) also happened to wield considerable social power in society as a whole, and so they were able to carve out a domain for their "representations of space" in the ocean even as those representations contradicted society's dominant "spatial practices." Other users of ocean-space who lacked these navies' social power – such as the Micronesians, who saw their waters mined and/or irradiated during World War II – have not been so fortunate. Nonetheless, as dialectical contradictions *within* the spatial practices of capitalism *and* contradictions *between* these spatial practices and the experiences of everyday users intensify, the ocean will probably continue to emerge as an arena for social conflict and a space for experimenting with social futures, themes that are explored in Chapters 5 and 6.

5 Ocean-space and postmodern capitalism

The spatiality of postmodern capitalism

Since around 1970, the world has begun a transition to a political–economic organizing system that some have termed postmodern capitalism. Although the postmodern era is driven by many of the same processes and structural imperatives that have underlain industrial capitalism, these processes have manifested themselves in distinct ways, creating a unique spatiality whose conflictual aspects are both more subtle and more intense (Harvey 1989).

As in industrial capitalism, the spatiality of postmodern capitalism can be analyzed through a focus on the dialectical nature of capitalist systems. Capitalism has advanced through the progressive homogenization and commodification of elements of social life, as is evidenced in Fordism, with its system of bulk production and bulk consumption. At the same time, and in contradiction to this tendency toward homogenization, capitalism thrives upon the creation of difference. Value is generated by moving capital from one location to another; investments pay off when new products are developed and marketed. Hence conservative theorists worry that a triumph of Fordism – in which a global mass of content producer–consumers has its every need met by bulk-produced goods – may portend lethargy, ennui, and capitalist dysfunction (Fukuyama 1992; Rostow 1960).

Postmodern capitalism is emerging in this context of triumphant Fordism, hypercommodification, and global homogenization. Even as the Fordist system extends to areas in the Third World through the diffusion of mass-produced goods and the commodification of previously non-commodified aspects of life, it has begun to take on new characteristics. Faced with market saturation for many goods in the First World and the tendency for profit rates to fall, capital increasingly orients itself to flexible production for niche markets. Indeed, capital devotes considerable effort to *creating* these niche markets, marketing signs of identity as well as actual consumable commodities.

Speed especially is important in postmodern capitalism. In their effort to identify, create, and satisfy new consumer identities in specific world-regions and in specific, globally dispersed social strata, enterprises have developed increasingly sophisticated transportation, communication, and logistical systems for rapidly transmitting capital, information, components, and products among far-flung production facilities and markets. Complex networks for outsourcing elements of the production process (from research and development to component production to assembly to marketing) as well as "just-in-time" inventory systems allow for short product development cycles and rapid retooling. Images, knowledge, money, and commodities transmitted by satellites and airplanes at an ever-increasing pace play a crucial role in giving postmodern capitalism its distinct character.

This importance of movement and speed (or "time–space compression" to use Harvey's term) has led some to suggest that the spatial fixity–mobility dialectic has been resolved, with mobility the clear winner. Proponents of this view paint a picture of compact and easily mobile First World command-and-control centers performing research-and-development and marketing functions, surrounded by an underutilized periphery of producer areas that are pitted against each other in a "race to the bottom." A component manufacturer in Malaysia can be played off against one in Mexico or a prefabricated plant may be moved from Haiti to Sri Lanka in response to the first signs of a union organizing drive or tax law change. Pundits on the right hail "the end of geography" (O'Brien 1992) while those on the left fear global capitalism as a "new leviathan" (Ross and Trachte 1990).

This argument is rejected here; what some view as a qualitative shift in the spatiality of capital is merely the continuation of an ongoing dialectic. As many geographers have noted, despite the claims of its promoters, footloose capital has not succeeded in annihilating space. Indeed, the complete annihilation of space is not in capital's interest. Even as individual firms and industries "globalize" and even as goods and capital move in increasing volume and at increasing speed around the world, place continues to matter (Cox 1997). The rapid product development cycles of the high-technology sector have led to a landscape of "territorial production complexes" in which firms rely on spatially entrenched networks of research, educational, and production institutions (Storper 1992; Storper and Walker 1989). The finance industry too, for all its globalization, is supported by communications infrastructures, social institutions, and cultural mores that "fix" it in such places as London, New York, and Tokyo (Sassen 1991; Leyshon and Thrift 1997). Postmodern capitalism is characterized by an increasing number of "manufactured places" that exist to be "consumed" and that generate much of the identity-based consumption of the era. These places – be they Disneyland, a theme-based urban redevelopment area, or a spectacle-oriented shopping mall – also represent significant investments of immobile capital. Furthermore, these manufactured places represent spatial fixity not only as places of immobile productive investments ("representations of space" resulting from "spatial practices," in Lefebvre's terminology) but also as places wherein consumption and everyday life irrevocably are embedded in locationally specific processes, signs, and meanings, as well as physical structures (Lefebvre's "spaces of representation") (Soja 1989, 1996).

A more complex version of the thesis that capitalism is undergoing a fundamental change in its spatiality is offered by Manuel Castells, who argues, "Capital and labor increasingly tend to exist in different spaces and times: the space of flows and the space of places, instant time of computerized networks versus clock time of everyday life" (Castells 1996: 475). While Castells (borrowing from the spatial dialectics theorists) acknowledges that "spaces of flows" always have been important to capitalism, he holds that postmodern society has reoriented itself to privilege flow-related activities and networked structures, and that this in turn is leading to fundamental changes in the organization of labor, cities, firms, etc. In particular, Castells claims that there used to be a close correspondence between the space of economic activity and the space of everyday life (both were "the city" or "the region"), but that in the new network society these spaces are becoming disjointed and there is decreasing correspondence between the space of flows and the everyday space of places.

Its insights into the changing spatiality of everyday life notwithstanding, Castells' thesis is hampered by an incomplete consideration of spaces of flows. Castells identifies three "layers" within the space of flows. The first layer is the material "between-space" (or transportation–communications infrastructure) within which movement transpires. Castells focuses on telecommunications and so he identifies this layer as "a circuit of electronic impulses" (Castells 1996: 412), but one could also include other channels of movement such as roadways, railways, and the dedicated transportation–communication surfaces of airspace and ocean-space. The second layer is the nodes of the network (e.g. world cities). It is at this layer where there is the greatest interaction between the space of flows and the space of places since New York, for instance, is both a *place* of labor and everyday life and a crucial *node* on the network of flows that is ever more prominent in world society. The third layer is the social space inhabited by managerial elites: "Airports' VIP lounges, designed to maintain the distance *vis-à-vis* society in the highways of the space of flows; mobile, personal, on-line access to telecommunications networks, so that the traveler is never lost; a system of travel arrangements, secretarial services, and reciprocal hosting that maintains a close circle of the corporate elite together through the worshipping of similar rites in all countries" (Castells 1996: 417).

While Castells recognizes all three layers of spaces of flows, his analysis is almost entirely restricted to the second and third layers – the places of nodal (urban) processes and the places wherein which the social dynamics of the space of flows are reproduced. The actual "fluvial" spaces of the network (the first layer of the space of flows) are dismissed as insulated from the processes that characterize the local places that are sites of social contestation: "Capital tends to escape in its hyperspace of pure circulation, while labor dissolves its collective entity into an infinite variation of individual existences" (Castells 1996: 475–476). While Castells acknowledges that spaces of flows have their origin in contested social processes, he fails to investigate the politics of their ongoing material construction (or reproduction), and as such he writes them off as "hyperspace[s] of pure circulation," fundamentally asocial and separated from everyday life. As has been stressed throughout this book, the "first layer" spaces of flows are not merely unfortunate spaces of movement that, while perhaps conceived by society, are then divorced from the social factors and conflicts that also construct the everyday places of experience. Rather, these spaces, like the discrete places that they join, have been and remain arenas of social contestation amidst the ongoing dialectic of fixity and mobility, a point that is developed further in Chapter 6.

Thus, it is argued here that postmodern capitalism, for all its outward differences from industrial capitalism, maintains a spatiality on land and at sea not unlike that of the industrial era. Places are important as locations for fixed investments. Movement of goods (and money and information) between these places is important as well. To a greater degree than ever before, the speed of this movement also is critical. As in the industrial era, postmodern capitalism revolves around the centrality of the "place" and the free flow of goods between places, and, as in the industrial era, the tendencies toward fixity and mobility are in dialectical opposition. However, these two spatial processes – the development/representation of places and the movement of commodities/information/money between places – are more intense under postmodern capitalism (Lash and Urry 1994), and this results in an intensification of the conflicts surrounding spatial constructions, including in those "first layer" spaces of flows that are noted – but largely ignored – by Castells.

The construction of postmodern ocean-space

The intensification of capitalism's spatial tendencies during the emergent era of postmodern capitalism has resulted in a parallel intensification of each of the elements of the industrial capitalist-era construction of ocean-space: the idealization of the deep sea as a great void of distance, suitable for annihilation by an ever-advancing tendency toward capital mobility; the portrayal of specific points in ocean-space as territories, extensions of land that may be developed through the application of spatially fixed investments; and the designation of specific elements or functions as special spaces of stewardship, suitable for systemic social regulation but to be insulated from state appropriation and territorial enclosure. As each element of the industrial-era ocean-space construction has intensified, each has also become more extensive, leading to frequent conflicts as incompatible elements literally overlap each other in space. The intensification of all three components of the industrial-era ocean-space construction – and the conflicts that this intensification engenders – is exemplified by the dramatic growth of the cruise ship industry in recent decades, from 1.4 million passengers in 1980 to 5.9 million in 1999 (CLIA 2000; Pattullo 1996). Cruise ships offer several distinct (and not necessarily complementary) marine experiences (Trist 1999), and each of these experiences may be linked with a component of the multifaceted ocean-space construction developed during the industrial capitalist era and intensified under postmodern capitalism. First, the tendency toward annihilation of ocean-space is seen in the cruise ship industry's tendency to promote the ocean as a mere surface. The ship itself, not the sea nor the ports, is promoted as the primary destination. This construction of the sea by the cruise ship industry first appeared in the early twentieth century, when "ships were . . . designed to nurture the illusion that one was not at sea" (Dickinson and Vladimir 1997: 6). As Arthur Davis, a designer for Cunard from this era, said:

> "The people who use these ships are not pirates, they do not dance hornpipes; they are mostly seasick American ladies, and the one thing they want to forget when they are on the vessel is that they are on a ship at all." (cited in Dickinson and Vladimir 1997: 6–7)

Likewise, the industry's resurgence in the 1970s was in part facilitated by a shift in marketing from promotion of the ship as a means for getting from one land-destination to another to promotion of the ship as itself a destination, a place of merriment within the non-space of the ocean (Dickinson and Vladimir 1997). Indeed, as Foucault (1986) suggests, it may be that the perceived (and constructed) placelessness of the sea allows for the ship, fundamentally unrooted in a space of society, to be constructed as a hedonistic haven.

While this "great void" construction of the sea has been strong within the cruise ship industry, the other two elements of the industrial-era construction also have been mobilized by industry marketing staffs and ship directors. The tendency toward territorialization can be seen in nostalgic references wherein specific areas of the sea are promoted as historically constructed places wherein, first, pirates and, later, early twentieth-century yachters frolicked. Finally, the tendency toward constructing the ocean as a place filled with resources can be seen in nature-oriented cruises (usually with a scuba diving component) and in coastal zone managers' efforts to preserve these marine resources so that the tourist industry will remain booming (even if that means declaring areas of ocean-space off limits to locally based fishers) (Nichols 1999; Trist 1999). The meteoric rise of cruise ship tourism in the past three decades is indicative of the intensification of each of these three tendencies during the era of postmodern capitalism.

The annihilation of ocean-space

With the era's emphasis on movement and speed, the dominant element of postmodern capitalism's ocean-space construction is a continuation of the great void ideal that characterized the industrial capitalist era. As was noted in the previous chapter, even the US navy, locked for so long in a mercantilist-era mindset, has come to construct the ocean not as an arena for contesting power and asserting control but as a void across which one must travel to project power on to land.

The new intensity of the great void ideal of ocean-space (and, indeed, transportation-space in general) is epitomized by the triumph of the container ship and the automated, intermodal container port. With containerization, movement by sea, rail, and truck is constructed as one continuous flow. The aim is to annihilate any unique characteristics of the environments across which the containers move. The vehicle carrying the containers is obscured, as are the commodities within the containers; trade is reduced to *movement*. Labor in the port and on the ship similarly is hidden from view. There is no longer a popular image of a sailor, maritime worker, or stevedore; work connections between port and city, formerly evident in the gritty, odorous maritime service area near the city center, now are hidden within the sterile robotic gantry cranes of the remote container port. The imagination of maritime life is restricted to consumption sites glorifying mercantilist pasts, and these sites rarely contain any cues to assist the tourist in connecting historic memories with functioning ports (Sekula 1995). Of course, outside this image lies an empirically rich world of individuals whose everyday lives revolve around entirely different encounters with the ocean as a friction surface (e.g. refugees whose lives are dictated by the agonizingly slow movements of smugglers' ships) and as a space of nature (e.g. fishers whose lives revolve around knowledge of distinct fish-rich places within the ocean). However, the existence of individuals and their alternate constructions of the ocean as a space of representation are denied by the representations of ocean-space that emanate from postmodern capitalism's dominant spatial practices.

In postmodern capitalism, capital denies the existence of the sea as a distinct place or environment (even as its actual use of the sea continues to grow). The spatial ideology of postmodern capital is one of flexibility, speed, and global coverage, and the ocean has a special place within this spatial ideology as a seemingly friction-free surface across which capital can move without hindrance:

> Water is capital's element . . . The bourgeois idealization of sea power and ocean-borne commerce has been central to the mythology of capital, which has struggled to free itself from the earth just as the bourgeoisie struggled to free itself from tilling the soil. Moving capital is liquid capital, and without movement, capital is a mere Oriental hoard . . . [The ocean] is capital's favored myth-element.
>
> (Connery 1995: 40, 56)

Thus, corporate imagery portrays the sea as an empty space across which capital flows with increasing ease as it seeks out profit-generating opportunities on land, Castells' "hyperspace of pure circulation." The geoeconomic region known as the Pacific Rim is notable for its imagery of discrete, decentered units (nation-states, world-cities, sweatshops, etc.) revolving around a space of (marine) emptiness: "The hegemonic construction of a Pascalian sublime whose 'circumference is everywhere and center nowhere' . . . [characterized by] the deterritorializing power of oceanic vastness" (Wilson and Dirlik 1995: 1), "a perfect image for a centeredness with no central power" (Connery 1995: 34; see also Dirlik 1993). For the corporate practitioner of capitalist globalization, the ocean that binds the rim (and more generally, the space of the world economy) is an unprofitable nuisance space to be progressively annihilated by capital in its search for complete freedom of movement and the conquest of distance. Corporate advertisements take this representation of the ocean to fantastic excess; in a 1990 Merrill Lynch advertisement a panoramic photograph of the ocean is accompanied by the caption, "For us, this doesn't exit" (reprinted in Roberts 1996), while a 1997 advertisement for the telecommunications firm Concert envisions a "global village" wherein the world has been impacted by a fortuitous act of tectonic convergence in which the continents have been squeezed together, eliminating practically all intervening ocean-space (reprinted in Steinberg 1999c). AT&T similarly advertises its international service with a slogan celebrating its ability to annihilate the marine divide: "Oceans separate. And we connect" (cited in Carvajal 1995).

The postmodern attempt to annihilate the ocean also can be seen in cultural products, including, ironically, the film *Waterworld* (1995). In one sense, the film is about the triumph of the ocean: the entire earth's surface has been submerged by the rising sea, with the possible exception of a rumored Shangri La known as Dryland. And yet the ocean is surprisingly non-existent as a place of production, consumption, or nature. Individuals in Waterworld neither act in harmony with, nor in opposition to, marine nature; they simply ignore nature because the sea is an environment without nature. On the ocean, the weather is always good and the sea is always calm. In an extensive underwater scene, there are no fish present. The only bit of marine life appearing in the film is a monster of sorts, introduced when the issue of food arises. Even here, the monster is slain off-screen in a presumably effortless battle, reappearing seconds later as a denaturalized, easily digestible fish fillet.

Of course, one natural element *is* ever present in Waterworld: water, but water is portrayed more as a damper that extinguishes nature than as an element of nature itself. The ocean is neither a site of resources nor a resource in itself. Drinking water is obtained not by purifying sea water but by purifying urine. Land, when it finally appears, is rich in variation and aesthetic signs (and its paradigmatic element – dirt – is a highly sought-after commodity in Waterworld), but the sea is a natureless environment: it is simply a surface across which individuals travel and fight as they search for Dryland. The only interesting objects within the sea itself are the ruins of past human civilizations, be they decaying buildings on the ocean floor or rusted hulks of twentieth-century oil tankers.[1]

In short, *Waterworld* presents Castells' vision. On the one hand, there are the spaces of existence (*places*) in which individual actors use the resources (nature) at their disposal to go about their everyday lives and constitute society. On the other hand, there are the natureless spaces of flows in which are orchestrated the acts of movement that are crucial to the continuation of society but which, in essence, are asocial. And yet, this idealization of spaces of flows (including ocean-space) as devoid of society, nature, or geographic differentiation represents neither the reality nor the interests of postmodern capitalism. If capital truly were able to transcend the barriers to seamless mobility imposed by the distance and nature of the ocean, the ocean no longer would have utility as a surface of distance that maintains the world of differentiation upon which capital thrives. The ocean's service in a world of capital fluidity lies in the *apparent* ability of Merrill Lynch, Concert, and AT&T to wish away both its nature and the very space it occupies. Capital triumphs through these individual acts that *approach* space-annihilation. If capital ever truly were to *succeed* in annihilating spatial friction and geographic difference, it would be deprived of these acts that mark and constitute one aspect of its success.

As political economists have long asserted, the ability to shift capital between "different" places provides a crucial mechanism for capital

---

[1] Portions of this analysis of *Waterworld* are derived from A. Sekula, personal communication, 1995. Although the protagonist, played by Kevin Costner, has made a crucial adaptation to the nature of the ocean, springing gills so that he can exist in its nature, he is ostracized by others for this act of sensitivity to his environment. In general, the transgressors in Waterworld are no more respectful of the ocean as a resource-space than are the members of the dominant society.

accumulation (Hilferding 1981; Lenin 1939; Luxemburg 1964), and the intervening distance of ocean-space amplifies difference. Capital's perverse desire to annihilate its "favored myth-element" – although perhaps rational from a short-run profit-maximization standpoint – runs the risk of also annihilating opportunities for the realization of value through movement, thereby reducing capital to the status of "a mere Oriental hoard."

Deleuze and Guattari shed further light on capitalism's complex construction of spaces of flows, or "smooth spaces," including the ocean, which they identify as "a smooth space par excellence" (Deleuze and Guattari 1988: 479). As sites of alterity, "smooth" spaces serve as necessary counterpoints to the "striated" spaces of capital whose physical and social features and points of friction enable investment, sedentarization, enclosure, surveillance, and other processes associated with modern life (Deleuze and Guattari 1988). Despite their utility, Deleuze and Guattari note that agents of capital progressively seek to absorb and "modernize" these "smooth" spaces because they are resistant to essential capitalist categories and institutions. Thus, the tendency to annihilate the formal independence of ocean-space is indicative of a more general tendency toward self-destruction, whether this annihilation is achieved through colonization by modernist institutions of navigation and militarism (as is depicted by Virilio (1986) as well as Deleuze and Guattari) or through physical obliteration (as is idealized by Merrill Lynch and Concert).

Finally, this capitalist fantasy of annihilating ocean-space is ironic because, despite its representation during the industrial capitalist era as a friction-free void, the ocean in fact may be the portion of the earth's surface least amenable to time–space compression. The triumph of speed is relative; the sea is still a space of nature, and it figuratively and literally contributes friction to the idealized free flow of goods between places of capital investment. Eurodollars move from New York to Tokyo in fractions of seconds, but hydrodynamics limit the speed of the ocean freighters that carry the bulk of the world's commodities to the same speed as at the end of World War I. This slowness, just as much as the rapidity of flows, contributes to the particular temporal and spatial characteristics of postmodern capitalism (Sekula 1995).

In summary, even as postmodern capitalism intensifies its ideal of ocean-space as a great void to be annihilated, the ocean remains important as a space both constituted by and constitutive of the social system. Within this construction of ocean-space, the sea is successfully *imagined* as annihilated, but it remains an important space in the actual workings of the world economy. Total tonnage shipped continues to increase and the vast majority of goods transported internationally still travel by ship. Furthermore, as the discussion of industrial capitalism demonstrated, even transportation uses of ocean-space require a degree of regulation. Although the ocean may, more than ever, be a "space of flows" and although movement across this space may have unprecedented significance for global society, it does not follow that one should write off the ocean as a "hyperspace of pure circulation" and direct one's focus entirely to the networked places that the spaces of flows connect. Rather, the construction of these spaces of flows is complex and thus laden with social tensions. Spaces of flows exist within the dialectical tensions of capitalism's dual needs for fixity and movement, homogenization and differentiation, time–space compression and distanciation. All socially constructed spaces, *including* the "first level" spaces of flows, are unstable because they serve as arenas for this dialectic. In addition, however, the ocean is a particularly unstable social construct because, besides serving as a "first level" space of flows, it also continues to serve other, non-flow-oriented functions.

The territorialization of ocean-space

Just as postmodern capitalism has intensified the Indian Ocean-style great void idealization that was one tendency of the industrial capitalist-era ocean-space construction, it also has intensified the era's Micronesian-style tendency toward territorialization and development of discrete marine places. During the industrial era, this territorialization of the sea was restricted to discrete coastal zones. Recently, however, there have been movements to extend this territorialization to ever larger areas of ocean-space. Thus, the stage has been set for conflict between the tendency to idealize the ocean as an "empty" space of flows and a countervailing tendency toward territorialization.

The territorialization and development of ocean-space continues to be most intense in coastal areas, but, even in the coastal areas, this territorialization is intensifying with new characteristics, commensurate with the spatiality of postmodern capitalism. During the industrial era, coastal spaces were constructed as developable territory, but these coastal developments generally were related to trade. Since trade was viewed as an activity subordinate to the development-oriented activities of production that characterized land-space, trade-based coastal development represented only a partial territorialization. Thus, Melville's Redburn (1849) remarks:

> Sailors go *round* the world without going *into* it; and their reminiscences of travel are only a dim recollection of a chain of tap-rooms surrounding the globe, parallel with the Equator. They but touch the perimeter of the circle; hover about the edges of terra-firma; and only land upon wharves and pier-heads. (Melville 1957: 127–128; emphasis in original)

The lives of long-distance sailors still revolve around a network of ports with little interaction with the hinterland, although containerization has diminished the number of individuals involved in port- or ship-based transport activities and it has shifted most docking activities to remote container ports. As a result, the former docklands near city centers have become available for more socially embedded development activities. In particular, many of these spaces have been developed as sites for tourism, the paradigmatic industry of postmodern capitalism (Baudrillard 1988; Urry 1990, 1994). From prototype developments in Boston and Baltimore to Cape Town, Sydney, and countless other cities, there has been a proliferation of the harborside festival marketplace, an urban redevelopment strategy that both reflects the spatiality of postmodern capitalism (Kilian and Dodson 1996) and provides an ideal backdrop for promoting consumption of commodities within the postmodern tourist economy (Goss 1996). In the harborside festival marketplace, the place's mercantile past is celebrated through the fetishization of human interactions with marine space, where tourists are encouraged to consume amidst an environment replete with nostalgic images pointing to the space's previous function (DeFilippis 1997; Sekula 1995).

Despite references to maritime transport, this image of ocean-space underlying the festival marketplace conflicts with the great void idealization. The festival marketplace portrays the ocean as a site to be consumed, an intriguing space with a rich past and a non-functional present that makes it safely available for appropriation by the tourist's gaze. Territorial control of coastal space facilitates the development that enables its commodification. In direct contrast, the great void idealization presents an ocean that has no appreciable past or future (it has no essence and ideally will be annihilated in the future), but that serves a definite present-day function (it serves as a surface for the movement of commodities). Designers of harborside developments selectively hide references to this latter-day, functional ocean, as they obscure container terminals, commercial fish markets, and other signs of contemporary marine activity, while historical referents that complicate the "official" history are sanitized or obliterated (Atkinson *et al.* 1997; Atkinson and Laurier 1998; Goss 1996; Sekula 1995). Thus, the construction of the sea as a developable space for consuming nostalgia, like its idealization as a great void to be annihilated, rests at a point of contradiction between the tendency to value individual places and the idealization of place-lessness, a contradiction that embodies capital's dual needs to engage simultaneously in fixity and mobility. The sea is to be gazed at and even celebrated, but as an actual place of production and transportation it is largely hidden.

Moving away from the harbor, one enters the nearshore waters. Like the harbor, this area of ocean-space was already defined during the industrial capitalist era as a territory amenable to land-like regulation and development, but its development now is being organized at a heightened pace. Governmental and nongovernmental agencies with the express mission of developing the coastal zone are calling for the implementation of integrated coastal management programs so as to maximize the region's development potential (Nichols 1999). Tourism too is increasing in coastal waters, as recreational fishing and scuba diving play an increasing role in national development plans (Orams 1999; Trist 1999). With the rise of development planning for the coastal zone, this area of ocean-space, politically incorporated within the territory of the state by the mid-nineteenth century, now is becoming fully incorporated socially as well.

Beyond a nation's territorial waters lies its exclusive economic zone (EEZ). As was discussed in the previous chapter, these zones were conceived of as spaces for implementing a Seldenian variant of stewardship; EEZs were not so much to be developed as a component of state territory as they were to be managed as a space wherein a single state had exclusive rights. Increasingly, however, EEZs are recognized as rich reserves of living and non-living resources, and in some cases the extraction of these resources requires the positioning of spatially fixed investments in discrete areas beyond territorial waters. Potential ocean uses here include semi-stationary off-shore fish farms, the harvesting of biological material from deep-sea heat vents, and the mining of a host of deep seabed minerals including polymetallic sulphides, gas-hydrate-rich underwater ice, ferromanganese- and cobalt-rich crusts, and, most notably, polymetallic manganese nodules, which are discussed in detail later in this chapter (Allen 1994; Broad 1997; Earle 1995; Earney 1990; Lemonick 1995; Norse 1993). Fixed investments in discrete places, however, require a strong territorial regime to guarantee their security. Thus the EEZs increasingly are constructed as extensions of state territory amenable to development, rather than as "special" spaces under state control so as to facilitate stewardship and management (Alexander 1983; Booth 1985; Grolin 1983). In the United States, evidence of this transformation can be seen in the Magnusson Fishery Conservation and Management Act of 1976 (PL 94-265, revised in 1997 as the Magnusson-Stevens Act), which, although maintaining the status of the EEZ as a distinct, federally con-trolled management zone, calls for its management to be guided and administered by regional fishery management councils whose mem-bers are largely nominees of the individual states and whose interests are thus tied to each state's development objectives.

The latest possible extension in the territorialization of ocean-space is occurring in waters beyond the 200 nautical mile limit of the EEZ. Faced with the problem of the overfishing of highly migratory species and species that straddle EEZs and adjacent portions of the high seas, the United Nations in 1993 convened the Conference on Straddling Fish Stocks and Highly Migratory Fish Stocks. As occurred during the UNCLOS fishing negotiations, the major divide at the conference was between states engaged in distant-water fishing[2] and states with sub-stantial fish stocks in the deep waters off their coasts.[3] In 1995 the confer-ence adopted the Agreement for the Implementation of the Provisions of the 1982 United Nations Convention on the Law of the Sea Relat-ing to the Conservation and Management of Straddling Fish Stocks and Highly Migratory Fish Stocks (United Nations 1995). This agreement gives each coastal state the authority to regulate exploitation of highly migratory species and straddling stocks in areas of the high seas adja-cent to its EEZ so as to conserve the abundance of these species within its EEZ. It also encourages coastal states to work with distant water fishing states which are already fishing in those adjacent waters so as to develop a regional regime acceptable to all. In effect, this agreement extends to the adjacent area of the high seas beyond 200 miles a regime similar to the "weak" EEZ originally proposed by the United States for the 12–200 mile zone at the first UNCLOS III meetings, a regime that in turn was modeled after the first Truman proclamation and the Conven-tion on Fishing and Conservation of the Living Resources of the High Seas adopted at UNCLOS I.

[2] Leaders of this group were China, the European Union, Japan, Poland, and South Korea.
[3] Major states in this group were Argentina, Canada, Chile, Iceland, Indonesia, New Zealand, Norway, and Peru.

At present, as was the case when the Truman proclamation was first issued, this regime more closely resembles state-implemented steward-ship than a further extension of land-like territorialization. However, a debate continues over whether or not this extension of coastal state authority over fishing beyond 200 miles from land marks a continuation of a "creeping enclosure movement" (Armas Pfirter 1995; Clingan 1993; Joyner and De Cola 1993; Orrego Vicuña 1993). Various proposals have been made for further implementing some form of formal governance in the deep sea. Juda and Burroughs (1990) propose that the current system of non-territorial resource regimes overlaying the high seas regime be replaced with a system of regional management organizations charged with the responsibility of regulating all ocean uses within a region's EEZs and adjacent high seas. Others go further, suggesting a wholesale rejection of the stewardship paradigm and a further extension of state territoriality into ocean-space. Hollick (1981) and Ball (1996) warn that a national enclosure movement is inevitable unless preventive action is taken, while others calculate that state enclosure would lead to the most efficient utilization of scarce ocean resources (Denman 1984; Eckert 1979). Booth calls further enclosure "technologically possible, econom-ically unavoidable, and politically tempting" (Booth 1985: 57; see also Grolin 1983; Oxman 1983; Pardo 1984), and a special supplement to *The Economist* declares:

> [The sea] is a resource that must be preserved and harvested. To en-hance its uses, the water must become ever more like the land, with owners, laws and limits. Fishermen must behave more like ranchers than hunters. (*Economist* 1998: 4)

Johnston (1993) suggests still another territorial alternative: enclosure by a superstate authority that would parcel out rights to exploit the "common heritage" of the sea, although he notes in another article that he has difficulties envisioning a scenario wherein the few powers with the capability to utilize fully the ocean's resources would grant territorial power to a higher, superstate authority (Johnston 1992).

Any of these territorial regimes for the deep sea is conceivable. Satya Nandan, UN Under-Secretary-General for Ocean Affairs and the Law of the Sea from 1983 to 1992, has noted that with the consolidation of the shipping industry, fewer states than ever have a direct interest in constructing the sea as a friction-free transportation surface while at the same time states' interest in enclosure of extractable ocean resources has grown (Nandan 1989). Zacher and McConnell (1990) have calculated the

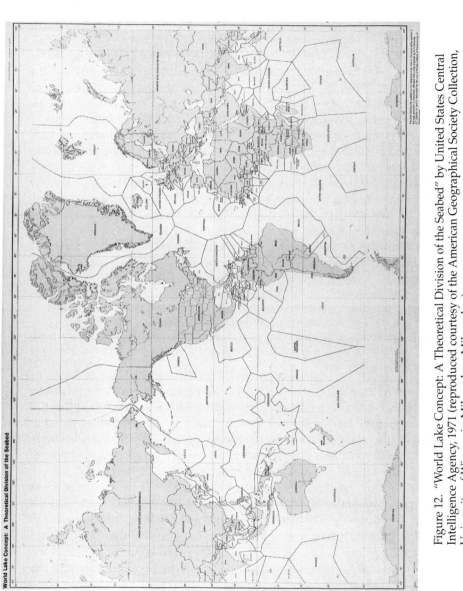

Figure 12. "World Lake Concept: A Theoretical Division of the Seabed" by United States Central Intelligence Agency, 1971 (reproduced courtesy of the American Geographical Society Collection, University of Wisconsin-Milwaukee, Milwaukee).

potential winners and losers and the relative strengths and interests of national players should the ocean commons be obliterated along the lines of the "World Lake Concept" map developed by the US Central Intelligence Agency in the early 1970s (Figure 12).[4] They conclude that in the long term this division of the ocean is at least as likely as one granting territorial authority to a superstate agency.

Proponents of dividing the entire ocean among sovereign, territorial states (e.g. Bernfeld 1967) point out that freedom of navigation could be guaranteed much as provisions are made for overflight over sovereign land-space. Or perhaps the air will increasingly take the place of the sea as transit-space, in which case the sea, like many non-European land-areas in the colonialist era, could be defined as *res nullius* and susceptible to appropriation. Landlocked states probably would object to this wholesale division of the sea (they would be able to make a claim to some of the riches from a superstate agency but would have no claim to riches from other nations' territory), but Zacher and McConnell suggest that they probably would not have the power significantly to influence the outcome.

While arguments may be made for the likelihood of an "enclosure movement," such a movement on either a national or a global scale would seriously challenge other, equally important, imperatives of capitalism. The "world lake" option would pose a threat to the free trade across ocean-space required by capitalism and maintained by the great void idealization (Christy 1968). Indeed, the United States, which has an especially strong interest in maintaining the ocean as a friction-free surface for trade and military mobility, produced the "World Lake Concept" map not as a preferred alternative but as a "'scare' example" (Buzan 1976: 82). Since World War II, each time the United States has taken a strong interest in intensifying ocean governance on a global scale or in the areas adjacent to its territorial waters, it has taken pains to distance itself from proposals supporting increased territorial enclosure that might endanger the high seas shipping and military norms that underpin US hegemony (Baer 1994; Cafruny 1987; Sullivan 1985).

As for the "common heritage" option whereby territorial control would be granted to a superstate entity, President Reagan and United Kingdom Prime Minister Margaret Thatcher made it clear in their opposition to a strong territorial regime for regulating manganese nodule

[4] This map, in turn, was based upon one created in 1967 by Francis Christy and presented to the Law of the Sea Institute (Alexander 1967).

mining (discussed below) that they perceived territorial control by an autonomous superstate authority as inimical to the workings of competitive, free-enterprise capitalism.

As Chase-Dunn notes:

> There are two main characteristics of the interstate system which need to be sustained [if the capitalist world-economy is to survive]: the division of sovereignty in the core (interimperial rivalry) and the maintenance of a network of exchange among the states.
>
> (Chase-Dunn 1989: 150)

The "world lake option" would challenge the second of these two prerequisites, as the elimination of an ocean commons would potentially interfere with capitalist free trade. The "common heritage" option would challenge Chase-Dunn's interimperial rivalry prerequisite by placing a space of production and "development" outside the network of competitive states that constitute the world-system.

Like the idealization of the ocean as a great void suitable for annihilation, the territorialization of ocean-space responds to a pressing imperative of postmodern capitalism – the need to commodify, invest in, and "develop" elements of nature and space that previously had existed outside political–economic competition and modernization. However, like the intensification of the great void ideal, this expansion of territorialization conflicts with other imperatives of capitalism. Advocates of marine development propose that this land-like territorialization be extended beyond its relatively unintensive application in narrowly defined coastal waters to "integrated development" programs in large portions of ocean-space. As this extension occurs, the territorialization aspect of the postmodern ocean-space construction is increasingly in conflict with both the idealization of the ocean as a great void and its management and stewardship as a special resource space.

The stewardship of ocean-space

The third aspect of the postmodern era's social construction of ocean-space – stewardship – fuses the late capitalist concern for nature with the concept of stewardship that characterized the Roman Mediterranean and mercantilist-era ocean-space constructions as well as elements of the industrial capitalist-era construction. Under the stewardship paradigm, the ocean is seen as a socially significant space providing crucial resources (whether these are resources of connection or material resources). To ensure access to these resources, the ocean (or areas thereof) is designated as off-limits to territorial appropriation, but individual states, the community of states, and/or non-state actors are permitted to exercise social power in the interest of stewarding marine resources.

The postmodern doctrine of marine stewardship continues and intensifies this construction, but with a key difference: In the mercantilist era, the sea was designated as a special space insulated from the norms of possession and property (*res extra commercium*) because of the special function that it served as a surface for trade. In the postmodern era, the basis for this designation has been expanded because the sea increasingly also serves as a special space of nature. In contrast to the intervening industrial era, when the sea was denigrated as a void between the terrestrial spaces of production and consumption, the ocean once again is constructed as a significant space wherein states and intergovernmental entities are permitted to exercise non-territorial power so as to manage the ocean's resources in a rational, efficiency-maximizing manner and to ensure continued access to resources deemed necessary for the long-term survival of the social system.

This "nature-space" (or "resource-space") perspective on the ocean, which expands upon some of the resource-specific non-territorial treaties of the late industrial era, can be seen in a number of recent intergovernmental initiatives, such as Part XII of the 1982 UN Convention on the Law of the Sea (United Nations 1983); Chapter 17 of *Agenda 21*, the report of the UN Conference on Environment and Development (United Nations 1993); and the events and programs surrounding the International Year of the Ocean, 1998. These programs and documents, especially the latter two, explicitly place the world-ocean within the discourse of sustainable development, a discourse that others have noted is devoted to the rational management of scarce resources so that nature can continue to serve as a material base for capital accumulation well into the twenty-first century (M. O'Connor 1994a). As the statement of objectives for the International Year of the Ocean (IYO) reads, in its entirety:

> The overall objective is to focus and reinforce the attention of the public, governments and decision makers at large on the importance of the oceans and the marine environment as resources for sustainable development. The major aim of the joint efforts during 1998 will be to create awareness and obtain commitments from governments to take action, provide adequate resources and give the priority to the ocean and coastal areas which they deserve as *finite economical assets*. This is most important, in view of the increasing threats of pollution,

> population pressure, excessive fishing, coastal zone degradation and climate variability to the finite resource the ocean represents. Without a healthy ocean, the life-supporting system of the earth would be seriously endangered.
>
> (IOC 1997b, emphasis added)[5]

An IYO planning document leaves little doubt about its overall orientation toward what Esteva (1992) calls "the reign of scarcity": "Finite size must be emphasized" in all IYO activities and publications (Intergovernmental Oceanographic Commission 1997a).

This application of the sustainable development discourse to the ocean at the intergovernmental level has been supported by representations of the ocean in the popular media. In 1995 alone, two major US publications, *Time* and *National Geographic Magazine*, featured cover stories celebrating the ocean as a resource-rich, but fragile environment (Lemonick 1995; Parfit 1995). *Time* tells an optimistic story: The sea is a frontier replete with opportunity, at last capable of being "conquered." *National Geographic Magazine* tells a more pessimistic story: The sea is an endangered environment wherein new technologies both respond to and reproduce scarcity. Both stories, however, place the sea within a discourse of sustainable development similar to that constructed by the promoters of the IYO: As the sea is a space of "finite economical assets," the commodification of its environment should be guided by long-term planning for maximum efficiency and productivity. Also associated with these efforts to promote investment in the sustained exploitation of the ocean's riches is a general campaign for what Leddy (1996) calls the "Cousteauization" of the oceans, a popular movement to cultivate public interest in the ocean's biota with the effect of generating support for further marine research and governmental and/or corporate stewardship of marine resources, similar to the "Audubonization" of birdlife identified by Luke (2000). In the United States, perhaps the most visible spokesperson for this movement has been publicist/author/bureaucrat/oceanographer Sylvia Earle, supported by a marine research and development military–industrial complex represented by individuals such as computer entrepreneur and former US Deputy Secretary of Defense David Packard and retired Admiral

---

[5] The IYO and affiliated programs involved a host of United Nations agencies and private foundations. Lead coordination was provided by the Intergovernmental Oceanographic Commission (IOC), a unit of the United Nations Educational, Scientific and Cultural Organization (UNESCO). Official information on the IYO and related programs and agencies may be found at the web site http://ioc.unesco.org/iyo.

James Watkins, a former US Chief of Naval Operations and US Secretary of Energy, who headed the Consortium for Oceanographic Research and Education to January 2001 (Broad 1997).

Like the other two aspects of the postmodern ocean-space construction, the rise of the stewardship principle reflects specific aspects of the spatiality of postmodern capitalism. Capitalism has a tendency to abstract space and time from nature (Lefebvre 1991) and, as Altvater (1994) notes, this abstraction has become exceptionally intense as the parameters of time and space within which individual capitalists make investment decisions collide with the reality of nature, which is variable, contingent, and unpredictable. The discourse of sustainable development is an attempt to bypass capitalism's "ecological contradiction" by incorporating the material obstacles of space and time into the business cycle, with corporate leadership providing environmental stewardship (M. O'Connor 1994b). The discourse of a resource-rich, but fragile ocean in need of comprehensive management and planning is the result (Nichols 1999). Thus, *National Geographic Magazine* asserts that individuals engaged in fishing must come to terms with "this world of inevitable limits" and give way to long-range planning undertaken by states and corporations (Parfit 1995: 29).

Although *National Geographic Magazine* regrets the loss of the independent fishing boat owner plying the ocean's wilds, the bureaucratization of ocean management and the privatization of rights to its resources is presented as the maturation of our attitudes toward nature. The stewardship of marine resources by agents of capital is naturalized through explicit parallels to the enclosure of agricultural land in the western United States: Fisheries, like post-Dust Bowl agriculture, must be allowed to evolve into "big industry: highly regulated, tidy," where rational management is applied for long-term sustainability (Parfit 1995: 37). A similar perspective is advocated by *The Economist*:

> If people want both to preserve the sea and extract the full benefit from it, they must now moderate their demands, and structure them. They must put aside ideas of the sea's immensity and power, and instead take stewardship of the ocean, with all the privileges and responsibilities that implies.
> (*Economist* 1998: 18)

While this element of the postmodern construction of ocean-space should meet some of the requirements of postmodern capitalism, it, like the other two elements, cannot offer a permanent solution to the problems that inspired its creation. Considering that every adjustment in capitalism's mechanism for (de)valuing nature implicitly poses a challenge to its means of ordering social relations (Harvey 1996), it appears unlikely that corporate decision-makers truly will be willing (or able) to adopt a calculus that incorporates the spatial and temporal conditions of production (J. O'Connor 1994).

Secondly, even if an ocean-management regime consistent with the stewardship principle were to negotiate successfully the ecological contradiction of capital, it still would need to negotiate capitalism's spatial contradiction. Under postmodern capitalism, this spatial contradiction is more intense than ever, as the ocean is increasingly used as an asocial space of movement (supported by the great void principle and the tendency toward annihilation), a social space of development (supported by the land-like principle and the tendency toward territorialization), and a non-possessible space that provides crucial resources for the social system (supported by the nature-space principle and the tendency toward stewardship). Each of these objectives leads to contradictory policies. The territorialization of the sea (whether by an intergovernmental authority or individual states) would probably interfere with its maintenance as a friction-free transport surface. A regime dedicated to the preservation of free trade and the annihilation of barriers in ocean-space would probably fail to provide sufficient security for potential investors in extra-state production sites where they seek to locate spatially fixed investments. And the granting of marine governance to a global ecocracy with the mission of stewarding marine nature would probably interfere both with development objectives and with the ideal of constructing the sea as a space immune to socially generated friction. During the industrial era, a blending of these three principles was possible because their associated activities were performed less intensively and – to a large extent – they were carried out in distinct areas of the ocean. Now, as the associated uses intensify and overlap, they are increasingly in conflict. To date, one of the most dramatic of these conflicts has been the controversy surrounding the establishment of a regime to govern the mining of manganese nodules from the deep seabed.

Manganese nodules and Part XI of the 1982 convention

While several emergent uses of ocean-space have captured the imagination of the popular press, none has attracted the attention of policy makers so much as deep seabed manganese nodules. Manganese nodules are naturally occurring, potato-size objects that occur throughout much of the deep sea beyond the continental shelf and lie on the seabed's surface or beneath a very thin layer of silt. Besides manganese, they contain substantial amounts of nickel, copper, and cobalt, and trace amounts of other valuable minerals. Researchers have known of the nodules' existence since 1868, but it was only in the 1960s that advances in underwater mining technology made the commercial extraction of nodules from these depths conceivable. The struggle to create a regime to facilitate nodule mining is illustrative of the intensifying conflict among the three aspects of the postmodern construction of ocean-space, and it is probably indicative of similar conflicts to emerge in the future.

Part XI and the implementation agreement

Shortly after manganese nodule mining emerged as a technologically feasible source of important industrial minerals, policy makers, particularly in the United States, became concerned with designing a regime that would enable the extraction of nodules while preserving the other elements of the contemporary ocean-space construction. Mining the nodules would involve huge investments in large, discrete areas of the ocean floor. By most estimates, prior to mining, an enterprise would have to prospect a site at least 30,000 sq km in area and then spend up to $2 billion custom-designing mining and processing equipment for the minerals of that specific site (United Nations 1987, 1989). It was recognized that enterprises, whether state-run or private, would require some sort of territorial governance system before "sinking" this magnitude of capital in a portion of the ocean (Christy 1968; Dubs and Cook 1977), but the world's powers were loathe to sanction any system that might imply the beginning of national enclosure of the deep sea (Comptroller General of the United States 1975). As an alternative, the United States suggested that the seabed and its resources be declared "the legacy of all human beings." This proposal first was made publicly by President Lyndon Johnson at a July 1966 ceremony commissioning an oceanographic research vessel:

> Under no circumstances, we believe, must we ever allow the prospects of rich harvest and mineral wealth [of the deep ocean seabed] to create a new form of colonial competition among maritime nations. We must be careful to avoid a race to grab and hold the lands under the high seas. We must ensure that the deep seas and the ocean bottoms are, and remain, the legacy of all human beings. (Johnson 1966: 930)

The following year, Arvid Pardo, the Maltese permanent representative, formally proposed this designation – rephrased as "the common heritage of mankind" – to the United Nations (Pardo 1967). Shortly thereafter, UNCLOS III began meeting to consider, among other issues, a proposal for seabed mining to be carried out under a UN-administered permitting system, with a percentage of revenues returned to the United Nations for global distribution to developing countries and/or to mineral-producing states likely to lose revenues due to competition from enterprises operating in global space.

Initially, Pardo's call received strong support, but as UNCLOS III convened substantial differences emerged between the First and Third World visions for the international seabed and its governing organ, the International Seabed Authority (ISA).[6] Third World states, recognizing the symbolic value of a commodifiable resource for the first time being designated as global property, proposed that the seabed be an opening wedge for a new international economic order (NIEO) that would lead the way toward breaking the overwhelming control of capital, technology, and resources believed to be the basis of First World global dominance. Lauding the radical nature of this initiative, Robles notes that

> For its advocates, the introduction of the common heritage principle . . . offered the opportunity to transform not only the traditional law of the sea but also the traditional international law deemed inadequate to meet the needs of the majority of states and of humanity.
>
> (Robles 1996: 70)

To translate this "common heritage" principle into a vehicle for social change, Third World negotiators proposed that production from the international seabed be carried out by a UN production company, operating in a globally governed territory, with technology and (at least initially) capital provided by the developed states. For the first time, economically productive space would be controlled by the whole of humanity, and a body representing the whole of humanity would have control over generating value from that space and determining allocation of profits.[7]

---

[6] The history of Part XI of the UN Convention on the Law of the Sea and examples of various parties' positions, can be found in greater detail in such works as Anand (1983), Buzan (1976), Friedheim (1993), Luard (1974), Oxman *et al.* (1983), Robles (1996), Sanger (1987), and Van Dyke (1985), as well as proceedings of the annual meetings of the Law of the Sea Institute.

[7] In fact, there has been considerable debate about the complementarity between the Third World states' agenda with reference to the seabed and the programmatic goals of the NIEO

Politicians and miners in the First World saw this proposal as fundamentally at odds with capitalism's assertion of the sanctity of production by competitive entities, mediated only by the system of multiple, sovereign states that territorially govern the spaces of production. As an alternative, the United States and its allies proposed that the ISA be little more than a global licensing agency that would receive claims, supervise production by national and private entities, and distribute "tax revenues" to less developed countries and those states that produced similar minerals on land and were losing revenue due to competition from the international seabed. Nonetheless, despite their reservations, the United States and its allies (as well as the Soviet Union) uncharacteristically were willing to negotiate with weaker, developing states, because the world's leaders were eager to codify other components of the Convention on the Law of the Sea that would limit territorial seas to twelve nautical miles and guarantee free transit through international straits (Comptroller General 1975; Galdorisi 1995a, 1995b; McDorman 1984; Richardson 1982).

As negotiations proceeded on Part XI of the convention (the section of the convention concerned with the international seabed area), all sides agreed to a compromise. A private or national mining company would prospect two potential mining sites of equal value. The ISA then would grant one site to the mining company/state and reserve the other to be mined by the Enterprise, the ISA's production company. The Enterprise would receive its initial capital and technology from mandatory contributions by mining entities, but soon it would become self-financing.

During the 1970s, as UN diplomats worked through the details of Part XI and the dual-site approach to the ISA, several events occurred that changed the context for negotiations. Already by the mid-1970s, exploration of the deep sea by mining interests had slowed down. Following basic research, further development of technology both for extracting nodules from the sea and for processing them had to be site-specific. Without a guarantee of what (if any) site in the ocean would be theirs, miners (especially private miners concerned with short-term profitability) had little incentive to invest in further research and development. Additionally, the global recession of the early 1970s reduced the amount of capital available for funding such speculative projects and

(Borgese 1977; Friedheim and Durch 1977; Laursen 1982; Morris 1977; Ogley 1981; Pardo 1978; Pardo and Borgese 1975; Simoes Ferreira 1979; White House 1983). Regardless, as McDorman (1984) notes, it was significant that the Third World agenda generally was *perceived* as an extension of the NIEO.

a declining demand for metals reduced the incentive for exploration of new production sites that at best would be marginally profitable for the foreseeable future (Shusterich 1982).

By 1982, when the convention, including Part XI, was ready for signature, this decline in the metals market and the decreased likelihood of deep sea mining occurring at any time soon had been joined by the ascendancy of the Reagan and Thatcher administrations in the United States and United Kingdom. Reagan and Thatcher were opposed to any agreement that might dent the sanctity of free-enterprise capitalism mediated through the system of sovereign states (Burke and Brokaw 1983; Goldwin 1983; White House 1983). Furthermore, the mining industry, a strong backer in the United States of the Reagan administration, opposed the treaty because it threatened to establish a global competitor and potentially opened the door to putting other resource-rich spaces under global stewardship, insulated from capitalist competition (Welling 1985). With the commencement of mining seemingly far off, First World governments and mining interests (and especially the United States and its miners) now were willing to reject the treaty and postpone future marine mining profits. From the perspective of the United States and its allies, much could be lost by signing the treaty and establishing a "dangerous" precedent. On the other hand, the "worst" that could happen if the United States and other mining states failed to sign would be that mining activities would be halted, but with commercially viable mining projected into the increasingly distant future, this would be no great loss.[8] In 1982, when the final draft of the convention came up for a vote, the United States voted against it and many other industrialized countries abstained. Some mining states – notably France and Japan – signed the convention, but they reserved ratification pending the adoption of

---

[8] Concurrently, most of the potential mining states – convention signatories and non-signatories alike – passed domestic legislation establishing procedures for domestic enterprises to register claims and carry out resource extraction in areas of the seabed beneath international waters. In each case these laws purported to be provisional, until an acceptable international regime was agreed upon. Most of these states' legislation also called for mining enterprises to pay into a seabed trust fund which would be turned over to the United Nations when an international regime was implemented. These municipal laws were followed by a series of bilateral and multilateral agreements whereby potential mining states agreed to notify each other as claims were filed and to settle peacefully overlapping claims. First World mining interests supported this informal regime as a challenge to the mining regime contained in the UN convention, but since no mining was commenced under the regime it is not known if it would have provided enough security for spatially fixed investments in the deep sea to satisfy investors. (For analysis of this informal regime see Breen (1984), Brown (1993), and Caron (1981).) Many of the relevant laws, regulations, and agreements are reprinted in Moore (1986).)

rules for the operation of the ISA and the Enterprise that would be to their liking.[9]

By the early 1990s world conditions had changed again, and, although seabed mining looked more distant than ever, all sides had a new desire to compromise. Metal prices remained low, and the end of the Cold War resulted in the NIEO losing an important (if sometimes lukewarm) proponent in the Soviet Union. Geopolitical changes intensified the US navy's concern with achieving universal ratification of the convention so as to guarantee rights of free transit, especially through narrow international straits (Galdorisi 1995a, 1995b, 1998; Schachte, 1993). Additionally, similar metal concentrations were discovered inside EEZs, where they could be mined at less expense and without the institution of the controversial UN regime (Paul 1985). Finally, it was revealed that nodule claims made in the 1970s by the US research ship *Glomar Explorer* had been inflated for the public to justify its presence in the Pacific Ocean where it was, in fact, attempting to raise a sunken Soviet submarine (Broad 1997; C. Higginson, personal communication, 1994).

In summary, by the early 1990s the political stakes of the Cold War were eliminated, the ideological battleground was diminished, and the likelihood of actually commencing commercial mining seemed more distant than ever. At the same time, the movement for global environmental management had been boosted by the 1992 UN Conference on Environment and Development (UNCED, the "Earth Summit") and passage of the convention was seen as being in keeping with its mandate for comprehensive management of environmental resources (Curtis 1983; Van Dyke *et al.* 1993). Practically all states had an interest in "burying" Part XI to make the convention acceptable to all, so that the rest of the document could be enshrined as universally accepted international law. As such, in 1990 the UN Secretary-General began holding a series of informal negotiations with signatories and non-signatories in an attempt to bring about universal acceptance by the time the convention achieved implementation (slated to occur one year after the sixtieth ratification). The sixtieth ratification was obtained in November of 1993 and in July 1994 the UN General Assembly considered Resolution 48/263, the Agreement Relating to the Implementation of Part XI of the United Nations Convention on the Law of the Sea of 10 December 1982 (hereafter, the "Implementation Agreement") (United Nations 1994).

---

[9] Three other states – Israel, Turkey, and Venezuela – also voted against the convention, but for reasons unrelated to Part XI.

Ostensibly, the Implementation Agreement worked within the guidelines laid out in the convention, reaffirming the status of the seabed as the "Common Heritage of Mankind." In practice, however, it introduced into the Law of the Sea "free market principles . . . which are fundamentally at variance with the common heritage principle" (Robles 1996: 70). The Implementation Agreement effectively reduced the Enterprise to an inoperable entity. It called for the elimination of mandatory technology transfers, the abolition of the site-reservation system, and limits on the Enterprise's ability to borrow money.[10] The agreement invited private and national miners to work with the Enterprise in joint ventures, but with no technology, no territory, and no capital to contribute to such a joint venture, it is difficult to see what incentive there would be for a miner voluntarily to seek out the Enterprise as a partner. After two days of debate – during which only one speaker, the permanent representative of Iran, denounced the impact that the agreement would have on the Enterprise (Kharrazi 1994) – The agreement was passed by the General Assembly by a vote of 121 to none, with seven abstentions.[11]

The lessons of Part XI

The rise and fall of the Part XI manganese nodule regime at first glance appears to indicate that the industrial capitalist-era ocean-space construction can adapt itself to the world of postmodern capitalism where there is intensified use of the ocean as a transport surface, intensified attempts at commodifying and developing individual marine resources and places, and intensified concern for sustainable, long-term management of the marine environment. In the seabed mining saga, these three imperatives temporarily conflicted with each other, leading some to propose a radical regime enshrining principles outside those traditionally incorporated within the industrial capitalist ocean-space construction: namely, that the ocean was a space that belonged to humanity and that all the world's inhabitants had a right not only to compete for access to its resources, but to a share of its resources. In the end, however, this radical regime was rejected and a restatement of the tripartite great void–land-like territory–stewarded resource-space construction was applied to the seabed.

[10] Other US demands also were obtained in the Implementation Agreement, including a change in the method for allocating seats on the ISA's governing body and the abolition of a requirement for a review conference.
[11] The seven abstaining states were Colombia, Nicaragua, Panama, Peru, Russia, Thailand, and Venezuela.

Although the saga appears to validate the continuing utility of the industrial capitalist ocean-space construction in the postmodern era, it is likely that the construction's victory in this instance masks deeper structural contradictions. In fact, the radical aspects of Part XI were "written away" only because manganese nodule mining failed to remain an important issue. When nodule mining was of interest – whether as a source of profits or as an ideological wedge – all sides entertained a regime that would have challenged the accepted construction of ocean-space. It was only when the prospects for nodule mining subsided that world powers reverted to their interest in maintaining the status quo, and they then were able to pressure the weaker states into acquiescing in their desire.

Should metal prices rise, however, it remains questionable whether a license from the ISA, a body lacking the sovereign territorial power of a state, would provide the security of tenure necessary to attract the huge quantities of high-risk capital required for commercial mining. This issue was avoided during the United Nations negotiations as mining interests argued in principle for a regulatory system with minimal intervention, but statements made by mining executives suggest the possibility that no license from a non-state authority would be sufficient to mollify the concerns of financiers (Brewer 1985; Shusterich 1982; Takeuchi 1979; Welling 1985). In the case of UNCLOS III's seabed mining provisions, the contradiction of capitalist spatiality in the ocean temporarily was resolved because the seabed lost its attraction as a site of fixed investment. But it is only a matter of time before a new ocean use requiring spatially fixed investments (or a resurgence of interest in manganese nodules) reopens this conflict (Earney 1990).

The lesson of the manganese nodule saga (or at least its first decade, when the issue was "alive") is that as opportunities for stationary capital investments emerge within the deep sea, they will not be incorporated easily within the existing ocean-space construction. Even the United States, with its strong interest in the preservation of the old regime, was willing to entertain an entirely new construction of ocean-space; indeed, it was the United States that originally proposed such innovations as an international licensing authority, a dual-site reservation system, and a global profit redistribution pool. The "traditional" industrial capitalist construction of the deep sea, premised upon a combination of the great void high seas principle with a series of non-territorial regulations for specific resources, is incapable of providing the territorial governance necessary for guaranteeing immobile capital investments in discrete

187

areas of ocean-space. And yet, as capital seeks out new investment sites and seeks to commodify new aspects of social life and nature, it appears drawn in this direction.

Thus, there is an intensifying dialectic in capitalism's marine spatial order. On the one hand, capital is drawn toward constructing ocean-space as a great void across which ships, commodities, labor, and capital travel with exceeding ease, a "hyperspace of pure circulation." On the other hand, capital is drawn toward constructing ocean-space as a series of potential "places" in the capitalist sense of the word: locations where value can be created by placing or removing immobile capital investment and where a high degree of territorial control is needed. Indeed, the progress of the first half of this dialectic supports the progress of the second, even as it increases the intensity of the conflict. As capital represents ocean-space as annihilated, it diminishes the identity of the ocean as *res extra commercium*, an "other" that plays a distinct role as a special space of movement within society. Thus, it becomes easier to conceive of the ocean as *res nullius*, space that is so devoid of any social content that it is available for appropriation and development, even though the appropriation of the sea necessarily conflicts with the "great void" idealization that makes this appropriation possible. Finally, each of these tendencies, besides conflicting with each other, intensifies the speed with which the ocean is transformed to obtain value. As a result, a third tendency – the mandate for rational management so as to extend the ocean's resource value – emerges amidst (and in contradiction to) the other two.

As in earlier eras of capitalism, the ocean-space construction of post-modern capitalism is rooted in the spatiality of the era's dominant political–economic processes. As the contradictions within postmodern capitalism's social institutions are more intense than in previous eras, so are the contradictions within the postmodern ocean-space construction. The manner in which these contradictions will resolve themselves will be intertwined with the manner in which other social contradictions will be resolved, and that is a topic beyond the scope of this study. Nonetheless, this history of the uses, regulations, and representations of ocean-space and the manner in which its construction has been embedded in social processes suggest a few options, and these are considered in Chapter 6.

6 Beyond postmodern capitalism, beyond ocean-space

Social change in the marine heterotopia

As capital pursues its mutually reinforcing but ultimately contradictory trajectories in ocean-space, one can expect a broad range of social constructions to be considered in the future. Small variations on the current set of management priorities will not, in the long run, diminish the conflicts within contemporary capitalist uses of ocean-space. As was demonstrated by the saga of the manganese nodule mining regime, contradictions within the social construction are increasingly intense, and, in an attempt to support their particular interests, fractions of capital may be expected to favor uncharacteristic regimes and to make unusual alliances. Some of these proposals may buttress the general organization of society, but some (perhaps inadvertently) may open cracks in its foundation.

At first glance one might question the likelihood that a marginal space, apparently on the fringe of social structures and institutions, would be a fertile location for imagining and actually constructing significant social change. Marxists might protest that relatively little value-added production occurs in ocean-space and little surplus labor is extracted there, so it is not likely to be a significant space of social transformation. Feminists similarly might protest that little of the social reproduction that characterizes everyday life transpires at sea. Here, these protests are met with two responses. The first response derives from the postmodernist assertion that any attempt to define a "center" to political (or social) economy inadvertently reinforces this center, even if the stated aim is to transform it (Gibson-Graham 1996). Although one's first instinct may be to direct efforts at social change toward processes (and spaces) that are central to existing power structures, postmodern theorists suggest that margins – where the "fit" of systemic practices is problematic – also may be fruitful locuses for social contestation. It is at the margins that actors struggle over individual, social, and spatial constructions that are both inside and outside the system. As zones of partial incorporation, margins provide fertile ground both for imagining and constructing alternative social futures (hooks 1984).

The second response derives from the insight of Henri Lefebvre (1991), who views all spaces as sites of contention. As Peet notes in his summary of Lefebvre:

> Every society, every mode of production, produces its own space. But the production of social space is not like the production of commodities, because space subsumes many different things, is both outcome and means (of fresh action), and is both product (made by repetitious labor) and work (i.e. something unique and original). It consists of objects (natural and social) and their relations (networks and pathways). Space contains things yet is not a material object; it is a set of relations between things. Hence, we are confronted with many, interpenetrated social spaces superimposed one on the other, a "hypercomplexity" in which each fragment of space masks not one social relationship but many. For Lefebvre, the "problematic" of space has displaced that of industrialization. (Peet 1998: 103)

As capitalism progresses, space increasingly becomes "abstract" (i.e. socially constructed), and as this happens there is increasing potential for the various elements that construct a space to conflict with each other. Thus, the production of space emerges as an arena for the implosion of the structural contradictions of capitalism.

Lefebvre presents a more robust model of socio-spatial construction than that offered by Castells. For Castells, social change may engender massive changes in spatial organization, but once those changes are implemented the new spatial formations are unstable only to the extent that there is instability in the social system underlying them. Thus certain spaces, such as the first layer of the space of flows, may be written off by Castells as relatively unproblematic. For Lefebvre, however, spaces require continual reproduction, and, because every space has multiple facets, the act of space construction inherently is dialectical, the intensity of this dialectic increasing commensurate with the level of a space's abstraction.

It follows that every socially constructed space – including the sea which, as the previous chapters have demonstrated, increasingly is constructed as a multi-faceted, abstract space – is a potential site and subject of social change. While the sea may not be a space where significant value is added and it may not be experienced directly by most individuals, it *is* a space of social construction, and as individuals construct the sea they are participating in the construction of the institutions and structures that govern their lives. Consumers of the Nike sneakers that remained on the *Hansa Carrier* during the 1990 storm referred to at the beginning of this book probably did not think of the sea when they purchased their pair of sneakers, but through this action they did more than reproduce the exploitative social relations at the factory in Asia where the shoes were made. They also reaffirmed the construction of the sea as a friction-free transport surface, a necessary counterpoint to the hierarchical division of the world into a series of developable investment sites that are at different rungs on the ladder of modernization. The social construction of ocean-space, like that of land-space, is a process by which axes of hierarchy, identity, cooperation, and community are contested, establishing bases for both social domination and social opposition.

There is a long history of marine-based social formations serving as models for social change in land-space. While the Grotius–Freitas–Selden debate was an exercise to construct a regime for a marginal area of the world-economy, it resulted in the establishment of a structure for all interaction among land-based states. Indeed, it was because of his contributions to the nascent Law of the Sea that Grotius is known as the "Father of the Law of Nations" (Colombos 1967: 8). Likewise, the efforts by sixteenth-century cartographers to draw lines through the ocean as they reinterpreted the 1494 Treaty of Tordesillas contributed to the establishment of the modern norm of the sovereign, territorial state (Steinberg 2000). In a similar vein, late mercantilist-era sailors established many of the norms and solidarities that went on to characterize the industrial capitalist-era proletariat (Rediker 1987). Early twentieth-century communists, anarchists, and syndicalists looked to the sea as a likely arena for developing new structures to govern social relations in land-space (Sekula 1995), and a number of contemporary anarchists and scholars continue to find inspiration in the communal, non-statist ethics of the mercantile-era pirate band (Kuhn 1997; Osborne 1998; Rediker 1987; Wilson 1995).

As a space that is almost universally represented as female but that is populated overwhelmingly by males, the ocean is an arena of intense gendering processes, which impact and reflect social conceptions of gender at sea and on land. Recent scholarship has demonstrated that eighteenth- and nineteenth-century marine culture was an important arena for forging modern gender identities (Creighton 1995; Creighton and Norling 1996) as well as transgressive racial and sexual identities (Burg 1983, 1994; Bolster 1990, 1996; Horton 1986). Particular attention has been directed toward women pirates of the era, high-profile class and gender transgressors who have been heralded as laying some of the groundwork for Enlightenment ideals of liberty (Rediker 1996) as well as being admired as inspirations for contemporary feminist–anarchist struggle (Klausmann and Meinzerin 1997). The sea historically has been – and remains – both a space where the norms of mainstream society are forged and a space where alternative futures are envisioned.

To inquire into the potentials and limits of the ocean as a space of social transformation, it is useful to consider the ocean as a heterotopia, a concept brought to the social sciences by Foucault (1986) and expanded upon by Hetherington (1997):

> Heterotopia [are] spaces of alternate ordering. Heterotopia organize a bit of the social world in a way different to that which surrounds them. That alternate ordering marks them out as Other and allows them to be seen as an example of an alternate way of doing things.
>
> (Hetherington 1997: viii)

Hetherington locates heterotopia within a broader modernist project wherein social control is advocated as a means for bringing about personal improvement (and, ultimately, personal freedom). Because this social project of freedom-through-control contains its own contradictions, it needs continual readjustment, a process that frequently occurs through the re-construction of society's marginal spaces.

Hetherington emphasizes that the construction of a heterotopia does not necessarily bring about far-reaching social change. As sites wherein both new modes of control and new modes of freedom are imagined and implemented, heterotopia are better defined as the cutting-edge arenas wherein modernity's control–freedom dialectic is played out, rather than the arenas wherein the dialectic is overthrown:

> In using the concept heterotopia, it would be wrong to privilege either the idea of freedom or control. Heterotopia act as obligatory points of passage that allow established modes of social ordering to be challenged in ways that might be seen as utopian . . . [However,] it would . . . be wrong to associate heterotopia just with the marginal and powerless seeking to use Other places to articulate a voice that is usually denied them. An Other place can be constituted and used by those who benefit from the existing relations of power with a society as in the case of the establishment of the workhouse or prison as a place of Otherness that becomes a site of social control through the practices

> associated with it and the meanings that develop around it. A certain
> amount of neutrality needs to be introduced when defining hetero-
> topia. This is why I define a heterotopia as a place of alternate order-
> ing. I use the word alternate to suggest that some form of difference
> is involved, a difference that involves the deployment of a utopian
> alternative. (Hetherington 1997: 52)

Constructed amidst the dialectics of modernity, heterotopia both reproduce order through the alternate organization of space and suggest
alternatives to that order. Thus, they are arenas in which the dominant
order of society is both challenged and reproduced.

This book has located the marine heterotopia within a series of contradictions within capitalism's material processes and spatial properties. First there is the dialectic highlighted by Lefebvre, wherein the
representations of space that support capitalism's spatial practices contradict the spaces of representation constructed by actual users of the
sea as they construct ocean-space in modernity through their everyday
actions. These contradictions are intensified, however, by a second set of
contradictions *within* capitalism's spatial practices, the contradiction between capitalism's tendency to construct value through spatial fixity and
its tendency to construct value through spatial mobility. Capitalism's
spatial logic requires an antithetical space of movement. However, a
unidimensional construction of the ocean as a non-space of movement is
in direct opposition to the dominant logic of development (and it fails to
facilitate the movement function, which requires a degree of regulation).
Given these contradictions, and given the ongoing tension that exists between various designs for the sea and the ongoing practices of everyday
users, there emerges a distinct marine heterotopia, a space of alternate
ordering. However, this marine heterotopia is unstable. Capitalism, as
a spatially dialectical system, has a tendency to commodify and ultimately annihilate its own heterotopia (e.g. the tendency to implement
a territorial regime so as to enable development in ocean-space). In the
vortex of this struggle – as some attempt to redefine the old heterotopia
according to new standards of "otherness," others attempt to annihilate
the heterotopia and make it "regular" space, and still others attempt to
preserve the old heterotopic construction – those utopian ideals that had
been part of the heterotopic construction may be seized upon by actors
wishing to make the marine heterotopia a site of social change.

Attempts to realize a heterotopia's utopian properties require the destruction of its antithetical functions, and this makes social struggle
within a heterotopia particularly problematic politically. Although

the long-term impact of destroying a functional heterotopia may be institutional dysfunction and social transformation, the short-term impact is a reduction in opportunities for alternative social formations. Thus, although Foucault (1986) identifies the ship at sea as the "heterotopia *par excellence*," Virilio (1986) holds that the ship, rather than incorporating the ocean's antithetical properties, colonizes this once resistant space through modernist institutions of navigation and militarism (see also Deleuze and Guatarri (1988)). Connery (1995) too is skeptical of those who would find liberation in "capital's favored myth-element." Rediker's early eighteenth century seamen provide a case in point: The utopia of maritime proletariat solidarity was co-opted and formed the basis for much of the system used a short time later to regulate land-based industrial capitalist workers.

A particularly early expression of regret over the destruction of the marine heterotopia was expressed by solo circumnavigator Joshua Slocum. In the 1890s, sailing off the coast of Africa, he remarked:

> People have hardly time nowadays to speak even on the broad ocean, where news is news, and as for a salute of guns, they cannot afford the powder. There are no poetry-enshrined freighters on the sea now; it is a prosy life when we have no time to bid one another good morning.
> (Slocum 1903: 54)

More recently, Sekula (1995) has critiqued the maritime world of postmodern capitalism, where the annihilation of ocean-space by means of speed and bureaucracy is expressed in the metaphor of the container ship. In this world, production is artificially separated from consumption and this separation is enforced by the erasure from the imagination of the connecting space in between – the sea. For Sekula, this denial of the marine heterotopia and the reduction of interaction with the sea to the standardized movement of sterile containers across abstract ocean-space deprives the individual of a critical weapon against the tyranny of society. As Foucault declares:

> In civilizations without boats, dreams dry up, espionage takes the place of adventure, and the police take the place of pirates. (Foucault 1986: 27)

While these cautions that attempts at realizing the marine heterotopia's utopian element will lead or have led to its co-optation are well taken, the historical narrative presented here – and particularly the manganese nodule mining saga presented in the previous chapter – suggests a more hopeful ending. Spatial practices themselves are dialectical, even (perhaps especially) in heterotopia, and heterotopia continually exist within this dialectic. Just as Castells undervalues the dialectical nature of the material activities and functions that continually construct spaces of flows, these theorists may be undervaluing the dialectical processes that underlie the reproduction of heterotopia. Although capitalism does have the tendency to annihilate its heterotopia, it also has the need to construct new ones. And in this process, the utopian element that is always embodied – if forever distant – in a heterotopia may be pushed closer to reality, either in a reconstructed ocean-space or in other emergent heterotopic spaces and social formations.

We have seen already how the seabed mining negotiations were used by some as an attempt to create an opening wedge for the new international economic order, a system of capitalism tempered by concern for global equity and global conservation. Such a system would have granted to a global, governing body the right to extract, commodify, and allocate world resources. Proponents of this view argued that the International Seabed Authority should serve as a prototype for a range of institutions dedicated to the conservation and equitable distribution of land resources, including those lying within state territory. Since the decline of the nodule regime, this theme has continued to be promoted by the Pacem in Maribus group, a network of diplomats and policy advocates who propose applying the common heritage model of ocean governance to other global issues, including climate change, outer space, energy, food, and science and technology (Borgese 1998, 1999; Pacem in Maribus 1992).[1]

A similar theme has been promoted by the environmentalist group Greenpeace in *Freedom for the Seas in the 21st Century: Ocean Governance and Environmental Harmony* (Van Dyke *et al.* 1993), the proceedings of a conference it held in 1990. In this volume, the ocean is hailed as an arena uniquely insulated from what Shapiro (1997) calls the "violent cartographies" of statism. As such, ocean-space is perceived as providing an opportunity for environmentalists and those concerned with global equity to insert new concepts (such as the "common heritage of mankind" and non-Western norms for owning property and stewarding nature)

---

[1] Since the Pacem in Maribus group's agenda is largely a liberal one centered around allocation and not production, its members generally supported the amendments to Part XI; the significance of the loss of the ISA's production arm paled in their view in comparison with the importance of the establishment of a new global entity with the power to authorize and limit exploitation and distribution of profits from a piece of the earth's surface. Like Robles (1996), I fail to share their enthusiasm for the post-Implementation Agreement version of Part XI, but this should not diminish the significance of their attempt to apply the "common heritage" concept to the global environment.

into debates around which policies and ideals are formed. Eventually, by "greening" the debate in the ocean (where it is occurring "out in the open," in part because of the ocean's unique political status and in part because powerful players have contradictory interests), Greenpeace and like-minded groups and individuals may also "green" broader social debates. As one contributor to the collection notes:

> Whatever the imperfections and limitations of the 1982 Convention, it can enter into the reality of international society as a powerful creative force, preparing the minds of all to manage a world in which global social problems call for solutions that far exceed the potentialities of traditional diplomacy and traditional international law. There is no better place than the universal social phenomenon of the sea to begin learning to integrate universal social phenomena into the self-socializing of the human species.　　　　　　　　　　　　　　　(Allott 1993: 68)

As with manganese nodule mining, global fisheries management is an area where the unique political status of the sea is forcing powerful entities to experiment with alternatives that push against the limits of accepted capitalist practice. Thus, for instance, the multinational food corporation Unilever has joined with the World Wide Fund for Nature to establish the Marine Stewardship Council (MSC), an "ecolabeling" system where certification will be given to processors who restrict their purchases to fisheries that are being managed sustainably. The MSC aims "to harness market forces and consumer power in favour of healthy, well-maintained fisheries for the future" (MSC 1997). Although the progressivism of the MSC may be limited (Constance and Bonanno 2000; Steinberg 1999a), the organization proposes shifting responsibility for regulating global fisheries from the community of states to the community of civil society. In the short run, such a shift would probably sanction greater corporate control of declining fish stocks, but in the long run it has the potential to extend liberal principles of equal rights of opportunity – and perhaps even more radical concepts of equal shares of ownership – to individuals in world-society, a principle that goes beyond conventional liberal norms of economic rights.

Looking ahead to future uses of ocean-space, legal scholar Kent Keith has posited that the construction of "floating cities" in the sea would pose an even greater threat to the existing legal order than that of seabed mining. Floating cities could not easily be classified as ships, structures (like oil platforms), or states equivalent to existing land-based states. Hence he foresees the emergence of unique, independent floating-city states, or "internations":

> Thus, the concept of the nation may begin to fade, just as the con-
> cept of the feudal state faded; and the lifestyles and values of the new
> floating-city states, international communities moving freely through-
> out the world, may begin to influence the creation of a truly transna-
> tional world order. (Keith 1977: 204)

Keith's scenario is highly speculative, as even he acknowledges. He
first projects a future technology, then imagines the legal structure that
would be created to accommodate this technology, and finally pre-
dicts the effect of this legal structure on the overall political make-up
of world-society. Nonetheless, his vision bears a striking resemblance
to those early twentieth-century anarcho-syndicalists who saw in the
international sailing class the roots of a new, non-nation-state-based social order created first on sea and then on land. Indeed, Gilroy (1993)
identifies just such a diaspora "internation" in the community of the
Black Atlantic. This nation of Africans and African emigrants is demarcated not by its ties to the African continent but by its ties to the
Atlantic Ocean that connects Africa with the world. Defining itself in
relation to the ocean rather than immobile land-space, Gilroy argues
that the Black Atlantic nation has a distinct set of social mores, structures, and outlooks, a construction that forms an alternative to the dominant, land-based society. While land-based nations look backward in
history to find a permanent, unifying essence, diaspora nations like the
Black Atlantic find their identity in change, movement, difference, and
opposition.

Similar constructions of the ocean as a site of potential opposition
can be found in fiction as well. As has been noted, Captain Nemo was
a particularly early example of the postmodern anti-hero. A subaltern
on land, Nemo had power and authority in his Indian land-kingdom,
but this power existed only in the context of his subservience to the
British. Each act of survival, even as it brought him closer to British
culture, was also an act of defiance in which he asserted his identity as
an Indian. Nemo was wrapped in contradictions: he was simultaneously
powerful and powerless, ruler and ruled, pliant and defiant. Eventually,
these contradictions led him to engage in his own personal mutiny for
self-identity (implemented within the broader context of the 1857 Indian
Mutiny), an event whose failure plunged him into depression and then
into the sea. In the sea, he was able to construct his own "internation"
(although it is not at all clear if the society that he established on the
Nautilus was any more equitable than that which he had left in India).

Nemo constructs an identity for himself, his crew, and his ship that exists in defiance of the nation-states that divide the land. In Verne's novel, escape proves impossible; Nemo is drawn into the nationalist conflicts that he so despises and in the end his ship literally is drawn into their whirlpool. Verne does not allow the reader to see what would happen if Nemo were to try to bring his ideal of the "internation" to land, but one can guess that the result would not be so rosy as the scenario imagined by Keith. As in Hetherington's heterotopia, Nemo's space is more one of alternate ordering than personal liberation. But it contains seeds of a utopia that, given enough instability in the underlying social structure, may be realized at least partially.

A more recent view of the sea as oppositional space can be found in the feminist science fiction of Joan Slonczewski. In *A Door Into Ocean* (1986) the all-female residents of a distant planet live in harmony with the ocean. Although the inhabitants live on rafts, these rafts are constructed out of seaborne grasses and must continually be maintained because they also serve as food for animals who swim in the ocean. Residents of the rafts spend much of their time swimming and harvesting fish and vegetables from the sea, simultaneously living off and replenishing the marine ecosystem. Theirs is an entirely different sea from the lifeless great void of *Waterworld*.

Conditioned by the rhythms of the sea, the society of this ocean-world is an idealized feminist republic: council meetings end in consensus; all do their part to maintain the rafts; individuals communicate by "sharing." Predictably, the ocean-world is invaded by the army of a distant, male-dominated planet that bears a disturbing resemblance to Earth: the key commodity is the cut stone – nonrenewable, inalterably manipulated by humans, and devoid of life. A war ensues between male guns and female passive resistance and medical skills. The aggressors are confounded by the ocean-women's refusal to "share death" and by their mastery of holistic, life-giving biological systems linked to the ocean. At the end of the book the future of the ocean-planet is uncertain, but the cultural interchange has left a lasting impression on the warriors from land.

Another liberatory feminist vision of the ocean may be found in Octavia Butler's *Wild Seed* (1980). In this novel, the goddess Anyanwu transforms herself into a dolphin and escapes to the ocean to seek temporary relief from the oppressive, patriarchal, land-bound god Doro. A similar ideal of the sea as a peaceful, liberatory space existing in contrast to land may be found in the musings of anthropologist

Loren Eiseley:

> If man had sacrificed his hands for flukes, he would still be a philoso-
> pher, but there would have been taken from him the power to wreak
> his thought upon the world. Instead, he would have wandered, like the
> dolphin, homeless across currents and winds and oceans, intelligent,
> but forever the curious observer of unknown wreckage falling through
> the blue light of eternity. This role would now be a deserved penitence
> for man. Perhaps such a transformation would bring him once more
> into the mood of child-like innocence in which he talked successfully
> to all things living but had no power and no urge to harm. It is worth
> a wistful thought that someday the whale might talk to us and us to
> him. It would break, perhaps, the long loneliness that has made man
> a frequent terror and abomination even to himself.
>
> (cited in Ellis 1995: 226–227)

The visions of Slonczewski, Eiseley, Keith, and Verne are of course
fanciful. Even the "common heritage" ideals of Greenpeace, Borgese,
Pardo, and the Pacem in Maribus group are difficult to imagine coming
to fruition. Each of these visions is based on a projection of what would
be possible (and desirable) in a world in which social power (and, in
some instances, technology) were different from what they are now.
Several of these visions could be challenged for their optimism. For
instance, Keith's deterritorialized "floating cities" might evolve not into
utopian "internations" characterized by peace and harmony but rather
into dystopic floating *maquiladoras* that use their freedom from land- and
state-based labor and environmental regulations to implement extreme
forms of labor exploitation.

The Preamble to the Constitution of the Federated States of Micronesia
presents what might be a more realistic depiction of the utopian element
that resides within the marine heterotopia:

> We affirm our common wish to live together in peace and harmony,
> to preserve the heritage of the past, and to protect the promise of the
> future.
>
> To make one nation of many islands, we respect the diversity of our
> cultures. Our differences enrich us. The seas bring us together, they do
> not separate us. Our islands sustain us, our island nation enlarges us
> and makes us stronger.
>
> Our ancestors, who made their homes on these islands, displaced no
> other people. We, who remain, wish no other home than this. Having
> known war, we hope for peace. Having been divided, we wish unity.
> Having been ruled, we seek freedom.
>
> Micronesia began in the days when man explored seas in rafts and
> canoes. The Micronesian nation is born in an age when men voyage

among stars: our world itself is an island. We extend to all nations
what we seek from each: peace, friendship, cooperation, and love in
our common humanity. With this Constitution we, who have been the
wards of other nations, become the proud guardian of our own islands
now and forever.   (reprinted in Leibowitz 1989: 599)

This document in many ways repeats the norm of state constitu-
tions. Sovereignty is claimed over land-space ("we . . . become the proud
guardian of our own islands") and it is achieved by recognizing the
status of Micronesia as one state among many, each of which claims
exclusive control over land-space. At the same time, because of the long
historic relationship between residents of Micronesia and the sea that
surrounds their islands, the sea is given a crucial role in the construction of that land-space, as the crucial thread that binds the islands of
Micronesia together. Thus, an "alternate ordering" is constructed for
Micronesia. This ordering operates within (and thereby reaffirms) the
global system of land-space sovereignty. But, at the same time, because
of Micronesia's unique nature and the unique everyday constructions of
ocean-space (spaces of representation) that continue to this day among
the islands' residents, it contains alternate values that subtly promote
visions of the ocean as a space that connects diverse elements. Ironically,
but in keeping with the designation of the ocean as a heterotopia, this
identification of the ocean as a connecting space that creates unity amidst
difference denaturalizes the territorial state and suggests a utopian
"internation" that runs counter to the very principles of the system of
sovereign, territorial, land-based states that the document reaffirms.

All of the visions of the marine heterotopia discussed in this chapter
contain a common perspective. Rather than viewing the ocean as a space
outside society, used by land-based social actors, they view the ocean as
a space *shaped by* society and that, in the process *shapes* society. Indeed,
they all note how the ocean's existence as a product of society, but outside its dominant categories, makes it an attractive arena for the escapist
imagination . . . but also for orchestrating social change through continual interventions in the social construction of the marine heterotopia.
The historical narrative presented in the previous chapters suggests
that this constructionist perspective provides a valid lens through
which to view the ocean's past. It follows that it also provides a valid
lens through which to view the ocean's future. Given this perspective, and given the finding that capitalism's own tendencies within the
sea increasingly contradict each other and necessitate continual policy

reformulation (and, more broadly, space construction), it follows that the sea may well emerge as an arena for contesting global-scale aspects of social organization.

Social conflict in spaces of movement

As postmodern political economy is defined by incessant circulation, it is increasingly difficult to accept the great void idealization of transportation/communication space as an asocial, formless surface traversed by goods and information, generated in the static places of "society." Increasingly, it is clear that the spaces within which goods and information flow – the cyberspace of the Internet, the airspace of airplanes, and the geostationary orbit of satellites, as well as the sea-lanes of the deep sea – are as "real" and as socially constructed as the "fixed" places of land-space. Among these "first level spaces of flows," the sea has the longest history as a space of intense use and social construction. However, the constructions of these other spaces are beginning to exhibit similar contradictions and, hence, they present similar opportunities as arenas for social change.

After the ocean, the earth's subterranean regions probably have the longest history of active use among the world's "other" spaces. Historically, however, they have seen much greater use as spaces of fixed investments and development (for extracting water and mineral resources) than as spaces of movement. Therefore, their regulatory history, at least on a global scale, has been less complex than that of the ocean, and the apportionment of underground space to territorial states has been relatively unproblematic. Nonetheless, as new uses have emerged, society has needed to adjust its social construction of this "other" space, a history that particularly is evident in changing literary representations (Williams 1990).

The conflict over the social construction of inner-atmospheric airspace is more analogous to that of ocean-space, and its social construction has engendered considerable debate (Jönsson 1987). However, in order to complement the example of the sea (a space of transportation, or the movement of goods), the rest of this chapter focuses on communication (the movement of information), and our attention is directed to the spaces of global communication flows that assume unprecedented importance under hypermobile, postmodern capitalism.

As with transportation spaces such as ocean-space and inner-atmospheric airspace, spaces of communication flows simultaneously serve as seemingly "external" spaces of movement relatively free from social barriers and regulations and as arenas that present opportunities for commodification, an activity that involves making spatially fixed investments and historically has required regulatory control by territorial states. As in the case of the sea, supporters of these two imperatives have been joined by a third force in the debate: those who favor stewardship at the intergovernmental level by a regime wherein communication spaces are constructed as susceptible to exertions of social power by states but immune to territorial claims that might interfere with continuance of their primary mobility-oriented function.

Turning first to outer-atmospheric airspace (outer space), increasingly the telecommunications industry finds that demand exceeds available satellite locations in geostationary orbit. Thus, this space has become valued and commodified as a scarce resource. The increasing regulation of outer space and the hoarding and trading of nationally allocated locations within geostationary orbit challenges the frictionless, great void construction that predominated early on in the era of satellite communication (Laver 1986; Soroos 1982). Conflicts over the regulation of outer space have been difficult to resolve for reasons that closely parallel the spatial dialectic in ocean-space. On the one hand, the limited space of geostationary orbit is a scarce resource whose exploitation requires the embedding of capital. On the other hand, the few states with the power to exploit this space cannot engage in an acquisitive "scramble for the skies" reminiscent of the late nineteenth-century "scramble for Africa," for fear that unwittingly they might challenge the social construction of outer space as a friction-free communication field on which its valorization depends.

Thus, there is a contradiction in outer space analogous to that in the ocean. The construction of outer space as friction free is crucial to the maintenance of its value and the profitability of its primary resource (communication). But these resources can be exploited only through the embedding of capital, which requires a regime that challenges the construction of outer space as an asocial space of open access and unimpeded movement. As Harvey notes, "Spatial organization is necessary to overcome space . . . [There is] a tension within the geography of accumulation between fixity and motion, between the rising power to overcome space and the immobile spatial structures required for such a purpose" (Harvey 1985: 145, 150).

The ongoing debate over privatization of the Internet can be viewed in similar terms. The Internet began as a US government-sponsored computer network to facilitate communication among researchers in the military and university communities. The aim was to create a virtual space of communication flows. Like the domains of ocean-space and air-space – but even more readily apparent since this space did not exist in a material sense prior to its social construction – the virtual space of the Internet was constructed as a frictionless surface to serve the flows of information that are crucial to global political economy. Like the ocean, the Internet has spawned a unique subculture of travelers (surfers) whose identity revolves around the "fluvial" nature of the space that they inhabit (Cooke 1999).

Among the first acts of the administration of U.S. President Bill Clinton after its taking office in 1993 was the establishment of the Information Infrastructure Task Force (IITF), chaired by the Secretary of Commerce and under the aegis of the Vice President. The IITF developed a vision for a national information infrastructure (NII), which later expanded into the Global Information Infrastructure–Global Information Society (GII–GIS) Initiative (Drake 1995). The GII–GIS Initiative is grounded in five principles: "Encouraging private sector investment; promoting competition; providing open access to the network for all information providers and users; creating a flexible regulatory environment that can keep pace with rapid technological and market changes; and ensuring universal service" (IITF 1995: 1). The IITF sees no contradiction between the Internet as a site of fixed investments (implied in the first two points) and the Internet as a site of flows (implied in the remaining three). Government intervention is to be limited to the creation of technical standards, basic research into state-of-the-art technologies, and enforcement of anti-trust regulations. Like the British and American navies during the heyday of industrial capitalism, the government's role is restricted to demolishing the barriers that might hinder access to and interaction among the sites of fixed investments; the goal is to create a "truly seamless 'network of [private] networks'" (IITF 1995: 30; see also IITF 1993), Castells' "hyperspace of pure circulation." Similarly, the Organization for Economic Co-operation and Development (OECD), which endorsed GII–GIS in 1995, proclaims:

> The concept of global information infrastructure–global information society (GII–GIS) encompasses the development and integration of high speed communication networks, and a set of core services and applications in digital format, into global integrated networks capable

> of seamless delivery. Such networks provide fully interactive access, to network-based services within countries and beyond national borders.
> (OECD 1997: 7)

The OECD goes on to maintain that this network of networks will come about by "facilitating the transition from closed markets with no, or limited competition, such as in telecommunication and broadcasting areas, to open and dynamic markets" (OECD 1997: 7; see also Kahin and Wilson 1996; Smith 1997).

Some of those involved in the Internet privatization debate question the GII–GIS promoters' confidence that the friction-free character of communication space, necessary to facilitate the movement of information, will be enhanced or even maintained under privatization. Aside from worries that increased access fees may keep some off the system, analysts fear that, in the process of embedding capital and establishing legal mechanisms to protect that capital and guarantee capture of profits, telecommunication firms inadvertently will establish barriers to communication. Analysts worry that firms, with the cooperation of states, will seek to protect their fixed investments and, in the process, threaten the "asocial" character of the Internet that has facilitated the network and given their investments value (Noam 1992; Sirbu 1992). Already, web browser manufacturers have begun to implement proprietary protocols that restrict access to high-end features on a site to viewers using the same software by which the site was created. While such developments increase the incentive for firms to enter the market and engage in product innovation, they run the risk of interfering with the seamless connectivity that gives cyberspace its value.

Even the US government, despite the IITF's rhetoric, effectively has acknowledged this contradiction in the GII–GIS dual mandate by funding construction of a second Internet system, the Next Generation Internet (NGI), a high-speed network to be devoted solely to non-commercial activities (MacKie-Mason and Varian 1996; White House 1996). By creating a second Internet, the original Internet (tellingly referred to as "the commodity Internet") increasingly may lose its identity as a free space of flows where a lack of barriers ensures maximum communication efficiency. Instead, the "commodity Internet" can be reconstituted as a space wherein those making fixed investments may reap profits under the protection of state regulation, while the NGI retains its friction-free purity.

This decision of the US government to abandon its attempt at constructing the Internet as a "pure" space of flows and to shift its funding to a separate system illustrates the contradiction between the construction of transportation–communication spaces as locations for placing investments and the construction of these spaces as surfaces for frictionless movement. It also demonstrates that some of these spaces present unique opportunities for diffusing the contradiction. In cyberspace, the US government simply created a new stratum of space. So long as the territorialization of the (commodity) Internet does not become so extreme that consumers clamor for government regulation to preserve the mobility function (e.g. consumer complaints that Microsoft-powered sites are inaccessible through Netscape browsing software), this solution may be fairly effective. Over time, however, it seems likely that commercial interests will begin clamoring for access to the higher-speed Next Generation Internet to market their high-performance communication products, at which point this conflict will be played out anew. A similar instance of outright space creation in the communication domain can be observed in outer space, where the US government has been promoting a network of low-Earth orbiting satellites, far below the 22,300 mile altitude of geostationary orbit that increasingly is being crowded with conventional satellites (OTA 1995).

In ocean-space, similar acts of space-creation or use-segmentation would be more difficult. In the industrial capitalist era, spatial segmentation of uses was achieved largely through the separation of coastal from deep seas, but present uses of the ocean have extensified and intensified to the point that they frequently overlap and impact each other. Conceivably, the ocean's movement functions could be moved to airspace, leaving the ocean available for land-like appropriation, but this is highly unlikely without major breakthroughs in the technology and pricing of air travel.

Most probably, in all of these spaces there will be a continual see-saw as those who regulate, invest in, consume, and produce representations of transportation–communication spaces attempt to achieve constructions that support the spaces' multiple, but contradictory, functions. In some cases, these constructions may be fairly stable. In other cases, however, like the manganese nodule mining regime, legal mechanisms implemented to enable short-term utilization of the space may, over the long term, introduce organizing principles that are detrimental to the continuation of the capitalist system. As a heterotopia, the ocean is a space of ordering and limits, but, as those orders and limits themselves stretch the bounds of social norms and systems, it is also a space for imagining and actualizing social change.

Conclusion: "The sea isn't a place . . ."

This history of the social construction of the ocean began with the story of the Nikes found floating in the Pacific Ocean. The Nike story provides a fitting end for the narrative as well, because in many ways the Nikes can be considered a metaphor for the ocean itself. Like the ocean, Nikes are encountered as images that, while rooted in function, tell only partial stories of the material relations that underlie their social construction. Nike, like the ocean, presents an image of freedom from the restrictions of place and society. Its advertisements focus on the creation of a Nike mystique wherein the shoe is associated with effortless athletic prowess, flippant antiauthoritarianism, and radical individuality (Korzeniewicz 1994), and the company itself has been called "something of a model of the global, postindustrial corporation" (Katz 1994: ix). Like the ocean, the image of the Nike shoe at times obscures its actual materiality, as form is elevated over function: At most, 40 percent of Nike customers use the shoes for their intended sport (Katz 1994). Finally, complementing this disjuncture between material reality and representation is a parallel separation between the representation and the actual conditions of production. While Nike's image is one of free-spirited individualism ("Just do it!"), it utilizes a "bloody Taylorist" system of subcontractors that the *Far Eastern Economic Review* describes as "ruthless" (Clifford 1992).

Countless political economists, including most notably Marx (1967), have argued that to interpret social processes one must examine commodities (such as Nikes) and analyze the processes of production beneath their surface. It has been argued here that a similar approach should be taken to the study of the production of the world's spaces, including seemingly asocial spaces such as the world-ocean. The message of the Nike advertisements notwithstanding, image is *not* everything.

Images play a crucial role in establishing the framework through which we encounter "reality," but there is always a process of production behind that image, a social construction. Uses, regulations, and representations impact and reproduce each other to form this social construction, which ultimately results in an image encountered by the consumer. Just as this process occurs for the social construction of commodities, it also occurs for the social construction of spaces.

Analysis of the processes behind the images of socially constructed spaces is crucial, in part because every image suggests a social policy. If the ocean is a friction-free transport surface outside society, then it should be managed with as few rules as possible to allow for maximum utilization. If the ocean is a set of developable places, then these places should be captured by sovereign states so that political authorities can institute regulations that will facilitate development through the placement of spatially fixed investments. And if the ocean is a resource-space too valuable to be squandered away by competitive states and their enterprises, then it should be stewarded (whether by individual states, the community of states, or civil society) so that all nations (or individuals) may be given an opportunity to benefit from its riches.

The sea is presented as a space "outside" society, a friction-free surface increasingly made obsolete (or at least suitable for being ignored) thanks to air travel and seamless container transport. The sea is presented as an abstract point on a grid, to be developed. The sea is presented as a repository of fragile, global nature, to be stewarded. Each of these images is accurate, but each is partial. Not only do the images tell partial stories; they obscure the material reality experienced by those who derive their living from the sea. These images obscure contemporary seafarers, dockworkers, artisanal fishers, and others who may be "managed" out of existence by the regulatory strategies with which each image is aligned. For the sea remains – as it has been since the advent of the modern era – a space constructed amidst competing interests and priorities, and it will continue to be transformed amidst social change.

Following an elaboration of the territorial political economy perspective, this book reviewed several ideal-type constructions of ocean-space: a non-territorial "Indian Ocean" construction in which the sea is constructed as an asocial space between societies, a highly territorial "Micronesian" construction in which the sea is perceived and managed as an extension of land-space, and a complex "Mediterranean" construction in which the sea is defined as non-possessible but nonetheless a legitimate arena for expressing and contesting social power. It was found that during the mercantilist era the primary construction of the sea was as a Mediterranean-style "force-field." Channeled circulation, taking place primarily at sea, was a defining political–economic activity under mercantilism, and so the states of the era constructed the sea as an arena in which they claimed stewardship rights to distinct ocean routes, but did not attempt outright possession.

In the industrial capitalist era, the key economic activity shifted from circulation across space to investment (and disinvestment) in specific production and consumption sites. Since these sites almost exclusively were on land, the deep sea became defined as a great void, idealized as outside society, a wild space of nature that was antithetical to the social places on land that could be planned, controlled, and developed. Thus, the deep sea was constructed as a space to be relished by romantics, studied by scientists, and made as friction-free and invisible as possible by capitalists, who saw the ocean as an empty surface between the terrestrial places that "mattered." As it had been in the Indian Ocean, the sea was constructed as an asocial space between societies.

Complementing this industrial capitalist idealization of the deep sea was a territorialization of the coastal sea reminiscent of the Micronesian construction. The coastal sea, like land, was perceived as a potential site of intensive investments, and so it was incorporated within the territory of the state. A third industrial capitalist-era perspective on the ocean – as a resource-space to be stewarded – emerged as there arose opportunities for intensive marine resource exploitation outside the territorialized coastal waters. Regimes were developed to regulate exploitation of material and commerce-oriented resources, but these were implemented in a manner that would not interfere with the prevailing great void idealization. To the extent that this third aspect of the industrial-era construction facilitated the exercising of social power, but not possession, it can be viewed as a variant of the Mediterranean ideal-type.

Finally, the postmodern era is beset by increasing contradictions in capitalist spatiality and, more specifically, capitalist constructions of ocean-space. The ocean is more important than ever as transport-space, and so there is increasing pressure – in keeping with the great void idealization – to make the ocean as friction-free a surface as possible. At the same time, however, the ocean increasingly is attractive as a space of development, and soon for the first time there will probably be opportunities for spatially fixed investments in the deep sea. Additionally, humanity has developed an unprecedented capacity to transform the nature of the sea so that it no longer provides the resources it once did, a phenomenon that has led some to support a stewardship system whereby the ocean is governed as a special space of nature. As various ocean uses and the contradictions among them intensify, and as each of these constructions conflicts with the spaces of representation being constructed by everyday actors outside the imperative of capitalism's dominant (and contradictory) spatial practices, it seems likely that the ocean will become a site for imagining and creating future social institutions and relations, for land as well as for sea. Indeed, similar contestations are likely to occur throughout the world's dedicated spaces of movement, as these spaces all become increasingly crucial to hyper-mobile capital but also increasingly lucrative as locations for placing spatially fixed investments and/or engaging in unsustainable rates of resource extraction.

The ocean certainly is not the only space where social contradictions are worked through, social change transpires, and future social relations are imagined. But it is one such space. As mobility takes on an increasingly important role in the world economy and as technologies emerge for exploiting previously inaccessible resources, it seems likely that the significance of conflict over ocean governance will only grow. As in previous eras, the social construction of ocean-space to emerge will be embedded in – and contribute to – the construction of a new social order for the land as well as the sea. On the one hand, the oppositional visions presented in Chapter 6 are merely visions. On the other hand, Grotius' declaration of *mare liberum* was radical in its day and made little sense in a world where states were attempting to monopolize trade routes. Now *mare liberum* is universally accepted in principle (if not always in practice). There is no reason to reject the possibility that one of the alternate visions of the late twentieth century may be appropriate for a later age in which land-based (and, perhaps, sea-based) social actors have another set of priorities.

Finally, one should not forget that the sea, besides being a socially constructed space, is also a material space of nature. The sea was taken for granted by Nike investors, producers, and consumers alike: the sea would be crossed; it would be transcended; it would be annihilated as a set of places and even as distance in the effort to profit from capital investment or (from the perspective of the consumer) to obtain cheap sneakers. And yet it was the sea that disrupted the shipment, decommodified the commodities, and distributed the liberated sneakers to distant shores. For a brief moment of reversal, the sea constructed social relations.

Mary Oliver writes:

> The sea
>   isn't a place
>   but a fact, and
>   a mystery
>
> under its green and black
>   cobbled coat that never
>   stops moving.
>   (Oliver 1986: 66)

Amidst the dynamic processes of global political economy, the sea is a space of contradictions and alternatives, of images and laws, of labor and dreams. The sea never stops moving.

References

Abbreviations used

CLIA	Cruise Lines International Association
FAO	Food and Agricultural Organization of the United Nations
IITF	Information Infrastructure Task Force
IOC	Intergovernmental Oceanographic Commission
ISEL	Institute of Shipping Economics and Logistics
MSC	Marine Stewardship Council
OECD	Organization for Economic Co-operation and Development
OTA	Office of Technology Assessment
UNCTAD	United Nations Conference on Trade and Development

Agnew, John 1994, "The territorial trap: the geographical assumptions of international relations theory," *Review of International Political Economy* 1: 53–80.

Alexander, Lewis M. (ed.) 1967, *The Law of the Sea: The Future of the Sea's Resources: Proceedings of the Second Annual Conference of the Law of the Sea Institute, June 26–29, 1967, Kingston, Rhode Island,* Kingston: University of Rhode Island.
  1983, "The ocean enclosure movement: inventory and prospect," *San Diego Law Review* 20: 561–594.

Alexander, Lewis M. and Hodgson, Robert D. 1975, "The impact of the 200-mile economic zone on the Law of the Sea," *San Diego Law Review* 12: 569–599.

Alexandrowicz, C. H. 1967, *An Introduction to the History of the Law of Nations in the East Indies (16th, 17th and 18th Centuries),* Oxford: Oxford University Press.

Allen, Scott 1994, "Harvesting the sea: salmon farm plan spawns interest, worry," *Boston Globe,* 12 August: 1, 32.

Allott, Philip 1993, "Mare nostrum: a new international law of the sea," in Jon M. Van Dyke, Durwood Zaelke, and Grant Hewison (eds.), *Freedom for the Seas in the 21st Century: Ocean Governance and Environmental Harmony,* Washington: Island, pp. 49–71.

Althusser, Louis 1971, "Ideology and ideological state apparatuses," in Louis Althusser, *Lenin and Philosophy and Other Essays,* trans. Ben Brewster, New York: Monthly Review Press, pp. 127–186.

References

Altvater, Elmar 1994, "Ecological and economic modalities of time and space," in Martin O'Connor (ed.), *Is Capitalism Sustainable? Political Economy and the Politics of Ecology*, New York: Guilford., pp. 76–90.

Amin, Samir, Arrighi, Giovanni, Frank, André Gunder, and Wallerstein, Immanuel 1982, *Dynamics of Global Crisis*, New York: Monthly Review Press.

Anand, Ram P. 1983, *Origin and Development of the Law of the Sea*, The Hague: Martinus Nijhoff.

Andrews, Kenneth R. 1984, *Trade, Plunder and Settlement: Maritime Enterprise and the Genesis of the British Empire, 1480–1630*, Cambridge: Cambridge University Press.

Armas Pfirter, Frida M. 1995, "Straddling stocks and highly migratory stocks in Latin American practice and legislation: new perspectives in light of current international negotiations," *Ocean Development and International Law* 26: 127–150.

Arunchalam, B. 1987, "The Haven-Finding Art in Indian Navigational Traditions and Cartography," in Satish Chandra (ed.), *The Indian Ocean: Explorations in History, Commerce, and Politics*, New Delhi: Sage, pp. 191–221.

Atkinson, David, Cook, Ian, Laurier, Eric, and Nash, Catherine 1997, "Bristol's International Festival of the Sea and a post-colonial politics of containment," paper presented at the Conference on Imperial Cities, Royal Holloway College, London, 2–3 May.

Atkinson, David and Laurier, Eric 1998, "A sanitised city? social exclusion at Bristol's 1996 International Festival of the Sea," *Geoforum* 29: 199–206.

Austin, Warren R. 1985, "Speech before the United Nations Security Council, 26 February 1947," in Francis X. Hezel and M.L. Berg (eds.), *Micronesia: Winds of Change: A Book of Readings on Micronesian History*, Agana: Omnibus Program for Social Studies Cultural Heritage, Trust Territory of the Pacific Islands, 1985, pp. 480–481.

Bach, Robert L. 1982, "On the holism of a world-system perspective," in Terence K. Hopkins and Immanuel Wallerstein (eds.), *World-Systems Analysis: Theory and Methodology*, Beverly Hills: Sage, pp. 159–180.

Baer, George W. 1994, *One Hundred Years of Sea Power: The U.S. Navy, 1890–1990*, Stanford: Stanford University Press.

Ball, Wayne S. 1996, "The old grey *mare*: national enclosure of the oceans," *Ocean Development and International Law* 27: 97–124.

Barnes, Trevor J. and Duncan, James S. 1992, "Introduction: writing worlds," in Trevor J. Barnes and James S. Duncan (eds.), *Writing Worlds: Discourse, Text and Metaphor in the Representation of the Landscape*, London: Routledge, pp. 1–17.

Bartlett, Christopher J. 1963, *Great Britain and Sea Power, 1815–1853*, Oxford: Clarendon.

Baudrillard, Jean 1988, *America*, trans. Chris Turner, London: Verso.

Bautista Payoyo, Peter (ed.) 1994, *Ocean Governance: Sustainable Development of the Seas*, Tokyo: United Nations University Press.

Bernfeld, Seymour S. 1967, "Developing the resources of the sea: security of investment," *International Lawyer* 2: 67–76.

Berrill, Michael 1997, *The Plundered Seas: Can the World's Fish be Saved?* San Francisco: Sierra Club Books.

Birnie, Patricia W. 1987, "Piracy: past, present and future," *Marine Policy* 11: 163–183.

Black's Law Dictionary 1990, 6th edn., St. Paul: West.

Blaikie, Piers 1985, *The Political Economy of Soil Erosion in Developing Countries*, Harlow: Longman.

Blomley, Nicholas K. 1994, *Law, Space, and the Geographies of Power*, New York: Guilford.

Bolster, W. Jeffrey 1990, "To feel like a man: Black seamen in the northern states, 1800–1860," *Journal of American History* 76: 1173–1199.

1996, "'Every inch a man': gender in the lives of African American seamen, 1800–1860," in Margaret S. Creighton and Lisa Norling (eds.), *Iron Men, Wooden Women: Gender and Seafaring in the Atlantic World, 1700–1920*, Baltimore: Johns Hopkins University Press, pp. 138–168.

Booth, Ken 1985, *Law, Force and Diplomacy at Sea*, London: Allen & Unwin.

Borgese, Elisabeth M. 1977, "The new international economic order and the law of the sea" in Don Walsh (ed.), *The Law of the Sea: Issues in Ocean Resource Management*, New York: Praeger, pp. 82–116.

1986, *The Future of the Oceans: A Report to the Club of Rome*, Montreal: Harvest House.

1998, *The Oceanic Circle: Governing the Seas as a Global Resource*, Tokyo: United Nations University Press.

1999, "Global civil society: lessons from ocean governance," *Futures* 31: 983–991.

Bose, Sugata (ed.) 1990, *South Asia and World Capitalism*, Delhi: Oxford University Press.

Bourne, Edward G. 1904, *Spain in America, 1450–1580*, New York: Harper & Brothers.

Bradbury, Ray 1962, "Introduction: the ardent blasphemers," in Jules Verne, *20,000 Leagues Under the Sea*, trans. Anthony Bonner, Toronto: Bantam, pp. 1–12.

Braudel, Fernand 1972, *The Mediterranean and the Mediterranean World in the Age of Philip II*, trans. Siân Reynolds, New York: Harper & Row.

1981, *Civilization and Capitalism, 15th–18th Century*, I: *The Structures of Everyday Life: The Limits of the Possible*, trans. Siân Reynolds, New York: Harper & Row.

1982, *Civilization and Capitalism, 15th–18th Century*, II: *The Wheels of Commerce*, trans. Siân Reynolds, New York: Harper & Row.

1984, *Civilization and Capitalism, 15th–18th Century*, III: *The Perspective of the World*, trans. Siân Reynolds, New York: Harper & Row.

Breen, James H. 1984, "The 1982 Dispute Resolving Agreement: the first step toward unilateral mining outside the law of the sea convention," *Ocean Development and International Law* 14: 201–233.

References

Brenner, Robert 1977, "The origins of capitalist development: a critique of neo-smithian Marxism," *New Left Review* 104: 15–91.

Brewer, William C. Jr. 1985, "The prospect for deep seabed mining in a divided world," *Ocean Development and International Law* 14: 357–361.

Broad, William 1997, *The Universe Below: Discovering the Secrets of the Deep Sea*, New York: Simon & Schuster.

Broadus, James M. and Vartanov, Raphael V. (eds.) 1994, *The Oceans and Environmental Security: Shared U.S. and Russian Perspectives*, Washington: Island.

Brower, Kenneth 1981, *Micronesia: The Land, the People, and the Sea*, Baton Rouge: University of Louisiana Press.

Brown, E. O. 1993, "'Neither necessary nor prudent at this stage': the regime of seabed mining and its impact on the universality of the U.N. Convention on the Law of the Sea," *Marine Policy* 17: 81–107.

Bryant, Raymond L. and Bailey, Sinéad 1997, *Third World Political Ecology*, London: Routledge.

Burg, Barry R. 1983, *Sodomy and the Perception of Evil: English Sea Rovers in the Seventeenth-Century Caribbean*, New York: New York University Press.

1994, *An American Sailor in the Age of Sail: The Erotic Diaries of Philip Van Buskirk*, New Haven: Yale University Press.

Burke, Edmund [1757] 1958, *A Philosophical Enquiry into the Origin of Our Ideas of the Sublime and Beautiful*, London: Routledge & Kegan Paul.

Burke, Joseph 1976, *English Art, 1714–1800*, Oxford: Clarendon.

Burke, W. Scott and Brokaw, Frank S. 1983, "Ideology and the law of the sea," in Oxman, Caron, and Buderi (eds.), pp. 43–58.

Butler, Octavia E. 1980, *Wild Seed*, New York: Popular Library.

Buzan, Barry 1976, *Seabed Politics*, New York: Praeger.

Cafruny, Alan F. 1987, *Ruling the Waves: The Political Economy of International Shipping*, Berkeley: University of California Press.

Campbell, Tony 1981, *Early Maps*, New York: Abbeville.

Caron, David 1981, "Deep seabed mining: a comparative study of U.S. and West German legislation," *Marine Policy* 5: 4–16.

Carson, Rachel 1951, *The Sea Around Us*, New York: Oxford University Press.

Carvajal, Doreen 1995, "Diversity pays off in a babel of yellow pages," *The New York Times*, 3 December: 1, 46.

Castells, Manuel 1996, *The Rise of the Network Society*, Oxford: Blackwell.

Chandra, Satish (ed.) 1987a, *The Indian Ocean: Explorations in History, Commerce, and Politics*, New Delhi: Sage.

Chandra, Satish 1987b, "Introduction," in Chandra (ed.), pp. 11–26.

Chase-Dunn, Christopher 1989, *Global Formation: Structures of the World-Economy*, Cambridge: Basil Blackwell.

Chaudhuri, K. N. 1985, *Trade and Civilisation in the Indian Ocean: An Economic History from the Rise of Islam to 1750*, Cambridge: Cambridge University Press.

Chesneaux, Jean 1972, *The Political and Social Ideas of Jules Verne*, trans. Thomas Wikeley, London: Thames & Hudson.

214

Christy, Francis T. Jr. 1968, "A social scientist writes on economic criteria for rules governing exploitation of deep sea minerals," *International Lawyer* 2: 224–242.

CLIA 2000, *The Cruise Industry: An Overview*. Available on-line via http://www.cruising.org/press/overview/industry%5Foverview.htm.

Clifford, Mark 1992, "Spring in their step," *Far Eastern Economic Review*, 5 November: 56–57.

Clingan, Thomas A. Jr. 1985, "Statement given at the signing of the Final Act of the Third United Nations Conference on the Law of the Sea, 9 December 1982," in Moore (ed.).

1993, "*Mar presencial* (the presential sea): *déja vu* all over again? – a response to Francisco Orrego Vicuña," *Ocean Development and International Law* 24: 93–97.

Cohen, Saul B. 1973, *Geography and Politics in a World Divided*, 2nd edn., New York: Oxford University Press.

Coleridge, Samuel T. [1798] 1961, "The rime of the ancient mariner," in Royal A. Gettmann (ed.), *The Rime of the Ancient Mariner: A Handbook*, San Francisco: Wadsworth, pp. 3–41.

Colombos, C. John 1967, *The International Law of the Sea*, 6th edn., New York: David McKay.

Columbus, Christopher [1493] 1991, "The First Letter of Columbus," in John A. Murray (ed.), *The Islands and the Sea: Five Centuries of Nature Writing from the Caribbean*, New York: Oxford University Press, pp. 27–32.

"Commercial and fiscal policy of the Venetian Republic, The" 1904, *Edinburgh Review* 200: 338–361.

Comptroller General of the United States 1975, *Information on U.S. Ocean Interests Together with Positions and Results of the Law of the Sea Conference at Caracas: Report to Congress, March 9, 1975*, Washington: Office of the Comptroller General.

Connery, Christopher L. 1995, "Pacific rim discourse: the U.S. global imaginary in the late cold war years," in Wilson and Dirlik (eds.), pp. 30–56.

1996, "The oceanic feeling and the regional imaginary," in Rob Wilson and Wimal Dissanayake (eds.), *Global/Local: Cultural Production and the Transnational Imaginary*, Durham, NC: Duke University Press, pp. 284–311.

Constance, Douglas H. and Bonanno, Alessandro 2000, "Regulating the global fisheries: the World Wildlife Fund, Unilever, and the Marine Stewardship Council," *Agriculture and Human Values* 17: 125–139.

Cooke, Miriam 1999, "Mediterranean thinking: from netizen to medizen," *Geographical Review* 89: 290–300.

Corbin, Alain 1994, *The Lure of the Sea: The Discovery of the Seaside in the Western World, 1750–1840*, trans. Jocelyn Phelps, Berkeley: University of California Press.

Cordell, John (ed.) 1989, *A Sea of Small Boats*, Cambridge, MA: Cultural Survival.

Cordingly, David 1973, *Marine Painting in England, 1700–1900*, New York: Clarkson N. Potter.

Costanza, Robert, d'Arge, Ralph, de Groot, Rudolf, Farber, Stephen, Grasso, Monica, Hannon, Bruce, Limburg, Karin, Naeem, Shahid, O'Neill, Robert V., Paruelo, José, Raskin, Robert G., Sutton, Paul, and van den Belt, Marjan 1997, "The value of the world's ecosystem services and natural capital," *Nature* 387: 253–260.

Couper, Alastair D. (ed.) 1989, *The Times Atlas and Encyclopaedia of the Sea*, New York: Harper & Row.

Cox, Kevin (ed.) 1997, *Spaces of Globalization: Reasserting the Power of the Local*, New York: Guilford.

Cox, Robert W. 1987, *Production, Power, and World Order: Social Forces in the Making of History*, New York: Columbia University Press.

Craib, Raymond B. 2000, "Cartography and power in the conquest and creation of New Spain," *Latin American Research Review* 35: 7–36.

Creighton, Margaret S. 1995, *Rites and Passages: The Experience of American Whaling, 1830–1870*, Cambridge: Cambridge University Press.

Creighton, Margaret S. and Norling, Lisa (eds.) 1996, *Iron Men, Wooden Women: Gender and Seafaring in the Atlantic World, 1700–1920*, Baltimore: Johns Hopkins University Press.

Cresswell, Tim 1996, "Writing, reading and the problem of resistance: a reply to McDowell," *Transactions of the Institute of British Geographers* 21: 420–428.

Crimson Tide 1995, dir. Tony Scott, Hollywood: Hollywood Pictures.

Curtis, Clifton 1983, "Sign the sea law treaty," *The New York Times* 21 February: A17.

Dana, Richard H. Jr. [1840] 1964, *Two Years Before the Mast: A Personal Narrative of Life at Sea*, Los Angeles: Ward Ritchie.

Davenport, Frances G. (ed.) 1917, *European Treaties Bearing on the History of the United States and its Dependencies to 1648*, Washington: Carnegie Institute.

Davies, Arthur 1967, "Columbus divides the world," *The Geographical Journal* 133: 337–344.

Davis, Ralph 1962, *The Rise of the English Shipping Industry in the Seventeenth and Eighteenth Centuries*, London: Macmillan.

Dawson, Samuel E. 1899, "The Lines of Demarcation of Pope Alexander VI and the Treaty of Tordesillas, A.D. 1493 and 1494," Transactions of the Royal Society of Canada, 2nd Series, 5: 467–546.

DeFilippis, James 1997, "From a public re-creation to private recreation: the transformation of public space at South Street Seaport," *Journal of Urban Affairs* 19: 405–417.

Deleuze, Gilles and Guattari, Félix 1988, *A Thousand Plateaus: Capitalism and Schizophrenia*, trans. Brian Massumi, London: Athlone.

Denman, Donald 1984, *Markets Under the Sea? A Study of the Potential of Private Property Rights in the Seabed*, London: Institute of Economic Affairs.

Derby, Charles Earl of 1671, *The Protestant Religion is a Sure Foundation and Principle of a True Christian, and a Good Subject, a Great Friend to Humane Society; and a Grand Promoter of all Virtues, Both Christian and Moral*, 2nd edn., London: William Cademan.

Dickinson, Bob and Vladimir, Andy 1997, *Selling the Sea: An Inside Look at the Cruise Industry*, New York: John Wiley.

Dirlik, Arif (ed.) 1993, *What is in a Rim? Critical Perspectives on the Pacific Region Idea*, Boulder: Westview.

Drake, William J. 1995, *The New Information Infrastructure: Strategies for U.S. Policy*, New York: Twentieth Century Fund.

Dubs, M. A. and Cook, C. F. 1977, "The law of the sea from the perspective of the hard rock mining industry," *Marine Technology Society Journal* 11: 8–11.

Dunford, Michael and Perrons, Diane 1983, *The Arena of Capital*, New York: St. Martin's Press.

Earle, Sylvia A. 1995, *Sea Change: A Message of the Oceans*, New York: G.P. Putnam.

Earney, Fillmore C. 1990, *Marine Mineral Resources*, London: Routledge.

Ebbesmeyer, Curtis C. and Ingraham, W. James Jr. 1992, "Shoe spill in the North Pacific," *Eos* 73: 361–365.

1994, "Pacific toy spill fuels ocean current pathways research," *Eos* 75: 425–431.

Eckert, Ross 1979, *The Enclosure of Ocean Resources: Economics and the Law of the Sea*, Stanford: Hoover Institute Press.

Economist, The 1998, Survey: "The deep green sea," 23 May.

Ellis, Richard 1995, *Monsters of the Sea: The History, Natural History, and Mythology of the Oceans' Most Fantastic Creatures*, New York: Alfred A. Knopf.

Epstein, Isidore (ed.) 1948, *The Babylonian Talmud*, London: Soncino Press.

Esteva, Gutavo 1992, "Development," in Wolfgang Sachs (ed.), *The Development Dictionary: A Guide to Knowledge as Power*, London: Zed, pp. 6–25.

Extavour, Winston C. 1979, *The Exclusive Economic Zone: A Study of the Evolution and Progressive Development of the International Law of the Sea*, Geneva: Institut universitaire de hautes études internationales.

FAO 1981, *Atlas of Living Resources of the Sea*, 4th edn., Rome: FAO.

FAO (various years), *Yearbook of Fishery Statistics*, Rome: FAO.

Fenn, Percy T. Jr. 1925, "Justinian and the freedom of the sea," *American Journal of International Law* 19: 716–726.

Fiske, John 1892, *The Discovery of America*, I, Boston: Houghton, Mifflin.

Foster-Carter, Aidan 1978, "The modes of production controversy," *New Left Review* 107: 47–78.

Foucault, Michel 1977, *Discipline and Punish: The Birth of the Prison*, trans. Alan Sheridan, New York: Vintage.

1986, "Of other spaces," trans. Jay Miskowiec, *Diacritics* 16: 22–27.

Freitas, Seraphim de [1625] 1882, *Freitas contre Grotius sur la question de la liberté des mers: Justification de la domination portugaise en Asie*, trans. Alfred Guichon de Grandpont, Paris: J. P. Aillaud.

[1625] 1925, *De como es justo el imperio que los Portugueses obtienen en Asia*, trans. José Zuita Neto, Valladolid: Impresso de la Casa social católica.

[1625] 1959, *Do justo império asiático dos portugueses*, Lisbon: Instituto de alta cultura.

Friedheim, Robert L. 1991, "Fishing negotiations at the Third United Nations Conference on the Law of the Sea," *Ocean Development and International Law* 22: 209–257.

Friedheim, Robert L. 1993, *Negotiating the New Ocean Regime*, Columbia: University of South Carolina Press.

Friedheim, Robert L. and Durch, William J. 1977, "The international seabed resources agency negotiations and the new international economic order," *International Organization* 31: 343–384.

Fukuyama, Francis 1992, *The End of History and the Last Man*, New York: Free Press.

Fulton, Thomas W. 1911, *The Sovereignty of the Sea*, Edinburgh: William Blackwood.

Galdorisi, George V. 1995a, "The United Nations Convention on the Law of the Sea: A national security perspective," *American Journal of International Law* 89: 208–213.

   1995b, "The United States and the law of the sea: a window of opportunity for maritime leadership," *Ocean Development and International Law* 26: 75–83.

   1998, "An operational perspective on the law of the sea," *Ocean Development and International Law* 29: 73–84.

Galdorisi, George V. and Stavridis, Jim 1993, "Time to revisit the law of the sea?" *Ocean Development and International Law* 24: 301–315.

Galdorisi, George V. and Vienna, Kevin R. 1997, *Beyond the Law of the Sea: New Directions for U.S. Oceans Policy*, Westport: Praeger.

Gambi, Lucio 1994, "Geography and imperialism in Italy: from the unity of the nation to the 'new' Roman Empire," in Anne Godlewska and Neil Smith (eds.), *Geography and Empire*, Oxford: Blackwell, pp. 74–91.

Gaunt, William 1975, *Marine Painting: An Historical Survey*, New York: Viking.

Geographical Review 1999, Special issue, "Oceans connect," 89: 161–313.

Gibson-Graham, J. K. 1996, *The End of Capitalism (as We Knew it): A Feminist Critique of Political Economy*, Cambridge, MA: Blackwell.

Gilroy, Paul 1993, *The Black Atlantic*, Cambridge, MA: Harvard University Press.

Gladwin, Thomas 1970, *East is a Big Bird: Navigation and Logic on Puluwat Atoll*, Cambridge, MA: Harvard University Press.

Gold, Edgar 1981, *Maritime Transport: The Evolution of International Marine Policy and Shipping Law*, Lexington: Lexington Books.

Golding, William 1991, *To the Ends of the Earth: A Sea Trilogy*, London: Faber & Faber.

Goldwin, Robert A. 1983, "Common sense vs. 'the common heritage'," in Oxman, Caron, and Buderi (eds.), pp. 59–75.

Gorenflo, L. J. 1993, "Changing regional demography in the Federated States of Micronesia: contrasting planning challenges in an emerging Pacific nation," *Environment and Planning C: Government and Policy* 11: 123–141.

Gormley, W. Paul 1963, "The development and subsequent influence of the Roman legal norm of 'freedom of the seas'," *University of Detroit Law Journal* 40: 561–595.

Goss, Jon 1996, "Disquiet on the waterfront: reflections on nostalgia and utopia in the urban archetypes of festival marketplaces," *Urban Geography* 17: 221–247.

Gottman, Jean 1973, *The Significance of Territory*, Charlottesville: University of Virginia Press.

Gottschalk, Paul (ed.) 1927, *The Earliest Diplomatic Documents on America: The Papal Bulls of 1493 and the Treaty of Tordesillas Reproduced and Translated*, Berlin: Paul Gottschalk.

Gramsci, Antonio 1971, *Selections from the Prison Notebooks*, trans. and ed. Quintin Hoare and Geoffrey N. Smith, New York: International.

Grieco, Joseph M. 1990, *Cooperation Among Nations: Europe, America, and Non-Tariff Barriers*, Ithaca: Cornell University Press.

Grolin, Jesper 1983, "The future of the law of the sea: consequences of a non-treaty or non-universal treaty situation," *Ocean Development and International Law* 13: 1–31.

Grotius, Hugo [1608] 1916, *The Freedom of the Seas, or the Right Which Belongs to the Dutch to Take Part in the East Indian Trade*, trans. Ralph Van Deman Magoffin, New York: Oxford University Press.

Haas, Peter M., Keohane, Robert O., and Levy, Marc A. (eds.) 1993, *Institutions for the Earth: Sources of Effective International Environmental Protection*, Cambridge, MA: MIT Press.

Harley, J. Brian 1988a, "Maps, knowledge, and power," in Denis Cosgrove and Stephen Daniels (eds.), *The Iconography of Landscape: Essays on the Symbolic Representation, Design, and Use of Past Environments*, Cambridge: Cambridge University Press, pp. 277–312.

1988b, "Silences and secrecy: the hidden agenda of cartography in early modern Europe," *Imago Mundi* 40: 57–76.

1989, "Deconstructing the map," *Cartographica* 26: 1–19.

Harlow, Bruce 1985, *Mission Impossible: Preservation of U.S. Maritime Freedoms*, Seattle: University of Washington Sea Grant Program.

Harper, J. E. T. 1930, Foreword to Geoffrey Parrat, *The Royal Navy: The Sure Shield of the Empire*, London: Sheldon, pp. vii–ix.

Harrisse, Henry 1897, *The Diplomatic History of America: Its First Chapter, 1452–1493–1494*, London: B.F. Stevens.

Hartshorne, Richard 1953, "Where in the world are we? geographic understanding for political survival and progress," *Journal of Geography* 52: 382–393.

Harvey, David 1978, "The urban process under capitalism: a framework for analysis," *International Journal of Urban and Regional Research* 2: 101–131.

1982, *The Limits to Capital*, Chicago: University of Chicago Press.

1985, "The geopolitics of capitalism," in Derek Gregory and John Urry (eds.), *Social Relations and Spatial Structures*, London: Methuen, pp. 128–163.

1989, *The Condition of Postmodernity: An Enquiry into the Origins of Cultural Change*, Oxford: Basil Blackwell.

1996, *Justice, Nature and the Geography of Difference*, Malden: Blackwell.

Hetherington, Kevin 1997, *The Badlands of Modernity: Heterotopia and Social Ordering*, London: Routledge.

Hezel, Francis X. 1983, *The First Taint of Civilization: A History of the Caroline and Marshall Islands in Pre-Colonial Days, 1521–1885*, Honolulu: University of Hawai'i Press.

Hilferding, Rudolf [1910] 1981, *Finance Capital: A Study of the Latest Phase of Capitalist Development*, trans. Morris Watnick and Sam Gordon, London: Routledge.

Hollick, Ann L. 1981, *U.S. Foreign Policy and the Law of the Sea*, Princeton: Princeton University Press.

hooks, bell 1984, *Feminist Theory from Margin to Center*, Boston: South End Press.

Hopkins, Terence K. 1982, "World-systems analysis: methodological issues," in Terence K. Hopkins and Immanuel Wallerstein (eds.), *World-Systems Analysis: Theory and Methodology*, Beverly Hills: Sage, pp. 145–158.

Horton, James O. 1986, "Freedom's yoke: gender conventions among antebellum free Blacks," *Feminist Studies* 12: 51–76.

Hourani, George F. 1963, *Arab Seafaring in the Indian Ocean in Ancient and Early Medieval Times*, Beirut: Khayats.

Howarth, David 1977, *Dhows*, New York: Quartet.

Hughes, Robert 1992, *Barcelona*, New York: Alfred A. Knopf.

Hugill, Peter J. 1993, *World Trade Since 1431: Geography, Technology, and Capitalism*, Baltimore: Johns Hopkins University Press.

Hunt for Red October 1989, dir. John McTiernan, Hollywood: Paramount.

Hutchins, Edwin 1995, *Cognition in the Wild*, Cambridge, MA: MIT Press.

IITF 1993, *The National Information Infrastructure: Agenda for Action*, Washington: Government Printing Office.

1995, *Global Information Infrastructure: Agenda for Cooperation*, Washington: Government Printing Office.

IOC 1997a, *Draft Dedicated Programme for 1998 International Year of the Ocean, IOC-XIX/2 Annex 3*, Paris: IOC. Available on-line via http://ioc.unesco.org/ioc19/ioc19doc2ann3/htframe.htm.

1997b, *1998 International Year of the Ocean: Statement of Objectives*. Available on-line via http://ioc.unesco.org/iyo/introduction.htm#The overall objective.

ISEL, previously Institute of Shipping Economics (various years), *Shipping Statistics Yearbook*, Bremen: ISEL.

Jackson, S. E. 1995, "The water is not empty: cross-cultural issues in conceptualising sea space," *The Australian Geographer* 26: 87–96.

Janis, Mark W. and Daniel, Donald C. F. 1974, *The USSR: Ocean Use and Ocean Law*, Kingston: Law of the Sea Institute.

Johnson, Lyndon B. 1966, "Effective use of the sea: address delivered July 11, 1966, at the launching of the research vessel *USC & GSS Oceanographer*,

Washington Naval Yard," *Weekly Compilation of Presidential Documents* 27: 930–932.

Johnston, Ronald J. 1989, "The state, political geography, and geography," in Nigel Thrift and Richard Peet (eds.), *New Models in Geography*, I, London: Unwin Hyman, pp. 292–309.

1992, "Laws, states, and superstates: international law and the environment," *Applied Geography* 12: 211–228.

1993, "Tackling global environmental problems," *Geography Review* 6: 27–30.

Jönsson, Christer 1987, *International Aviation and the Politics of Regime Change*, New York: St. Martin's Press.

Joyner, Christopher C. and De Cola, Peter N. 1993, "Chile's presential sea proposal: implications for straddling stocks and the international law of fisheries," *Ocean Development and International Law* 24: 99–121.

Juda, Lawrence and Burroughs, R. H. 1990, "The prospects for comprehensive ocean management," *Marine Policy* 14: 23–35.

Kahin, Brian and Wilson, Ernest J. 1996, *National Information Infrastructure Initiatives: Vision and Policy Design*, Cambridge, MA: MIT Press.

Katz, Donald 1994, *Just Do It: The Nike Spirit in the Corporate World*, New York: Random House.

Keith, Kent M. 1977, "Floating cities: a new challenge for transnational law," *Marine Policy* 1: 190–204.

Kemp, Peter (ed.) 1988, *The Oxford Companion to Ships and the Sea*, corrected edn., Oxford: Oxford University Press.

Kennedy, Paul M. 1976, *The Rise and Fall of British Naval Mastery*, New York: Charles Scribner.

Kerouac, Jack [1955] 1976, *On the Road*, New York: Penguin.

Kharrazi, Kamal 1994, "Statement by HE Dr. Kamal Kharrazi, ambassador and permanent representative of the Islamic Republic of Iran to the United Nations in the plenary meeting of the General Assembly on the law of the sea, July 28," New York: Permanent Mission to the United Nations, Islamic Republic of Iran.

Kilian, Darryll and Dodson, Belinda J. 1996, "Forging a postmodern waterfront: urban form and spectacle at the Victoria and Alfred Docklands," *South African Geographical Journal* 78: 29–40.

Klausmann, Ulrike and Meinzerin, Marion 1997, "Women pirates," in Ulrike Klausmann, Marion Meinzerin, and Gabriel Kuhn (eds.), *Women Pirates and the Politics of the Jolly Roger*, Montreal: Harvest House, pp. 3–223.

Knight, W. S. M. 1925, "Seraphin de Freitas: critic of *Mare Liberum*," *Transactions of the Grotius Society* 11: 1–9.

Koh, Tommy T. B. 1983, "A Constitution for the Oceans," in United Nations, pp. xxxiii–xxxvii.

Korzeniewicz, Miguel 1994, "Commodity chains and marketing strategies: Nike and the global athletic footwear industry," in Gary Gereffi and Miguel Korzeniewicz (eds.), *Commodity Chains and Global Capitalism*, Westport: Praeger, pp. 247–265.

References

Krasner, Stephen D. (ed.) 1983, *International Regimes*, Ithaca: Cornell University Press.

Kratochwil, Friedrich 1986, "Of systems, boundaries, and territoriality: an inquiry into the formation of the state system," *World Politics* 39: 27–52.

Kuhn, Gabriel 1997, "Life Under the Death's Head: Anarchism and Piracy," in Ulrike Klausmann, Marion Meinzerin, and Gabriel Kuhn (eds.), *Women Pirates and the Politics of the Jolly Roger*, Montréal: Harvest House, pp. 225–280.

Kurlansky, Mark 1997, *Cod: A Biography of the Fish That Changed the World*, New York: Penguin.

Laclau, Ernesto 1971, "Feudalism and capitalism in Latin America," *New Left Review* 67: 19–38.

Lane, Frederic C. 1973, *Venice: A Maritime Republic*, Baltimore: Johns Hopkins University Press.

Lash, Scott and Urry, John 1994, *Economies of Signs and Space*, London: Sage.

Latour, Bruno 1986, "Visualization and cognition: thinking with eyes and hands," in Henrika Kuklick and Elizabeth Long (eds.), *Knowledge and Society: Studies in the Sociology of Culture Past and Present, Volume Six*, Greenwich: JAI Press, pp. 1–40.

Laursen, Finn (ed.) 1982, *Toward a New International Marine Order*, The Hague: Martinus Nijhoff.

Laver, Michael 1986, "Public, private and common in outer space: *res extra commercium* or *res communis humanitatis* beyond the high frontier?" *Political Studies* 34: 359–373.

Law, John 1986, "On the methods of long-distance control: vessels, navigation and the Portuguese route to India," in John Law (ed.), *Power, Action and Belief: A New Sociology of Knowledge?* London: Routledge, pp. 234–263.

Leddy, George 1996, "Televisuals and environmentalism: the dark side of marine resource protection as global thinking". Paper presented at the Annual Meeting of the Association of American Geographers, Charlotte, 9–13 April.

Lefebvre, Henri 1991, *The Production of Space*, trans., Donald Nicholson-Smith Oxford: Basil Blackwell.

Leibowitz, Arnold H. 1989, *Defining Status: A Comprehensive Analysis of United States Territorial Relations*, Norwell: Kluwer.

Lemonick, Michael D. 1995, "The last frontier: lured by the promise of major scientific breakthroughs and great mineral wealth, researchers mount an assault on the bottom of the sea," *Time*, 14 August: 52–60.

Lenček, Lena and Bosker, Gideon 1998, *The Beach: The History of Paradise on Earth*, New York: Viking.

Lenin, Vladimir I. [1917] 1939, *Imperialism: The Highest Stage of Capitalism*, New York: International.

Levathes, Louise 1994, *When China Ruled the Seas: The Treasure Fleet of the Dragon Throne, 1405–1433*, New York: Simon & Schuster.

Lewis, Martin W. 1999, "Dividing the ocean sea," *Geographical Review* 89: 188–214.

Leyshon, Andrew and Thrift, Nigel 1997, *Money/Space: Geographies of Monetary Transformation*, London: Routledge.

Lipietz, Alain 1986, "New tendencies in the international division of labor: regimes of accumulation and modes of regulation," in Allen J. Scott and Michael Storper (eds.), *Production, Work, Territory: The Geographical Anatomy of Industrial Capitalism*, Boston: Allen & Unwin, pp. 16–39.

Lobingier, Charles S. 1935, "The maritime law of Rome," *Juridical Review* 47: 1–32.

Luard, Evan 1974, *The Control of the Sea-Bed: A New International Issue*, London: Heinemann.

Luke, Timothy W. 2000, "Beyond birds: biopower and birdwatching in the world of Audubon," *Capitalism, Nature, Socialism* 11: 7–37.

Luxemburg, Rosa [1913] 1964, *The Accumulation of Capital*, trans. Agnes Schwarzchild, New York: Monthly Review Press.

McCay, Bonnie K. and Acheson, James M. (eds.) 1987, *The Question of the Commons: The Culture and Ecology of Communal Resources*, Tucson: University of Arizona Press.

McDorman, Ted L. 1984, "The 1982 Law of the Sea Convention: the first year," *Journal of Maritime Law and Commerce* 15: 211–232.

McDowell, Linda 1996, "Off the road: alternative views of rebellion, resistance and 'the beats'," *Transactions of the Institute of British Geographers* 21: 412–419.

Mack Smith, Denis 1976, *Mussolini's Roman Empire*, New York: Viking.

Mack Smith, Denis 1982, *Mussolini*, New York: Alfred A. Knopf.

MacKie-Mason, Jeffrey K. and Varian, Hal R. 1996, "Some economics of the Internet," in Werner Sichel and Donald L. Alexander (eds.), *Networks, Infrastructure, and the New Task for Regulation*, Ann Arbor: University of Michigan Press, pp. 107–136.

Mackinder, Sir Halford J. 1904, "The geographical pivot of history," *The Geographical Journal* 23: 421–437.

Mahan, Alfred T. 1890, *The Influence of Sea Power Upon History, 1660–1783*, Boston: Little, Brown.

Majid al-Sadi, Ahmad ibn 1971, *Arab Navigation in the Indian Ocean Before the Coming of the Portuguese: Being a Translation of Kitab al-Fawaid fi usul al-bahr wal-qawaid of Ahmad b. Majid al-Naji*, trans., Gerald R. Tibbets, London: Royal Asiatic Society of Great Britain and Ireland.

Malone, James L. 1985, "Address before the Mentor Group, 10 March 1983," in Jon M. Van Dyke (ed.), *Consensus and Confrontation: The United States and the Law of the Sea Convention*, Honolulu: Law of the Sea Institute, pp. 554–557.

Mann, Michael 1984, "The autonomous powers of the state: its origins, mechanisms, and results," *Archives Européennes de Sociologie* 25: 185–213.

Marcuse, Herbert 1969, *An Essay on Liberation*, Boston: Beacon.

Marsh, George P. [1864] 1965, *Man and Nature: Or, Physical Geography as Modified by Human Action*, Cambridge: Belknap.

Marx, Karl [1867] 1967, *Capital; a Critique of Political Economy. Edited by Frederick Engels*, trans. from the 3rd German edn. by Samuel Moore and Edward Aveling, New York: International.

Meillasoux, Claude 1981, *Maidens, Meal, and Money: Capitalism and the Domestic Community*, Cambridge: Cambridge University Press.

Melville, Herman [1849] 1957, *Redburn: His First Voyage*, Garden City: Doubleday Anchor.

[1851] 1988, *Moby Dick, or the Whale*, Evanston: Northwestern University Press.

Mignolo, Walter 1995, *The Darker Side of the Renaissance: Literacy, Territoriality, and Colonization*, Ann Arbor: University of Michigan Press.

Modelski, George and Thompson, William R. 1988, *Seapower in Global Politics, 1494–1993*, Houndsmills: Macmillan.

Mollat du Jourdin, Michel 1993, *Europe and the Sea*, Teresa Lavender Fagan (trans.), Oxford: Blackwell.

Moore, John N. (ed.) 1986, *International and United States Documents on Oceans Law and Policy*, Buffalo: William S. Hein.

Morgenthau, Hans J. and Thompson, Kenneth W. 1985, *Politics Among Nations: The Struggle for Power and Peace, Sixth edn.*, New York: Oxford University Press.

Morris, Michael A. 1977, "The new international order and the law of the sea," in Karl P. Sauvant and Hajo Hasenpflug (eds.), *The New International Economic Order: Confrontation or Cooperation Between North and South?* Frankfurt: Campus.

MSC 1997, *Newsletter 1*. Available on-line via http://www.panda.org/endang eredseas/msc/page1.htm.

1998, *Principles and Criteria for Sustainable Fishing: Airlie House Draft*, London: MSC. Available on-line via http://www.msc.org.

Murphy, Alexander B. 1996, "The sovereign state system as political-territorial ideal: historical and contemporary considerations," in Thomas J. Biersteker and Cynthia Weber (eds.), *State Sovereignty as Social Construct*, Cambridge: Cambridge University Press, pp. 81–120.

Nakayama, Masao and Ramp, Frederick L. 1974, *Micronesian Navigation, Island Empires and Traditional Concepts of Ownership of the Sea*, Saipan: Fifth Congress of Micronesia.

Nambiar, O. K. 1975, *Our Seafaring in the Indian Ocean*, Bangalore: Jeevan.

Nandan, Satya N. 1989, "The 1982 UN Convention on the Law of the Sea: at a crossroad," *Ocean Development and International Law* 20: 515–518.

Nichols, Karen 1999, "Coming to terms with 'integrated coastal management': problems of meaning and method in a new arena of resource regulation," *The Professional Geographer* 51: 388–399.

Nijman, Jan 1994, "The VOC and the expansion of the world-system, 1602–1799," *Political Geography* 13: 211–227.

Noam, Eli M. 1992, "Beyond the golden age of the public network," in Harvey M. Sapolsky, Rhonda J. Crane, W. Russell Newman, and Eli M. Noam (eds.), *The Telecommunications Revolution: Past, Present, and Future*, London: Routledge, pp. 6–10.

Norse, Elliott A. (ed.) 1993, *Global Marine Biological Diversity: A Strategy for Building Conservation into Decision Making*, Washington: Island.

Nowell, Charles E. 1945, "The Treaty of Tordesillas and the diplomatic background of American history," in Adele Ogden and Engel Sluiter (eds.), *Greater America: Essays in Honor of Herbert Eugene Bolton*, Berkeley: University of California Press, pp. 1–18.

Nunn, George E. 1948, *The Diplomacy Concerning the Discovery of America*, Jenkintown: Tall Tree Library.

O'Brien, Richard 1992, *Global Financial Integration: The End of Geography*, New York: Council on Foreign Relations Press.

O'Connell, Daniel P. 1982, *The International Law of the Sea*, Oxford: Clarendon.

O'Connor, James 1994, "Is sustainable capitalism possible?" in O'Connor (ed.), pp. 152–175.

O'Connor, Martin (ed.) 1994a, *Is Capitalism Sustainable? Political Economy and the Politics of Ecology*, New York: Guilford.

O'Connor, Martin 1994b, "On the misadventures of capitalist nature," in O'Connor (ed.), pp. 125–151.

OECD (various years), *Maritime Transport*, Paris: OECD.

OECD, Committee for Information, Computers, and Communications Policy 1997, *Global Information Infrastructure – Global Information Society (GII-GIS) Policy Requirements*, Paris: OECD.

Ogley, Roderick 1981, "The law of the sea draft convention and the new international economic order," *Marine Policy* 5: 240–251.

Oliver, Mary 1986, "The waves," in Mary Oliver, *Dream Work*, Boston: Atlantic Monthly Press, pp. 66–67.

Olson, Charles 1947, *Call Me Ishmael*, New York: Reynal & Hitchcock.

Orams, Mark 1999, *Marine Tourism: Development, Impacts and Management*, London: Routledge.

Orrego Vicuña, Francisco 1993, "Toward an effective management of high seas fisheries and the settlement of the pending issues of the law of the sea," *Ocean Development and International Law* 24: 81–92.

Osborne, Lawrence 1998, "A pirate's progress: how the maritime rogue became a multicultural hero," *Lingua Franca*, March: 35–42.

Ostrom, Elinor 1990, *Governing the Commons: The Evolution of Institutions of Collective Action*, Cambridge: Cambridge University Press.

OTA 1995, *Wireless Technologies and the National Information Infrastructure*, *OTA-ITC–622*, Washington: Government Printing Office.

Ó Tuathail, Gearóid 1996, *Critical Geopolitics: The Politics of Writing Global Space*, Minneapolis: University of Minnesota Press.

Ó Tuathail, Gearóid and Agnew, John 1992, "Geopolitics and discourse: practical geopolitical reasoning in American foreign policy," *Political Geography* 11: 190–204.

Oxman, Bernard H. 1983, "The two conferences," in Oxman, Caron, and Buderi (eds.), pp. 127–144.

1985, "Summary of the law of the sea convention," in Richard Falk, Friedrich Kratochwil, and Saul H. Mendlovitz (eds.), *International Law: A Contemporary Perspective*, Boulder: Westview, pp. 559–570.

Oxman, Bernard H., Caron, David D., and Buderi, Charles L. O. (eds.) 1983, *Law of the Sea: U.S. Policy Dilemma*, San Francisco: Institute for Contemporary Studies Press.

Paasi, Anssi 1996, *Territories, Boundaries, and Consciousness: The Changing Geographies of the Finnish-Russian Border*, New York: Wiley.

Pacem in Maribus 1992, "Ocean governance: a model for global governance in the 21st century?" Background paper prepared for Pacem in Maribus XX, 1–5 November, Malta.

Panel on the Law of Ocean Uses 1990, "U.S. interests and the United Nations Convention on the Law of the Sea," *Ocean Development and International Law* 21: 373–410.

Panel on the Law of Ocean Uses 1994, "United States interests and the law of the sea convention," *American Journal of International Law* 88: 167–178.

Pardo, Arvid 1967, "Address to the General Assembly, 1 November 1967," in *General Assembly Official Records, 22nd Session (1515ᵗʰ and 1516ᵗʰ Meetings), A/C.1/PV.1515 and 1516 (1967)*, New York: United Nations.

1978, "The evolving law of the sea: a critique of the Informal Composite Negotiating Text (1977)," in Elizabeth M. Borgese and Norton Ginsburg (eds.), *Ocean Yearbook 1*, Chicago: University of Chicago Press, pp. 9–37.

1983, "An opportunity lost," in Oxman, Caron, and Buderi (eds.), pp. 13–25.

1984, "The law of the sea: its past and its future," *Oregon Law Review*. 63: 7–17.

Pardo, Arvid and Borgese, Elisabeth M. 1975, *The New International Economic Order and the Law of the Sea*, Malta: International Ocean Institute.

Parfit, Michael 1995, "Diminishing returns: exploiting the ocean's bounty," *National Geographic Magazine*, November: 2–37.

Parker, Geoffrey 1985, *The Development of Western Geopolitical Thought in the Twentieth Century*, London: Croom Helm.

Pattullo, Polly 1996, *Last Resorts: The Cost of Tourism in the Caribbean*, London: Cassell.

Paul, R. 1985, "Development of metalliferous oxides from cobalt-rich manganese crusts," *Marine Technology Society Journal* 19: 45–49.

Pearce, David W. and Turner, R. Kerry 1990, *Economics of Natural Resources and the Environment*, Hemel Hempstead: Harvester Wheatsheaf.

Peet, Richard 1998, *Modern Geographical Thought*, Oxford: Blackwell.

Peet, Richard and Watts, Michael (eds.) 1996, *Liberation Ecologies: Environment, Development, Social Movements*, London: Routledge.

Pérez de Cuéllar, Javier 1983, "International law is irrevocably transformed," in United Nations, *The Law of the Sea: Official Text of the United Nations Convention on the Law of the Sea with Annexes and Index, A/CONF.62/122*, New York: United Nations, pp. xxix–xxxii.

Phillipson, Coleman 1911, *The International Law and Custom of Ancient Greece and Rome*, London: Macmillan.

Pineo, Huguette Ly-Tio-Fane 1985, *Chinese Diaspora in Western Indian Ocean*, Mauritius: Editions de l'Océan Indien/Chinese Catholic Mission.

Piore, Michael and Sabel, Charles 1984, *The Second Industrial Divide: Possibilities for Prosperity*, New York: Basic.

Pontecorvo, Giulio 1988, "The enclosure of the marine commons: adjustment and redistribution in world fisheries," *Marine Policy* 12: 361–372.

Powell, Corey S. 1992, "Flotsam footwear," *Scientific American*, November: 26.

Prager, Herman 1993, *Global Marine Environment: Does the Water Planet Have a Future?* Lanham: University Press of America.

Professional Geographer, The 1999, Focus Section: "The geography of ocean-space," 51: 366–450.

Pryor, John H. 1988, *Geography, Technology, and War: Studies in the Maritime History of the Mediterranean, 649–1571*, Cambridge: Cambridge University Press.

Psuty, Norbert P., Steinberg, Philip E. and Wright, Dawn 2002, "Coastal and marine geography," in Gary Gaile and Cort Wilmott (eds.), *Geography in America at the Dawn of the 21st Century*, Oxford: Oxford University Press.

Raban, Jonathan 1992, "Introduction," in Jonathan Raban (ed.), *The Oxford Book of the Sea*, Oxford: Oxford University Press, pp. 1–34.

Raffles, Sir Stanford 1879, "The maritime code of the Malays," *Journal of the Royal Asiatic Society – Straits Branch* 3: 62–84.

Raleigh, Sir Walter 1829, *The Works of Sir Walter Raleigh*, Oxford: Oxford University Press.

Ramos Perez, Demetrio 1974, *Los Criterios Contrarios al Tratado de Tordesillas en el Siglo XVIII: Determinantes de la Necesidad de su Anaulacion*, Coimbra: Junta de Investigações do Ultramar.

Ratzel, Friedrich 1896, *The History of Mankind*, trans. A. J. Taylor, London: Macmillan.

Ray, Haraprasad 1987, "China and the 'western ocean' in the fifteenth century," in Chandra (ed.), pp. 109–124.

Reagan, Ronald 1990, "Statement by the president on United States ocean policy, 10 March 1983," in Burns H. Weston, Richard A. Falk, and Anthony D'Amato (eds.), *International Law and World Order: A Problem-Oriented Coursebook*, 2nd edn., St. Paul: West, pp. 226–228.

Rediker, Marcus 1987, *Between the Devil and the Deep Blue Sea: Merchant Seamen, Pirates, and the Anglo-American Maritime World, 1700–1750*, Cambridge: Cambridge University Press.

1996, "Liberty beneath the Jolly Roger: the lives of Anne Bonny and Mary Read, pirates," in Creighton and Norling (eds.), pp. 1–33.

Rees, Judith 1990, *Natural Resources: Allocation, Economics and Policy*, 2nd edn., London: Routledge.

Reuters 1991, "Drifting Nikes may lead science to mysteries of the sea," *The Boston Globe*, 17 November: A4.

Richardson, Elliot L. 1982, "Law of the sea: navigation and other traditional national security issues," *San Diego Law Review* 19: 553–576.

Roberts, Susan M. 1996, "The world is *whose* oyster?" unpublished manuscript.

Robles, Alfredo C. Jr. 1996, "Universality vs. the common heritage of humanity? the 1994 agreement on deep seabed mining," *World Bulletin* 12: 20–70.

Roe, Emery M. 1994, *Narrative Policy Analysis: Theory and Practice*, Durham, NC: Duke University Press.

Ross, Robert J. S. and Trachte, Kent C. 1990, *Global Capitalism: The New Leviathan*, Albany: State University of New York Press.

Rostow, Walt W. 1960, *The Stages of Economic Growth: A Non-Communist Manifesto*, Cambridge: Cambridge University Press.

Rounsefell, George A. 1975, *Ecology, Utilization, and Management of Marine Fisheries*, Saint Louis: C. V. Mosby.

Ruggie, John G. 1993, "Territoriality and beyond: problematizing modernity in international relations," *International Organization* 47: 139–174.

Ryan, Simon 1996, *The Cartographic Eye: How Explorers Saw Australia*, Cambridge: Cambridge University Press.

Sachs, Wolfgang (ed.) 1992, *The Development Dictionary: A Guide to Knowledge as Power*, London: Zed.

Sack, Robert D. 1986, *Human Territoriality: Its Theory and History*, Cambridge: Cambridge University Press.

Safina, Carl 1998, *Song for the Blue Ocean: Encounters Along the World's Coasts and Beneath the Seas*, New York: Henry Holt.

Said, Edward W. 1978, *Orientalism*, New York: Pantheon.

1993, *Culture and Imperialism*, New York: Vintage.

1994, "Response," *Social Text* 40: 20–24.

Sanger, Clyde 1987, *Ordering the Oceans: The Making of the Law of the Sea*, Toronto: University of Toronto Press.

Sassen, Saskia 1991, *The Global City: New York, London, Tokyo*, Princeton: Princeton University Press.

Sauer, Carl O. 1963, *Land and Life: A Selection From the Writings of Carl Ortwin Sauer*, Berkeley: University of California Press.

Schachte, William L. Jr. 1993, "International straits and navigational freedoms," *Ocean Development and International Law* 24: 179–195.

Scott, Allen J. and Storper, Michael 1986, "Industrial change and territorial organization: summing up," in Allen J. Scott and Michael Storper (eds.), *Production, Work, Territory: The Geographical Anatomy of Industrial Capitalism*, Boston: Allen & Unwin, pp. 301–311.

Sekula, Allan 1995, *Fish Story*, Düsseldorf: Richter.

Selden, John [1635] 1972, *Of the Dominion, or Ownership of the Sea: Two Books*, New York: Arno.

Semple, Ellen C. 1911, *Influences of Geographic Environment*, New York: Henry Holt.

1931, *The Geography of the Mediterranean Region: Its Relation to Ancient History*, New York: Henry Holt.

Shannon, Thomas 1989, *An Introduction Toward the World-System Perspective*, Boulder: Westview.

Shapiro, Michael J. 1997, *Violent Cartographies: Mapping Cultures of War*, Minneapolis: University of Minnesota Press.

Shusterich, Kurt 1982, "Mining the deep seabed: a complex and innovative industry," *Marine Policy* 6: 175–192.

Simoes Ferreira, Penelope 1979, "The role of African states in the development of the law of the sea," *Ocean Development and International Law* 7: 89–129.

Sirbu, Marvin A. 1992, "The struggle for control with the telecommunications networks," in Harvey M. Sapolsky, Rhonda J. Crane, W. Russell Newman, and Eli M. Noam (eds.), *The Telecommunications Revolution: Past, Present, and Future*, London: Routledge, pp. 140–148.

Slocum, Joshua 1903, *Around the World in the Sloop Spray*, New York: Scribner.

Slonczewski, Joan 1986, *A Door Into Ocean*, New York: Avon.

Smith, Gordon S. 1997, "Cyberspace's frontier," *Vital Speeches of the Day* 63: 591–595.

Smith, Neil 1990, *Uneven Development: Nature, Capital, and the Production of Space*, 2nd edn., Oxford: Basil Blackwell.

Soja, Edward W. 1971, *The Political Organization of Space*, Washington: Association of American Geographers.

1980, "The socio-spatial dialectic," *Annals of the Association of American Geographers* 70: 207–225.

1985, "Regions in context: spatiality, periodicity, and the historical geography of the regional question," *Environment and Planning D: Society & Space* 3: 175–190.

1989, *Postmodern Geographies: The Reassertion of Space in Critical Social Theory*, London: Verso.

1996, *Thirdspace: Journeys to Los Angeles and Other Real-and-Imagined Places*, Oxford: Blackwell.

Soroos, Marvin S. 1982, "The commons in the sky: the radio spectrum and geosynchronous orbit as issues in global policy," *International Organization* 36: 665–677.

Spykman, Nicholas J. 1944, *The Geography of the Peace*, New York: Harcourt, Brace.

Steensgaard, Niels 1987, "The Indian Ocean network and the emerging world-economy, circa 1500–1750," in Chandra (ed.), pp. 125–150.

Steinberg, Philip E. 1994a, "Comment: territory, territoriality and the new industrial geography," *Political Geography* 13: 3–5.

1994b, "Territorial formation on the margin: urban anti-planning in Brooklyn," *Political Geography* 13: 461–476.

1998, "Transportation space: a fourth spatial category for the world-systems perspective?" in Paul S. Ciccantell and Stephen G. Bunker (eds.), *Space and Transport in the World-System*, Westport: Greenwood, pp. 19–35.

1999a, "Fish or foul: investigating the politics of the Marine Stewardship Council," paper presented at Conference on Multilateral Ocean Governance, Institute of International Studies, Berkeley, April 30–May 2.

1999b, "Lines of division, lines of connection: stewardship in the world ocean," *Geographical Review* 89: 254–264.

1999c, "The maritime mystique: sustainable development, capital mobility, and nostalgia in the world ocean," *Environment and Planning D: Society & Space* 17: 403–426.

1999d, "Navigating to multiple horizons: toward a geography of ocean-space," *The Professional Geographer* 51: 366–375.

2000, "Sixteenth-century cartography and the establishment of state territoriality," paper presented at the Annual Meeting of the Southeast Division of the Association of American Geographers, Chapel Hill, November 19–21.

Steinberg, Philip E. and McDowell, Stephen D. 2000, "Transportation, communication, and the post-statism of cyberspace: a spatial constructivist view," unpublished manuscript.

Stevens, William O. and Westcott, Allan 1942, *A History of Sea Power*, New York: Doubleday.

Stevenson, John R. and Oxman, Bernard H. 1994, "The future of the United Nations Convention on the Law of the Sea," *American Journal of International Law* 88: 488–499.

Storper, Michael 1992, "The Limits to Globalization: Technology Districts and International Trade," *Economic Geography* 68 : 69–93.

Storper, Michael and Walker, Richard 1989, *The Capitalist Imperative: Territory, Technology, and Industrial Growth*, New York: Basil Blackwell.

Strabo 1917, *Geography*, trans. Horace L. Jones, Cambridge, MA: Harvard University Press.

Sullivan, Walter 1992, "If the shoe floats, follow it," *The New York Times*, 22 September: C1.

Sullivan, William L. Jr. 1985, "Is there a national ocean policy?" *Ocean Development and International Law* 15: 77–88.

Taggart, Stewart 1999, "The 20-ton packet: ocean-shipping is the biggest real-time datastreaming network in the world," *Wired* 9: 246–255.

Takeuchi, T. K. 1979, "Exploitation of manganese nodules: future problems," in *Proceedings of the Third International Ocean Symposium: The Deep Seabed and Its Mineral Resources*, Tokyo: Ocean Association of Japan, pp. 105–109.

Taylor, Peter J. 1989, "The world-systems project," in Ronald J. Johnston and Peter J. Taylor (eds.), *A World in Crisis? Geographical Perspectives*, 2nd edn., Oxford: Basil Blackwell, pp. 333–354.

1991, "Territoriality and hegemony, spatiality and the modern world-system," unpublished report submitted to the Fernand Braudel Center, Binghamton, New York.

1993, "*Contra* political geography," *Tijdschrift voor Economische en Sociale Geografie* 84: 82–90.

1995, "Beyond containers: internationality, interstateness, interterritoriality," *Progress in Human Geography* 19: 1–15.

Thomas, William L. Jr. (ed.) 1956, *Man's Role in Changing the Face of the Earth*, Chicago: University of Chicago Press.

Thomson, Janice E. 1994, *Mercenaries, Pirates, and Sovereigns: State-Building and Extraterritorial Violence in Early Modern Europe*, Princeton: Princeton University Press.

Thongchai Winichakul 1994, *Siam Mapped: The History of the Geo-Body of a Nation*, Honolulu: University of Hawai'i Press.

"Today's pirates pose double trouble" 1994, *Parade Magazine*, 3 April: 16.

Trist, Carolyn 1999, "Recreating ocean space: recreational consumption and representation in the Caribbean marine environment," *The Professional Geographer* 51: 376–387.

Tsamenyi, Martin and Herriman, Max 1998, "Ocean energy and the law of the sea: the need for a protocol," *Ocean Development and International Law* 29: 3–19.

Turnbull, David 1989, *Maps are Territories, Science is an Atlas*, Geelong: Deakin University Press.

Turner, Billie L. II, Clark, William C., Kates, Robert W., Richards, John F., Mathews, Jessica T., and Meyer, William B. (eds.) 1990, *The Earth as Transformed by Human Action: Global and Regional Changes in the Biosphere Over the Past 300 Years*, Cambridge: Cambridge University Press.

UNCTAD (various years), *Review of Maritime Transport*, New York: UNCTAD.

United Nations 1958a, *Convention on the Continental Shelf, A/CONF.13/L.55*, New York: United Nations.

1958b, *Convention on Fishing and Conservation of the Living Resources of the High Seas, A/CONF.13/L.54*, New York: United Nations.

1958c, *Convention on the High Seas, A/CONF.13/L.53*, New York: United Nations.

1958d, *Convention on the Territorial Sea and the Contiguous Zone, A/CONF.13/ L.52*, New York: United Nations.

1983, *The Law of the Sea: Official Text of the United Nations Convention on the Law of the Sea with Annexes and Index, A/CONF.62/122*, New York: United Nations.

1987, *Delineation of Mine-Sites and Potential in Different Sea Areas*, London: Graham & Trotman.

1989, *Selection of Sites for Seabed Manganese Nodule Processing Plants*, London: Graham & Trotman.

1993, *Agenda 21: Program of Action for Sustainable Development*, New York: United Nations.

1994, *Agreement Relating to the Implementation of Part XI of the United Nations Convention on the Law of the Sea of 10 December 1982, U.N. General Assembly Resolution 48/263*, New York: United Nations.

1995, *Agreement for the Implementation of the Provisions of the 1982 United Nations Convention on the Law of the Sea Relating to the Conservation and Management of Straddling Fish Stocks and Highly Migratory Fish Stocks, A/CONF.164/ 22/Rev. 1*, New York: United Nations.

United States 1945a, "Presidential proclamation no. 2667: concerning the policy of the United States with respect to the natural resources of the subsoil and the sea-bed on the continental shelf (September 28)," *Federal Register* 10: 12303.

1945b, "Presidential proclamation no. 2668: concerning the policy of the United States with respect to coastal fisheries in certain areas of the high seas (September 28)," *Federal Register* 10: 12304.

References

United States Navy 1992, *From the Sea: Preparing the Naval Service for the 21st Century*, Washington: U.S. Department of the Navy.

Urry, John 1990, *The Tourist Gaze*, London: Sage.

1994, *Consuming Places*, London: Routledge.

Vallega, Adalberto 1999, "Ocean geography vis-à-vis global change and sustainable development," *The Professional Geographer* 51: 400–414.

Vallega, Adalberto, Augustinus, Pieter G. E. F., and Smith, Hance D. 1998, *Geography, Oceans and Coasts: Towards Sustainable Development*, Milan: Franco Angeli.

Van Dyke, Jon M. (ed.) 1985, *Consensus and Confrontation: The United States and the Law of the Sea Convention*, Honolulu: Law of the Sea Institute.

Van Dyke, Jon M., Zaelke, Durwood, and Hewison, Grant (eds.) 1993, *Freedom for the Seas in the 21st Century: Ocean Governance and Environmental Harmony*, Washington: Island.

Vander Linden, H. 1916, "Alexander VI and the demarcation of the maritime and colonial domains of Spain and Portugal, 1493–1494," *The American Historical Review* 22: 1–20.

Vandergeest, Peter and Peluso, Nancy L. 1995, "Territorialization and state power in Thailand," *Theory and Society* 24: 385–426.

Varela Marcos, Jesús (ed.) 1994, *El Tratado de Tordesillas en la Cartografía Histórica*, Valladolid: Sociedad V Centenario del Tratado de Tordesillas.

Varela Marcos, Jesús 1997, *El Tratado de Tordesillas en la Política Atlántica Castellana*, Valladolid: Secretariado de Publicacaciones e Intercambio Científico, Univerdisad de Valladolid.

Verlinden, Charles 1987, "The Indian Ocean: the ancient period and the middle ages," in Chandra (ed.), pp. 27–53.

Verne, Jules [1875] 1959, *The Mysterious Island*, trans. W. H. G. Kingston, New York: Heritage.

[1870] 1962, *20,000 Leagues Under the Sea*, trans. Anthony Bonner, Toronto: Bantam.

Virilio, Paul 1986, *Speed and Politics: An Essay on Dromology*, trans. Mark Polizzoti, New York: Semiotext(e).

Walker, R. B. J. and Mendlovitz, Saul H. 1990, *Contending Sovereignties: Redefining Political Community*, Boulder: Lynne Rienner.

Wallerstein, Immanuel 1979, *The Capitalist World-Economy*, Cambridge: Cambridge University Press.

1983, *Historical Capitalism*, London: Verso.

1984, *Politics of the World Economy*, Cambridge: Cambridge University Press.

1991, *Geopolitics and Geoculture: Essays on the Changing World-System*, Cambridge: Cambridge University Press.

Waterworld 1995, dir. Kevin Reynolds, Hollywood: Universal.

Watt, Donald C. 1979, "First steps in the enclosure of the oceans: the origins of Truman's proclamation on the resources of the continental shelf, 28 September 1945," *Marine Policy* 3: 211–224.

Watts, Michael 1993, "Development I: power, knowledge, discursive practice," *Progress in Human Geography* 17: 257–272.

Wedgwood, Ruth 1995, "US should ratify the law of the sea treaty," *The Boston Globe*, 4 August: 19.

Welling, Conrad 1985, "A view from the industry," in Van Dyke (ed.), pp. 233–235.

West, Niels 1989, "Coastal and marine geography," in Gary L. Gaile and Cort J. Willmott (eds.), *Geography in America*, Columbus: Merrill, pp. 141–154.

White House 1983, "The law of the sea convention, position paper from the White House Office of Policy Information, 15 April," *Oceanus* 26: 74–76.

   1996, "Background on Clinton–Gore administration's Next-Generation Internet Initiative," news release, October 10.

Whitfield, Peter 1996, *The Charting of the Oceans: Ten Centuries of Maritime Maps*, Rohnert Park: Pomegranate.

Will, George F. 1995, "New tools for new navy," *The Boston Globe*, 25 August: 23.

Williams, Mary W. 1922, "The Treaty of Tordesillas and the Argentine-Brazilian boundary settlement," *Hispanic American Historical Review* 5: 3–23.

Williams, Rosalind 1990, *Notes on the Underground: An Essay on Technology, Society, and the Imagination*, Cambridge, MA: MIT Press.

Wilson, Peter L. 1995, *Pirate Utopias: Moorish Corsairs and European Renegadoes*, Brooklyn: Autonomedia.

Wilson, Rob and Dirlik, Arif (eds.) 1995, *Asia/Pacific as Space of Cultural Production*, Durham: Duke University Press.

Wolpe, Harold (ed.) 1980, *The Articulation of Modes of Production: Essays from Economy and Society*, London: Routledge.

Wood, Denis 1992, *The Power of Maps*, New York: Guilford.

Young, Oran R. (ed.) 1997, *Global Governance: Drawing Insights from the Environmental Experience*, Cambridge, MA: MIT Press.

Zacher, Mark W. and McConnell, James 1990, "Down to the Sea with Stakes," *Ocean Development and International Law* 21: 71–103.

Zacher, Mark W. and Sutton, Brent A. 1996, *Governing Global Networks: International Regimes for Transportation and Communications*, Cambridge: Cambridge University Press.

Index

234

CAMBRIDGE STUDIES IN INTERNATIONAL RELATIONS

Learning Resources
Centre